Martin Evertz
Visual Prosody

Linguistische Arbeiten

Band 570

Martin Evertz

Visual Prosody

The Graphematic Foot in English and German

DE GRUYTER

ISBN 978-3-11-070965-0
e-ISBN (PDF) 978-3-11-058344-1
e-ISBN (EPUB) 978-3-11-058119-5
ISSN 0344-6727

Library of Congress Control Number: 2018945766.

Bibliografische Information der Deutschen Nationalbibliothek
Die Deutsche Nationalbibliothek verzeichnet diese Publikation in der Deutschen Nationalbibliografie; detaillierte bibliografische Daten sind im Internet über http://dnb.dnb.de abrufbar.

This volume is text- and page-identical with the hardback published in 2018.
Printing: CPI books GmbH, Leck

www.degruyter.com

Acknowledgements

I would like to say a heartfelt thank-you to all those people who have supported me in completing this book.

Firstly, I would like to express my sincere gratitude to my advisor Beatrice Primus for the continuous support of my Ph.D study and related research, for her patience, motivation, and immense knowledge. Her guidance helped me in all the time of research and writing of this thesis. I cannot thank her enough for the opportunity she gave me.

Besides my first advisor, I would like to thank my second supervisors, Ulrike Domahs and Daniel Bunčić. Their comments and encouragement were invaluable.

A special thank goes to my colleagues at Beatrice Primus' chair and the whole institute for German language and literature I at the University of Cologne. I would like to especially thank Sven Alberg, Frank Kirchhoff, Timo Röttger, Tim Graf and Patrick Brandt. They helped me in various ways – through stimulating discussion, helpful advises and moral support.

Last but not the least, I would like to thank my family: my mother and late father and my brothers and their families and – of course – Manuel and his family for supporting me spiritually throughout writing this thesis and my life in general.

https://doi.org/10.1515/9783110583441-201

Contents

1 Introduction

According to well-established views, language has several subsystems where each subsystem (e.g. syntax, morphology, phonology) operates on the basis of hierarchically organised units. Importantly – and as is widely acknowledged – the linear structures of language are not all there is to grammar; instead it is the hierarchical structure that really determines what we perceive.

When it comes to the graphematic structure of words, however, the received view appears to be that linear structure is all that matters. Contrary to this standard view, a sub-field of writing systems research emerged that can be called non-linear or *supra-segmental graphematics*. Drawing on parallels with supra-segmental phonology, supra-segmental graphematics claims the existence and relevance of cross-linguistically available building blocks, such as the syllable and the foot, in alphabetical writing systems, such as the writing systems of German and English.

While some supra-segmental units, mostly the graphematic syllable and the graphematic word, gained some attention in the literature, the unit corresponding to the phonological foot, the *graphematic foot*, has been largely neglected. However, recent works, primarily Primus (2010) for German and Evertz & Primus (2013) for English and German, explore this category.

This work is devoted to the graphematic foot in English and German and examines its relevance, structure, and function. With the graphematic foot, it is possible to fill a gap in supra-segmental graphematics. As I will show in §1.3, it is possible to establish a graphematic hierarchy parallel to the phonological hierarchy, as for instance proposed by Nespor & Vogel (1986). Importantly, I will show in this work that the whole graphematic hierarchy can be established independently by inner-graphematic constraints in opposition to approaches in which graphematic units are derived from phonological ones.

The remainder of this chapter is organised as follows: First, I will discuss basic assumptions about writing systems and the linguistic approach towards them. Then I will present the phonological hierarchy (e.g. Nespor & Vogel 1986). Two of the categories of the phonological hierarchy, the foot and the syllable, will be examined a bit closer. Thereafter, I will give a definition of the graphematic hierarchy, which is the graphematic counterpart to the phonological hierarchy. The graphematic hierarchy will be the theoretic background of the analysis of the graphematic foot proposed in this work. The chapter concludes with a brief in-

1 I thank Rosa Jackson for proofreading the manuscript. Also I would like to thank the anonymous reviewer, who gave valuable input. All remaining mistakes are, of course, mine.

https://doi.org/10.1515/9783110583441-001

troduction to (unidirectional) Optimality Theory (OT), which will provide the primary formal framework of this work (I will offer in chapter 4 also an analysis of the graphematic foot within bidirectional Optimality Theory (biOT, Blutner 2000); I will introduce this variant of the OT there), and with a brief outline of the rest of this work.

1.1 Basic Properties of Graphematics

1.1.1 The Relation of Spoken and Written Language

Modern linguistics in the first half of the twentieth century has viewed upon the written representation of language as a phenomenon secondary to speech, while spoken language has been seen as 'real' language. Following quotes from various researchers are exemplary for this point of view:

> "Language and writing are two distinct systems of signs; the second exists for the sole purpose of representing the first" (de Saussure 1916, trans. Baskin 1959: 23).
> "Writing is not language, but merely a way of recording language by visible marks" (Bloomfield 1933: 21).
> "Speech is fundamental and writing [...] only a secondary derivative" (Hall 1964: 8-9).
> "[It is] the undoubtedly correct observation that spoken language is 'true' language, while written language is an artifact" (Aronoff 1985: 28).

In the literature, this view is referred to as *derivational* or *dependency hypothesis*. This hypothesis states that written language is derived from spoken language and that it is designed solely as a visible recording of speech that, however, is a mere imperfect and corrupt reflection of spoken language without or with only marginal systematicity of its own (cf. Coulmas 1996: 27).

Advocates of this hypothesis justify their approach by the claim that spoken language takes a fourfold priority over written language: i) phylogenetic priority, i.e. writing developed later than speech; ii) ontogenetic priority, i.e. a person acquires spoken language (normally) earlier than written language, iii) functional priority, i.e. speech serves a wider range of purposes; and iv) structural priority, i.e. writing is a representation of speech (Lyons 1972: 62f.).

Some of these priorities are – at least partially – disputable. But even if all claims of priority hold, one can argue that it "does not follow from any of the four [priorities] that the use of vocal sound as a medium of expression must be treated as critical, to the exclusion of writing, in defining either language or languages, except in the case of those languages which happen to have no written form" (Harris 2009: 55).

Of course, there is a logical dependency of written language that cannot be ignored. A writing system represents language. This distinguishes writing systems from other forms of graphical means of human communication like e.g. pictographs or staves (cf. Harris 1995). This means that every writing system is dependent on its corresponding spoken language: There is no written language without corresponding spoken language, but there are spoken languages without written languages (In fact, the majority of languages have been and are unwritten.). To put it differently, a spoken language is the necessary (but not sufficient) condition for a corresponding written language (cf. e.g. Neef & Primus 2001, Neef 2005).

This logical dependency, however, does not determine the particular kind of relation between spoken and written language. Neef (2005: 5) points out that once a writing system is established it can have an influence on the corresponding spoken language. It is even possible that a writing system survives its corresponding spoken language.

The alternative to the derivational hypothesis is the so called *autonomy hypothesis*. Its strong form denies any close connection between spoken and written language. I do not support this form. Instead, I plead for a weaker or relative position that can be called *interdependency* or *correspondence hypothesis*. As the names suggest, this hypothesis assumes that spoken and written language are interdependent: spoken language influences written languages but written language also influences spoken language.

Neef & Primus (2001: 15) summarise the following observations and assumptions of the interdependency theory:

i. There are not only phonology-based derivational rules (or rather constraints, see below) but also rules (or constraints) based on written language, and bidirectional correspondences.
ii. Phonology-based rules are generally neither simpler nor more general than rules based on written language.
iii. There are autonomous units and rules (or constraints) of writing systems that do not have correspondents in spoken language.
iv. There is non-predictable information concerning spelling and writing in the mental lexicon. This means that there is a graphematic component within the mental lexicon.
v. There is psycholinguistic evidence supporting the interdependence theory.

Let us go very briefly through these points. We will start with the last point. Psycholinguistic studies show that graphematic competence can be impaired by aphasia while speech remains unaffected (cf. Badecker 1996, Sucharowksi 1996, Miceli et al. 1997, Cuetos & Labos 2001). Furthermore, the dependency theory predicts that the acquisition of written language requires independently acquired phonological competence, especially the ability to segment words into phonemes and the ability to identify phonemes. Several studies, however, indicate that these aspects of phonological competence are indeed consequences and not conditions of the acquisition of written language (cf. e.g. Morais et al. 1987, Wimmer et al. 1991, Faber 1992; for a theoretical diachronic approach cf. Olson 1993, 1994). Additionally, psycholinguistic evidence suggests that there are several ways of word recognition in silent reading. Phonological decoding is only one of them and is not necessarily involved in word recognition (cf. Günther 1988, de Bleser 1991).

Let us now turn to points i. to iv., which concern the system itself. Neef & Primus (2001) discuss the occurrence of <h> in German. According to accounts within the framework of dependency theory (e.g. Ossner 1996, 2001), the occurrence of <h> must always be motivated by phonological correspondence. Neef & Primus (2001), however, give some examples in which this is not possible.

According to phonological theories, the sound [h] occurs in German only foot-initially, i.e. in the onset of a stressed syllable (Wiese 2000: 60); according to Neef (2000: 75) even only at the beginning of a phonological word. Words like in (1), in which [h] appears foot-medially, are thus a problem for a dependence theoretic approach: where does the <h> come from?

(1) *kohärent* 'coherent', *Mahagoni* 'mahogany', *Alkohol* 'alcohol'

As shown above, the occurrences of <h> are not explicable by phonology-based rules, i.e. by derivation from an underlying /h/ in the phonological form (Neef & Primus 2001). But it gets even worse for the dependency theory: these words can indeed be seen as evidence for sounds induced by the written representation of a word. Let us have a closer look at the words in (1).

Neef & Primus (2001) argue that the word *kohärent* [ko.hɛ.ˈʀɛnt] derives from Latin and is traceable in German since the 18th century (Kluge 1999: 23). Because Latin was already a dead language in the 18th century, the occurrence of [h] in the pronunciation of the word did clearly not derive from Latin pronunciation. Rather, it is motivated by the written form of the word.[2] We see a similar picture in the word *Alkohol* [al.ko.hoːl], which derives from Spanish *alcohol* [al.ko.ol]. In Spanish, the <h> is mute. Therefore, it seems that the German pronunciation is not influenced by the original Spanish pronunciation but by the written form.

2 It has to be noted, however, that *kohärent* can be seen as morphologically complex: *ko+härent*, which might be a relevant factor.

While a dependency theoretic model is struggling to account for the presence of <h> in these words (and may even fail to do so), these occurrences of [h] and <h> are not problematic at all for a interdependency theoretic approach: the <h> in these words is part of the graphematic form that can be interpreted phonographically (Neef & Primus 2001: 14).

The authors also point to the fact that <h> serves a writing system specific function in words such as in (1), that is, <h> marks a syllable boundary. If the words above lacked <h>, i.e. if the form of the graphematic words were <Maagoni> or <Alkool>, the syllable boundaries would be ambiguous for a reader; the words could be read as bisyllabic or trisyllabic words.

As we will see in chapter 3, the distribution of <h> in German can be accounted for by graphematic distribution constraints referring to the graphematic syllable (cf. Primus 2000). The most important of the distributional constraints is that <h> only appears in syllable margins. In a graphematic syllable model in which nuclei of strong syllables are obligatorily branching (cf. §3.4), this distributional constraint leads to the mapping of a syllable containing <h> in the rhyme, such as <lahm> 'lame', to a phonological syllable that also has a branching nucleus, e.g. [laːm]. Graphematic constraints like these can thus capture the function of <h> as a marker of tense/ long vowels (in this function it is commonly called lengthening-<h>) but also its function as syllable boundary marker.

Another example which shows how writing systems can influence spoken language is illustrated by the examples in (2):

(2) a. *Adler* 'eagle', *Magnet* 'magnet', *eklig* 'disgusting', *widrig* 'adverse'
b. [ʔaː.dlɐ], [ma.gneːt], [ʔeː.klɪç], [viː.dʀɪç]
c. [ʔaːt.lɐ], [mak.neːt], [ʔeːk.lɪç], [viːt.ʀɪç]
d. <Ad-ler>, <Mag-net>, <ek-lig>, <wid-rig>

The words in (2a) have ambiguous syllable boundaries. The syllable divisions in (2b) follow onset-maximisation (i.e. the onset is built as large as possible while codas are avoided, cf. §1.2). The boundaries in (2c) do not follow onset-maximization and disregard the preference for avoiding codas. Though the forms in (2c) are more marked than those in (2b), literate speakers of German sometimes tend to divide syllables like in (2c) when explicitly asked about phonological syllable boundaries. This ambiguity in syllable division may be explicable by the influence of the writing system, to be more precise, by the influence of word division (2d). The divisions in (2c) are not optimal for phonology, but they are perfect if the words in (2c) were written and not spoken, cf. the indicated line breaks in (2d) (cf. Günther 1992, Neef & Primus 2001).

Neef & Primus (2001) and Primus (2003) assume on basis of the evidence in favour of the interdependency hypothesis that a writing system is one modality of one paramount, modality-unspecific language system. The modalities of the language system correspond to each other, cf. (3).

(3) *Interface-Model of language systems* (Primus 2003: 4, my translation)

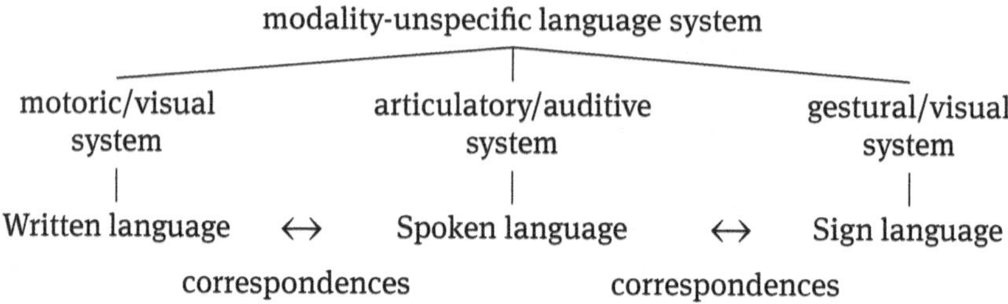

The evidence I sketched here and that will be presented in this work, are clearly in favour of the interdependency hypothesis. Units such as the syllable and the foot are thus perceived in this work as cross-medial available building blocks that can be found in all three modalities of language: sign language, written language and spoken language (for a recent overview of a cross-modality phonology cf. Domahs & Primus 2015).

I will thus assume that there is a bidirectional mapping relation between spoken and written language and that there are graphematically and phonologically based mapping rules that are used in reading and writing respectively (cf. Venezky (1970) for an early influential approach using grapheme-based mapping rules). Although the units in written and spoken language (as, for instance, the syllable and the foot) correspond to each other, they are modality-specific and, hence, independent of each other in this respect. The existence of the two types of units is also a prerequisite for any mapping approach to writing systems since a mapping relation presupposes two distinct units (unless it is a reflexive relation).

The graphematic mapping constraints proposed in this work are thus not derivational rules that derive phonological units from graphematic ones or vice versa. Rather, they are logical statements about mappings that are in conformity with the logical dependence hypothesis, as mentioned above (cf. Evertz & Primus 2013).

1.1.2 Graphematics vs. Orthography

The terms *graphematics* and *orthography* reflect the differentiation of norm vs. system that can also be found in other fields of linguistics. We will define these terms as follows (cf. Coulmas 1996, Dürscheid 2012):

(4) *Graphematics* is the linguistic study of writing systems.

(5) An *orthography* is a normative selection of the possibilities of the writing system of a particular language for writing that language in a uniform and standardised way.

The graphematics of English and German as linguistic fields include segmental graphematics (analogously to segmental phonology), supra-segmental graphematics (analogously to supra-segmental phonology), lexical graphematics or morpho-graphematics, and finally the syntax-graphematics interface (e.g. punctuation research) (Eisenberg 1989: 59).

If we understand orthography as linguistic field, it is a sub-field of graphematics, i.e. the field that is concerned with (5), that is, the normative writing of a particular language. Graphematics, on the other hand, is concerned with the whole system; this includes, for example, regularities that can be found in non-standardised writing.

Like in other fields of linguistics, the names of the scientific fields are synonymously used for the object of research. Thus, the graphematics of German and English simultaneously denote the writing systems of the two languages and the research on these systems. Neef (2005) exemplifies the distinction of orthography and graphematics in this sense with the help of the coding of the phonological form [va:l] in German, cf. table 1.1.

Tab. 1.1: Graphematic solutions for [va:l] (excerpt) (Neef 2005: 12)

Val	Vaal	Vahl
Wal	Waal	Wahl

Table 1.1 depicts potential codings of the phonological form [va:l] in German. These six graphematic forms (it is easy to think of many more, like e.g. <Waaal> or <Vhal> although forms like these are very unlikely) represent possibilities that are attested for other words in German. Thus, we can say that all of these potential codings conform to the graphematic systems. Orthography selects for each

word exactly one graphematic form. The German words for election and whale are homophones and pronounced [va:l], but the German word meaning election is coded <Wahl> and the German word meaning whale is coded <Wal>.

1.2 The Phonological Hierarchy

The theory of prosodic phonology (e.g., Selkirk 1980, 1981; Nespor & Vogel 1986) holds that speech is arranged into hierarchically organised constituents. These constituents form the domains for phonological rules or constraints, which are joined together into a hierarchical structure known as the prosodic or *phonological hierarchy*. Most theories agree that the phonological hierarchy contains at least the syllable, the foot, the phonological word and one or more constituents above the word (cf. Shattuck-Hufnagel & Turk 1996 for a comparison of the constituent inventories of some of the most influential theories). I will focus in this work on the constituents on word level and below.

The structure in (6) exemplifies the phonological hierarchy with the word *shouter*[3]; additionally to the mentioned categories of the prosodic hierarchy, segments, features, and subsyllabic constituents are displayed although most theories do not include them into the hierarchy (see below).

(6)

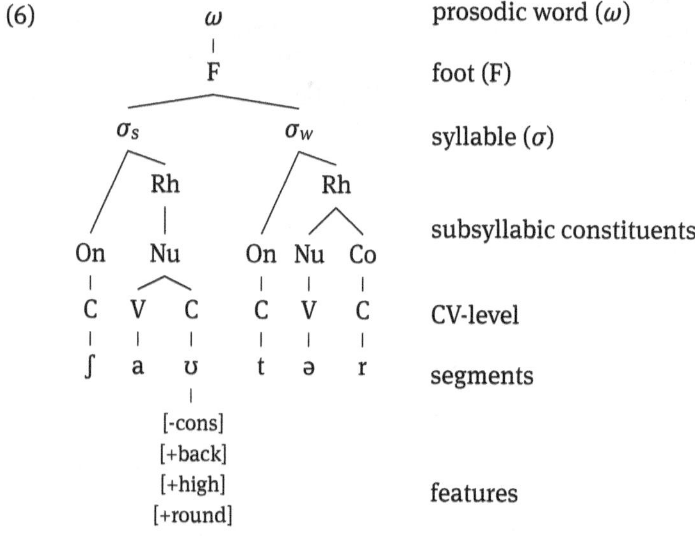

3 Please note that in some varieties of English, the second syllable of *shouter* is open. The illustration in (6) is fairly close to American English [ʃaʊtɚ], cf. Jones (2006)

This hierarchy is accompanied by the *Strict Layer Hypothesis* (Selkirk 1984, 1986). The following statement of this hypothesis is taken from Nespor & Vogel (1986: 7), cf. (7).

(7) a. A given nonterminal unit of the prosodic hierarchy X^p is composed of one or more units of the immediately lower category, X^{p-1}.
b. A unit of a given level of the hierarchy is exhaustively contained in the superordinate unit of which it is a part.

This means that the Strict Layer Hypothesis demands that a word is parsed exhaustively at all relevant levels of the prosodic hierarchy. Thus, (6) is an example of exhaustive parsing because in (6) every unit is contained in a unit of a higher level. The word in (6) therefore conforms to the Strict Layer Hypothesis.

The second principle of the strict layer hypothesis in (7) is the reason why Nespor & Vogel (1986: 13) do not consider the segment to be the lowest constituent in the prosodic hierarchy: segments may be ambisyllabic and thus not always be exhaustively contained in the constituent that immediately dominates it.

The Strict Layer Hypothesis is generally accepted as guiding principle for prosodic organisation, however, it is less clear to which degree it should be satisfied. Let us consider words such as *agree* and *Magie* 'magic' in which the last syllables constitute monosyllabic feet and the first syllables are unstressed. Since the Strict Layer Hypothesis states that every syllable has to be contained in feet and since feet are head-initial (cf. §1.2.2), the first syllable seems not to be dominated by a foot-node. This phenomenon is commonly dubbed extrametricallity (Hayes 1982, cf. §1.2.2 below).

There are basically three lines of explanation: a) the superfoot theory, b) the degenerate foot theory, and c) the weak layering theory. In the superfoot theory, the prosodic hierarchy is enriched with a higher-level footlike constituent F' (cf. e.g. Prince 1980, Selkirk 1980, McCarthy 1982a). In this theory, every syllable in words such as *agree* and *Magie* or in trisyllabic words is dominated either by F or by F'. The degenerate foot theory, on the other hand, analyses light syllables outside of feet as prosodic constituents by themselves; they are seen as non-moraic feet. The superfoot theory and the degenerate foot theory thus try to maintain strictly layered representations.

Itô & Mester (1992), however, doubt that these theories can be independently motivated. They propose that a prosodic word may directly dominate a syllable, in other words, strict layering does not always hold, but rather constitutes a prosodic ideal. This is referred to as the weak layering theory. Selkirk (1996) proposes an optimality-theoretic implementation (cf. §1.4) of the weak layering theory. She argues that the Strict Layer Hypothesis should not be seen as a monolithic whole but rather as a set of constraints, each with an independent status in the grammar. She proposes four constraints on prosodic domination, cf. (8).

(8) *Constraints on Prosodic Domination*
(where C^n = some prosodic category)
i. *Layeredness* No C^i dominates a C^j, $j > i$,
e.g. "No σ dominates a F."
ii. *Headedness* Any C^i must dominate a C^{i-1} (except if $C^i = \sigma$),
e.g. "A PWd must dominate a F."
iii. *Exhaustivity* No C^i immediately dominates a constituent C^j, $j < i\text{-}1$,
e.g. "No PWd immediately dominates a σ."
iv. *Nonrecursivity* No C^i dominates C^j, $j = i$,
e.g. "No F dominates a F."

According to Selkirk (1996), *Layeredness* and *Headedness*, which together embody the essence of the Strict Layer Hypothesis, are universally inviolable. This means that they hold in all phonological representations in all languages. *Exhaustivity* and *Nonrecursivity*, on the other hand, turn out not to hold of all instances of phonological structure. This notion of violability can account for structures that contain syllables which are not dominated by a foot node.

In the remainder of this section, we will take a look at the syllable and the foot in English and German. In §1.4, I will present an optimality-theoretic approach to phonological foot assignment in German (that can also be transferred to English) by Knaus & Domahs (2009).

1.2.1 The Syllable

The syllable seems to be a quite natural and intuitive unit of language. Speakers of English and German can usually agree on the number of syllables of a word, regardless whether those speakers are children or adults, literate or illiterate. Illiterate speakers find it even easier and more natural to segment words into syllables than into single sounds (Wiese 2000: 33).

Evidence for the existence of a unit syllable can be drawn from structural linguistic patterns. Moulton (1962: 65), for example, notes that the sounds [ɪ] and [i̯] are complementarily distributed, i.e. that they are allophones of one phoneme. Their complementary distribution, however, is only describable with recurrence to the syllable. Wiese (2000: 34) gives the following examples from German for this observation, cf. (9).

(9) [daː.lɪ̯e] *Dahlie* 'dahlia' - [tal.ʝə] *Taille* 'waist'
[ʃpaː.nɪ̯ər] *Spanier* 'Spaniard' - [ʃam.pan.ʝər] *Champagner* 'champagne'
[liː.lɪ̯ə] *Lilie* 'lily' - [vaː.nɪl.ʝə] *Vanille* 'vanilla'

The allophone [ʝ] appears only in the initial position of the syllable, while [ɪ̯] cannot be found syllable-initially.

Another argument for the existence of the unit syllable can be drawn from phonotactics. The distribution of segments is constrained: in any language, the set of occurring sequences of segments is only a small fragment of all potential combinations of the members of a segment inventory. In order to account for restrictions on segment distribution, a constituent is posited that serves as a domain of phonotactics.

The sequence /tm/, for example, is not a possible segment cluster in German; there is no word that starts or ends with this sequence.[4] In words such as *atmen* '(to) breath' or *widmen* '(to) dedicate', however, this sequence is allowed since in both words, /t/ and /m/ are in different syllables. An explanation employing the morpheme, which is another domain for phonotactic regularities, cannot account for the occurrence of /tm/ in these cases (cf. Wiese 2000: 34).

Let us now turn to the structure of the syllable. Under minimal assumptions, the principal subparts of the syllable are the syllable peak and the two margins, which can be called onset and coda. The syllable peak contains the most sonorous segment, where sonority is an abstract property of a segment (Zec 2007).

The sonority of segments is commonly represented by means of a scale like (10), which corresponds to an ordering of segments ranging from those highest in sonority, i.e. vowels, to those lowest in sonority, i.e. stops. The scale in (10) is a slightly simplified version of the sonority scale in Zec (2007: 178) and valid for German and English (cf. Giegerich 1992, Wiese 2000). The upper-case letters denote groups of sounds, V(owels), L(iquids), N(asals) and O(bstruents).

(10) *Sonority scale*

V	low vowel
	mid vowels
	high vowels
L	rhotics
	laterals
N	nasals
O	fricatives
	stops

4 An exception to this phonotactical constraint is the greek loanword *Tmesis* 'tmesis'.

It has to be noted, however, that it is under debate whether sonority has a phonetic correlate or not. Although there are some findings from articulatory and acoustic phonetics (e.g. Dogil 1989, Clements 1990, Hume & Odden 1996; Price 1980, Pompino-Marshall 1995, Hurch & Maas 1998, Lavoie 2001), there is no phonetic model capable of providing a fully satisfying account of sonority (cf. Neef 2002). The sonority hierarchy should thus be regarded as a *phonological* construct derived from distributional properties.

The syllable peak is defined as the (sole) sonority peak of a syllable and represented as a structural position V. V does not necessarily dominate a vowel. In languages such as English and German, the V-slot can also be occupied by liquids and nasals. Non-peak positions are denoted by C and must not necessarily dominate a consonant; this is, for instance, the case in the representation of diphthongs, in which the second vowel of the diphthong is dominated by C (cf. Clements & Keyser 1983).

English and German are languages which allow complex syllable margins, that is, they allow syllable margins that comprise more than one C-position, cf. (11).

(11) *Syllable template for English and German p-syllables* (cf. Wiese 2000: 38, Giegerich 1992: 144, 149-150)

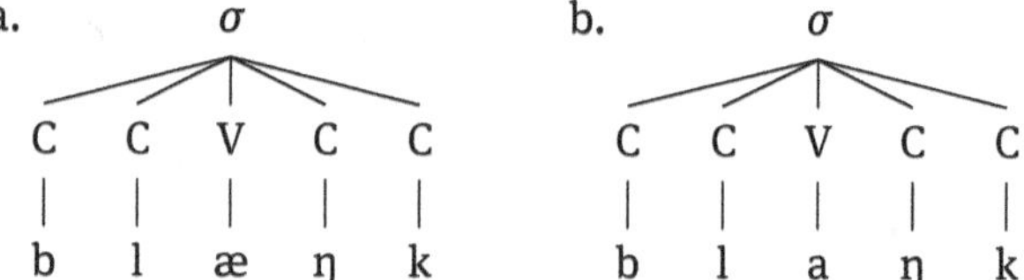

The sonority sequencing principle captures the relation of the structural positions of syllables to each other in terms of sonority.

(12) *Sonority Sequencing Principle* (SSP)
The preferred syllable is structured in a way such that consonantal strength decreases monotonously from the onset and the coda towards the nucleus. It reaches its minimum in the nucleus (Vennemann 1982: 283).

In Vennemann's formulation of SSP above, we can regard consonantal strength as the inversion of sonority. Another formulation of the SSP is based on Clements (1990): Between any member *x* of a syllable and the syllable peak *p*, only sounds of higher sonority rank than *x* are permitted.

A non-linear syllable model such as the CV-model can represent vowel opposition between long/ tense and short/ lax vowels in languages such as English and German by the association of long/ tense vowels with two structural positions while short/ lax vowels are associated with one structural position, cf. (13a) in which the vowel of the first syllable is dominated only by V, while in (13b) the vowel of the first syllable is dominated by V and C. Note that the structural representations of *filler* and *poker* in (13) hold for German and English.[5]

In English, some tense vowels are realised as diphthongs in many varieties, including Received Pronunciation and General American English (cf. Giegerich 1992: 44-47). A diphthong as in the received pronunciation of *poker* is analysed and represented as an underlying tense vowel, as shown in (13b). Tense vowels and diphthongs alternate, as in *line – linear, provoke – provocative* and *bathe – bath.* The phonetic correlate of the vowel contrast under discussion is a matter of debate and the terminology varies considerably (e.g., tense – lax, long – short, free – checked). Due to the structural property of tense vowels and diphthongs to occupy two structural positions, I will call them *binary* vowels. Lax vowels occupy one structural position and, hence, are *unary.*

In addition to the CV-tier, most phonologists assume that there is a richer structure with mediate constituents between the CV-tier and the σ-node. I will adopt a syllable structure model in which a syllable necessarily comprises a rhyme (Rh) which dominates a nucleus (Nu) that in turn dominates the V-position. Optional subsyllabic constituents are the onset (On) and the coda (Co), cf. the figures in (13).

(13) a. b.

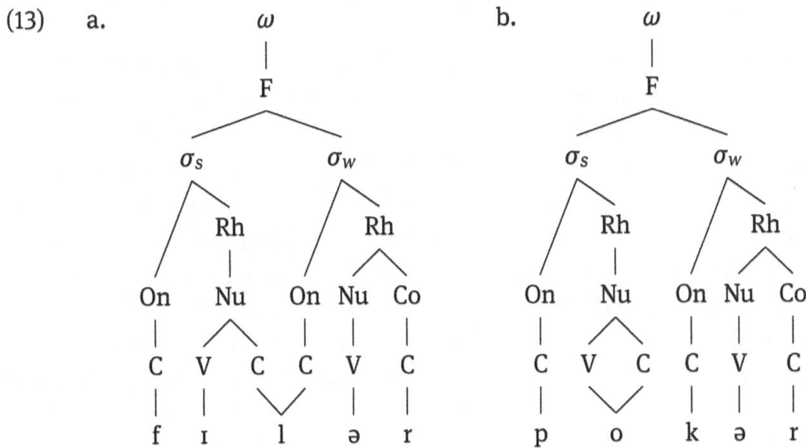

5 In Standard German, the last syllable of *Poker* and Filler is open and contains [ɐ]; in American English, both words end in [ɚ]. The illustrations in (13) are approximations.

A second vowel contrast (next to the contrast between unary and binary vowels) exists between full and reduced vowels in English and German. The first syllables in (13) each contain a full vowel, whereas the second syllables each contain a reduced one. Reduced syllables always have a non-branching nucleus.[6] Furthermore, reduced syllables are unstressable and skipped in stress rules (Wiese 2000: 280).

An important observation for English and German is that in both languages stressed syllables may never end in a unary vowel. A stressed syllable or even a monosyllabic word like */pɪ/ or */pɛ/ is ill-formed in English and German. This property of stressed syllables in English and German can be accounted for by a syllable structure constraint demanding that the nucleus of a stressed syllable is obligatory branching (cf. Becker 1996). According to Wiese (2000: 46-47) all full, stressed or unstressed, syllables have a branching nucleus that dominates V and C. A similar restriction is formulated by Giegerich (1992: 182) in terms of a branching rhyme.

Because of the nucleus constraint as sketched above, a unary vowel in a stressed syllable in English and German needs a closing consonant. This may lead to ambisyllabicity in English and German (Giegerich 1992: 170-172; Wiese 2000: 46-47; McMahon 2001: 111-112).

Let us have a brief look at ambisyllabicity. An ambisyllabic consonant is a consonantal segment that simultaneously belongs to the rhyme of one syllable and to the onset of the immediately following syllable. Early influential accounts promoting this concept include Kahn (1976) and Gussenhoven (1986) for English, and Vennemann (1982) for German. The concept of ambisyllabicity, however, is not undisputed (cf. Picard 1984, Goldsmith 1999).

Let us begin with a brief survey of the arguments for and against ambisyllabicity. Some of the earliest arguments for ambisyllabicity in the literature are drawn from the distribution of sounds, i.e. from allophony (e.g. Anderson & Jones 1974, Kahn 1976, Gussenhoven 1986). According to Kahn (1976), allophonic processes such as aspiration, glottalization, and tapping (reduction of alveolar stops to a tap) of word-medial stops in American English can be described in terms of syllable structure. According to Kahn (1976), [t^h] occurs only in syllable-initial position, glottalised [^ʔt] occurs only in syllable-final position, and tapped [ɾ] only occurs as ambisyllabic consonant. Anderson & Jones (1974) demonstrate with the help of the allophones of /t/ overlapping structure: "A medial sequence like [tr] in *petrol*

6 In one model of Wiese (among several other suggestions), reduced syllables do not have a nucleus at all (Wiese 2000: 108).

has 'syllable-initial and syllable-final characteristics'. In particular, the [r] is voiceless as in initial [tr] clusters, but there is also glottal reinforcement of the [t], as in final position" (Anderson & Jones 1974:8).

These arguments have been rejected by Kiparsky (1979), who analyses flapping as occurring foot-medially, while the other allophones occur at the margins of a foot. This analysis, however, is not incompatible with an ambisyllabicity-based approach, in fact, ambisyllabicity is tightly connected to the foot, as I will show below.

A more serious objection to ambisyllabicity is that it lacks consistent phonetic correlates (cf. Picard 1984). However, as Elzinga & Eddington (2013) point out, it can be seen as psychologically real. A number of psycholinguistic studies using methods such as the pause-break-task (Briere et al. 1968, Derwing 1992) in which participants are asked to say a word with a pause between the syllable (e.g. *lemon* – ***lem*** (pause) ***mon***), the syllable reversal task (Treiman & Danis 1988) in which participants are asked to switch the syllables in bisyllabic words (e.g. *lemon* – ***monlem***), or the syllable doubling task (Fallows 1981) in which participants double the first and last syllable of a bisyllabic word (e.g. *lemon* – ***lem****lemon*, *lemon****mon***), strongly advocate the existence of ambisyllabicity. Psycholinguistic studies also confirm the predictions of phonological theories on ambisyllabicity: ambisyllabic consonants occur preferably after unary vowels (cf. Derwing 1992, Treiman & Danis 1988, Treiman et al. 2002, Treiman & Zukowski 1990) and after stressed syllables Treiman & Danis 1988, Treiman & Zukowski 1990); for an overview in greater depth, cf. Elzinga & Eddington (2013).

The cause of ambisyllabicity can be described by the interaction of two constraints. I have sketched the first constraint above: nuclei of stressed syllables are obligatory branching. The second constraint is usually called *onset maximisation*, cf. e.g. the following syllable-boundary rule from Giegerich (1992: 170):

(14) Within words, syllable boundaries are placed in such a way that onsets are maximal (in accordance with the phonotactic constraints of a language).

In a word with a unary vowel in the first syllable and a single intervocalic consonant, such as *filler*, the nucleus constraint and the onset maximisation constraint are in conflict. A stressed syllable with unary vowel must be closed in order to be well-formed; thus the first syllable of *filler* should be [fɪl]. Onset maximisation, on the other hand, requires that the second syllable builds a maximal onset and thus should be [lər]. The conflict is solved by analysing /l/ as being part of both syllables simultaneously, cf. (13a).

Ambisyllabicity is thus related to foot structure since only stressed syllables, i.e. heads of feet, are subject to the nucleus constraint. I will discuss stress and phonological feet in the next section.

1.2.2 The Foot

The foot as a linguistic unit was introduced in metrical phonology. Based on the theory that the stress of syllables is the linguistic realisation of the rhythmic structure of language (e.g. Liberman 1975, Liberman & Prince 1977), feet are defined as constituents of this rhythmic structure.

The stress of a syllable (and in consequence the foot that dominates a sequence of syllables) in early metrical phonology like Liberman & Prince (1977) depends on the segmental feature [±stress] (Chomsky & Halle 1968). In Liberman & Prince's approach, an algorithm assigns the feature [+stress] to some vowels and builds up a structure called foot with a [+stress] vowel as head. The metrical structure serves to determine the relative degree of stress but it does not determine the assignment of stress itself.

According to McCarthy (1982b), the foot as a fully non-segmental respectively non-linear unit was introduced by Prince (1976). Prince argues that the foot is directly assigned to words. The terminal nodes of feet are syllables or morae in his conception.

Kiparsky (1979) and Selkirk (1980) propose that the foot is to be treated as an independent unit within a supra-segmental hierarchy and not as a mere result of foot assignment rules. The establishment of the foot as independent unit has several advantages. First, with the unit foot there is no need to rely on the feature [stress]. The foot structure suffices to determine vowel reduction in English.

Selkirk demonstrates this advantage with the words *modest* and *gymnast*. Both words have primary stress on the first syllable, but *gymnast* also has a secondary stress on the second syllable while the second syllable of *modest* is unstressed.

(15) *Vowel reduction in English* (Liberman & Prince 1977 vs. Selkirk 1980)

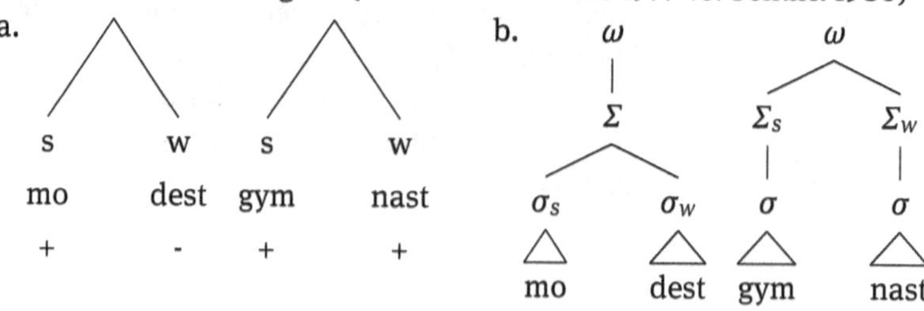

According to the approach of Liberman & Prince (1977) the first syllable of *modest* and *gymnast* is s(trong) and the second *w*(eak): The supra-segmental structure assigned to these words is therefore identical. In order to capture the secondary stress of *gymnast*, Liberman & Prince have to recur to the segmental feature [stress] as indicated by '+' and '-', in (15a).

Selkirk (15b) proposes that the prosodic categories *syllable* (*σ*), *stress foot* (*Σ*) and *prosodic word* (*ω*) play a fundamental role (Selkirk 1980: 565). The basic idea of her approach is that a syllable that is the only element of a foot cannot be interpreted as weak, i.e. stressless, even if the foot that dominates it is weak. In other words, heads of feet are never weak. The distinction between *-nast* in *gymnast* and *-dest* in *modest* is represented in terms of feet and thus supra-segmental and not segmental.

A second advantage is that the foot as independent unit is available as a domain for phonological rules (for example, glottal stop insertion in German, cf. Wiese 2000).

A third advantage is that the foot can be used for typological considerations. One of the most influential early accounts regarding the foot was that of Hayes (1981). Based on his work, several parameters which define prosodic systems are proposed in the literature. Among the most important parameters are the following:

(16)
a. *Foot type*
Feet are left-headed (trochee) vs. feet are right-headed (iamb).
b. *Direction*
Feet are built left-to-right vs. right-to-left.
c. *Quantity-sensivity*
Heavy syllables are heads of feet.
d. *Structural properties of heavy syllables*
closed rhyme vs. bimoraic syllable
e. *Extrametricality*
The rightmost syllable is not stressed.
f. *Word level labeling*
Head-feet are at the left vs. right margin of a word.

It is generally accepted that English and German have trochaic feet. Furthermore, it is uncontroversial that in both languages one of the last three syllables is stressed in monomorphemic polysyllabic words, and that stress is assigned from the right to the left (for English cf. e.g. Hayes 1982, Giegerich 1985, Trommelen & Zonneveld 1999: 149; for German cf. e.g. Jessen 1999, Janßen 2003).

Most phonologists assume that English is a weight-sensitive language (e.g. Chomsky & Halle 1968, Liberman & Prince 1977, Giegerich 1985, 1992, Hayes 1982, Kager 1989, Trommelen & Zonneveld 1999). Most of these accounts state that the stress position primarily depends on the structure of the penultimate syllable. If the penult is heavy (i.e. the rhyme of the syllable is either closed or open with a binary vowel), the penult is stressed; otherwise the antepenult receives main stress. The last syllable is regarded as extrametrical in these approaches.

This rule, however, does not capture cases in which the final syllable is stressed, e.g. *kangaˈroo, refuˈgee, lemoˈnade*. Thus, words with binary vowels in the rightmost syllables are exceptions to extrametricality. Hayes (1982) therefore formulates a rule that states that final syllables containing binary vowels form monosyllabic feet and receive primary (e.g. *ˌHalloˈween*) or secondary (e.g. *ˈmisanˌthrope*) stress. In contrast, final syllables containing short vowels are analysed as being extrametrical (cf. Domahs et al. 2014).

Whether German is quantity-sensitive or not is under debate. Eisenberg (1991), Kaltenbacher (1994), and Wiese (2000), for example, argue that syllable weight is irrelevant for the assignment of stress or foot structure in German. Wiese (2000: 282), for instance, formulates a foot rule according to which bisyllabic trochees are assigned from right to left. The last foot of a word is strong, which results in penultimate stress (e.g. *Biˈkini* 'bikini'). Deviations from this rule are explained by lexical specifications (such as lexically specified final stress as in *Samuˈrai* 'samurai').

In contrast, many researchers assume that syllable weight is decisive for German stress assignment (e.g. Wurzel 1970, 1980, Giegerich 1985, Vennemann 1990, Féry 1986, 1998, Ramers 1992). Janßen (2003) proposes that syllable weight influences foot structure assignment. In her approach, syllable weight is thus not directly linked to stress but mediated through foot structure. Experimental and neurolinguistic data support this assumption (e.g. Janßen 2003, Domahs et al. 2008, Röttger et al. 2012, Domahs et al., 2014).

In approaches towards English stress and foot assignment, syllable weight is usually defined in terms of morae, i.e. every structural position in the rhyme corresponds to one mora. Thus, syllables ending in a binary vowel and syllables ending in a unary vowel followed by one consonant are equally heavy. Syllables comprising more than two morae are usually called super-heavy.

In German, on the other hand, there are several definitions of heavy syllables. Féry (1998) states that only syllables that would be seen as super-heavy in English count as heavy in German. In Vennemann's theory (1990, 1991, 1995) every closed syllable and every syllable containing a diphthong is heavy, while every open syllable is light. Thus, a syllable such as /pat/ is light in Féry's but heavy in

Vennemannn's approach. Experimental and neurolinguistic studies (Janßen 2003, Knaus & Domahs 2009, Röttger et al. 2012, Domahs et al. 2014) support Vennemann's definition (1990, 1991, 1995) of syllable weight in German.

Especially interesting with respect to the question whether German is quantity-sensitive or not is a recent study of Domahs et al. (2014), which compares the word stress systems of English, German, and Dutch[7] with data from a pseudoword production experiment and lexical data retrieved from the CELEX database (Baayen et al. 1995). The authors found compelling evidence that German and English are quantity-sensitive languages; to be more specific, the structures of the penultimate and ultimate syllable are decisive for foot assignment in trisyllabic monomorphemic words, cf. (17).

(17)
i. Heavy and superheavy final syllables build monosyllabic feet that allow trisyllabic words to consist of two feet; main stress may fall on the ultimate or antepenultima syllable.
ii. If the penultimate syllable is heavy or the ultimate syllable is light, the penult builds a foot with the following ult, which results in a structure consisting of one foot.

The structures in (18) illustrate the prosodic structure of a trisyllabic word with one foot. We may call these structures *1-foot structures.*

(18)

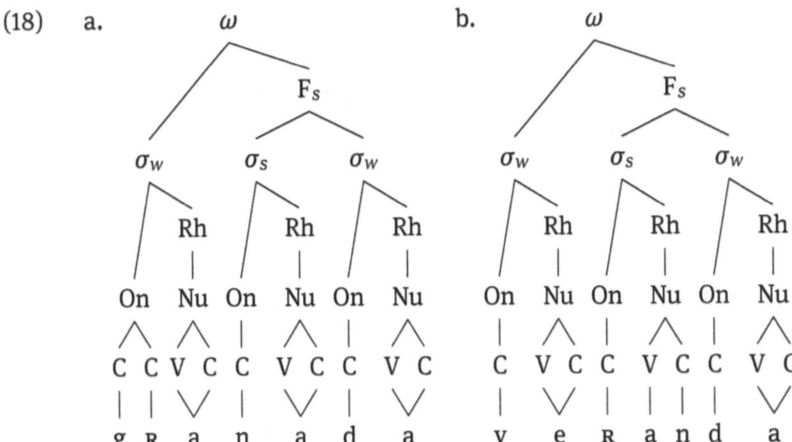

The structures in (19) are examples of 2-foot structures. In 2-foot structures, all syllables are parsed into feet and the last syllable constitutes a monosyllabic foot.

7 I will omit the results for Dutch; the results for Dutch, however, are very similar to those for German and English.

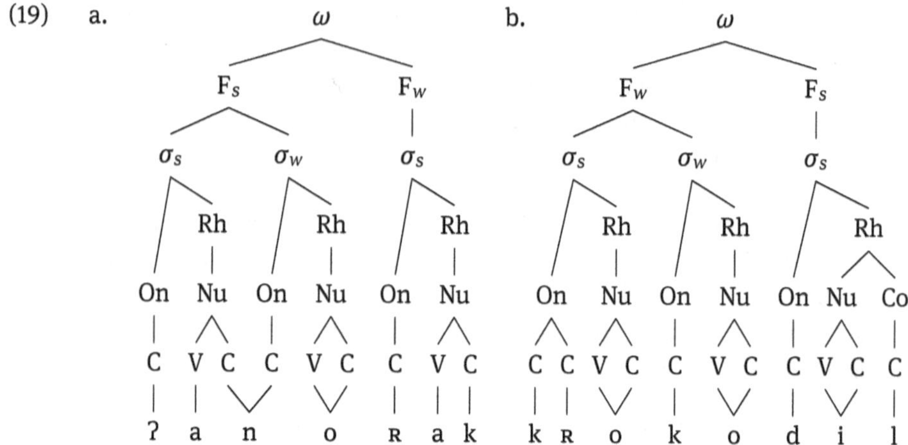

Domahs et al. (2014) did not find evidence for the assumption that final syllables are extrametrical in German or English on foot level; however, they found evidence that the last syllable in English is least likely to receive main stress, which can be seen as evidence for extrametricality on word level.

Table 1.2 summarises the main findings of Domahs et al. (2014) regarding metrical parameters of foot assignment in German and English.

Tab. 1.2: Metrical parameters of foot assignment in German and English (cf. Domahs et al., 2014)

Parameters	German	English
Foot type	trochee	trochee
Direction	right-to-left	right-to-left
Quantity-sensitive	yes	yes
Structural properties of heavy syllables	closed rhyme	bimoraic syllable
Extrametricality	no	yes (word-level)
Word level labeling	head right	head right

Both languages prefer trochees that are aligned with the right edge of a word. Among the bisyllabic trochees is the one that ends in a reduced syllable (that is a syllable with schwa or syllabic sonorant consonant as syllable peak (in English there are also reduced syllables with /ɪ/ as peak of reduced syllables)) the preferred or *canonical* foot. Because of the right-to-left-direction in both languages, canonical structures end in a bisyllabic trochee with reduced syllable; Evertz & Primus (2013: 4) summarise:

(20) The canonical foot in German and English is a trochee. If it is bisyllabic, it ends in a reduced syllable. The canonical phonological word in German and English ends in a trochee with a reduced syllable.

1.3 The Graphematic Hierarchy

With a category like the graphematic foot, it is possible to construct a complete graphematic counterpart to a phonological hierarchy (cf. §1.2), the *graphematic hierarchy*, cf. (21).

(21)

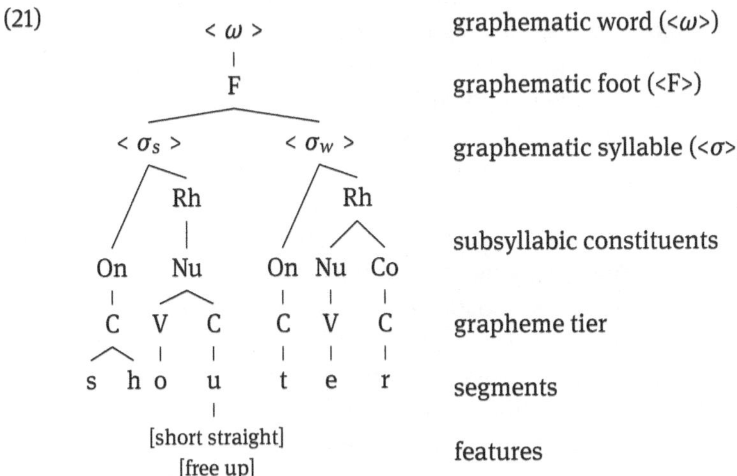

The graphematic hierarchy in this form was proposed first by Primus (2010) for German and by Evertz & Primus (2013) for English and German. I will adopt their terminology henceforth. The names of some graphematic units in (21) are the same as the names of the phonological units they correspond to. In order to avoid confusion, I will use “g” as a prefix referring to a graphematic unit and “p” as a prefix for a phonological element in case of doubt.

Let us have a brief overview of the units within the graphematic hierarchy. The graphematic word is the highest unit we will discuss (for a discussion whether clauses or other elements bordered by commas correspond to intonational phrases, cf. Kirchhoff (2016)).

There is no debate that the graphematic word is relevant and a real unit. The simplest definition is that a g-word is a continuous sequence of letters bordered by spaces. This definition suffices for our purpose; for a discussion of definitions of the graphematic word, cf. Evertz (2016). The correspondent of the graphematic word in spoken language, however, is not entirely clear. For German, the most likely candidates are the syntactic and the morphological word (Fuhrhop 2008, Bredel 2009), but not the phonological word. The compound *Tier+art* 'animal species', for instance, is realised as one graphematic word, <Tierart>. The presence of a glottal stop in [ˈtiːɐ̯.ʔaːɐ̯t] suggests, however, that the word actually comprises two phonological words.

The correspondent of English graphematic words is harder to determine since there is, especially in the spelling of compounds, a considerable degree of variation; for example, there are three parallel spellings for compounds, e.g. <secondhand>, <second hand>, and <second-hand>. The choice of spelling seems often to be a matter of taste, although the use of hyphens or the choice to write a compound as one graphematic word serves disambiguation, cf. *old furniture dealer* vs. *old-furniture dealer*. This may suggest that the graphematic word in English corresponds to morphological and syntactical words as well.

We will see, however, that the graphematic word has some properties that can be derived from the graphematic hierarchy, that is, it comprises at least one graphematic foot (cf. §4.3.2).

The next lower unit, the graphematic foot, is a sequence of at least one graphematic syllable. Exactly one g-syllable of this sequence is the head of the g-foot. Heads of feet are the most salient constituents of their units. The head of a p-foot is the stressed syllable, also called *strong* syllable. Other constituents of the foot are unstressed and called *weak*. I will employ this notion also for g-feet.

It is fair to say that the graphematic foot has been neglected in written language research (but cf. Primus 2010, Evertz & Primus 2013, Fuhrhop & Peters 2013, Evertz 2016). It is the primary aim of this dissertation to provide structural, distributional and experimental evidence for the independent existence and the internal structure of the graphematic foot. I will provide an analysis of graphematic foot assignment and mapping relations to the phonological correspondents of graphematic feet in the framework of unidirectional and bidirectional Optimality Theory (cf. §1.4 and §4.4.3.1). Chapter 4 is devoted to the analysis of the graphematic foot.

Graphematic syllables have been subject to previous research (cf. e.g. Butt & Eisenberg 1990, Roubah & Taft 2001, Domahs et al. 2001, Primus 2003, Rollings 2004, Weingarten 2004, Eisenberg 2006). As the structure in (21) shows, I assume that the graphematic syllable comprises constitutes that mediate between the syllable node and the grapheme tier. These constitutes include the (on)set, the (rh)yme, the (nu)cleus, and the (co)da. I will discuss those aspects of the structure of graphematic syllables that are relevant for the analysis of graphematic foot structure in chapter 3.

The next tiers in the graphematic hierarchy contain graphemes and letters. The existence of these units is uncontroversial in written language research. Letters can be defined as the segmental symbols of a phonemic writing system that may form strings of (in principle) any length. The inventory of those symbols is called alphabet (Günther 1988: 67, Rogers 2005: 14). In accordance with recent literature on letter decomposition (cf. Primus 2004, 2006, Fuhrhop & Buchmann 2009, Fuhrhop et al. 2011, Fuhrhop & Buchmann 2016, Berg et al. 2016), I will argue that letters are not holistic units but internally structured. Letters can be described by letter features as indicated in (21). The grapheme is the smallest supra-segmental unit in the graphematic hierarchy proposed in this work (cf. Berg et al., 2016). Letters, letter features and graphemes will be discussed in chapter 2.

In supra-segmental phonology, the phonological hierarchy is accompanied by the *Strict Layer Hypothesis* (cf. (7)). This hypothesis states in its strong form that each unit of a non-terminal category is composed of one or more units of the immediately lower category. The second part of the Strict layer hypothesis states that a unit of a given level of the hierarchy is exhaustively contained in the superordinate unit of which it is part (Nespor & Vogel 1986).

I assume that this hypothesis also holds in graphematics, although I advocate an interpretation of the Strict Layer Hypothesis that allows the first principle to be violated. In §1.2, I discussed the reason why this principle is deemed to be violable in phonology: it allows for a simple treatment of extrametrical syllables.

As for the second principle, one of the reasons why Nespor & Vogel (1986: 13) do not include the segment as lowest unit in the graphematic hierarchy is that segments may be ambisyllabic. Ambisyllabic segments, however, are not properly bracketed, that is, ambisyllabic segments have more than one mother node in a tree diagram and thus do not conform to the second principle of the Strict Layer Hypothesis. The situation in graphematics is different. According to Primus (2003: 34) there are no ambisyllabic elements in the writing system of German (cf. §4.1). I will show in chapter 4 that this is also the case for the writing system of English. This means that there is no reason (at least not in the English and German writing system) to exclude the segment from the graphematic hierarchy.

In accordance with the Strict Layer Hypothesis as sketched here, we may assume that the graphematic word, the graphematic foot, the graphematic syllable, the grapheme, and the letter are proper categories of the graphematic hierarchy.

1.4 Optimality Theory

Optimality Theory (OT) was introduced in the early nineties (Prince & Smolensky 1993, McCarthy & Prince 1993a,b) and was originally employed in phonology, where it became one of the predominant frameworks. Its scope of application did not remain limited to phonology; OT was also applied in morphology (e.g. McCarthy & Prince 1995), syntax (e.g. Legendre et al. 2001), semantics (e.g. Hendricks & de Hoop 2001) and graphematics (Geilfuß-Wolfgang 2007, Primus 2004, Wiese 2004, Song & Wiese 2010, Baroni 2013).

By now there are many variants of OT. In this section I will introduce a variant of OT, which can be called the "Standard Variant."

There are two fundamental properties of OT which differentiates it from rule-based, derivational frameworks. First, in OT there are no rules, but universal and violable *constraints*. Second, the grammatical output is not generated by rule-ordering but by *constraint interaction*. This entails that OT is not a derivational but a declarative framework. Derivational frameworks like generative phonology (e.g. Chomsky & Halle 1968) assume that there is an underlying abstract representation which is affected by rules. These rules apply in a specific order. Every application of a rule generates an intermediate output. These intermediate outputs constitute levels between the underlying representation and the eventual output. OT, on the other hand, has one input and one output but no intermediate levels of representation. A potential output, i.e. a candidate, is evaluated by its performance with respect to all relevant constraints at the same time, and in comparison to all competing candidates.

There are basically two kinds of constraints, *faithfulness constraints* demanding that the input of an evaluation is identical to its output and vice versa and *wellformedness/ markedness constraints* demanding that the output is unmarked (e.g. 'syllables must not have codas'). These kinds of constraints are generally in conflict with each other. Constraints are generally violable; this means that the violation of one constraint does not necessarily result in ungrammaticality. However, although constraints are violable, violation must be minimal (cf. Kager 1999: 12).

There are constraints whose violation is more costly than the violation of other constraints. In other words, there is a hierarchy or *ranking* of constraints. Constraints are universal, this means that every constraint is part of the grammar of every language. Languages differ in the ranking of the constraints, not in the set of the constraints.

The OT model assumes that a part of the grammar, the component called *Generator*, generates an infinite set of candidates related to an input, which can be retrieved from the *Lexicon* or by perception. Another part of the grammar, the

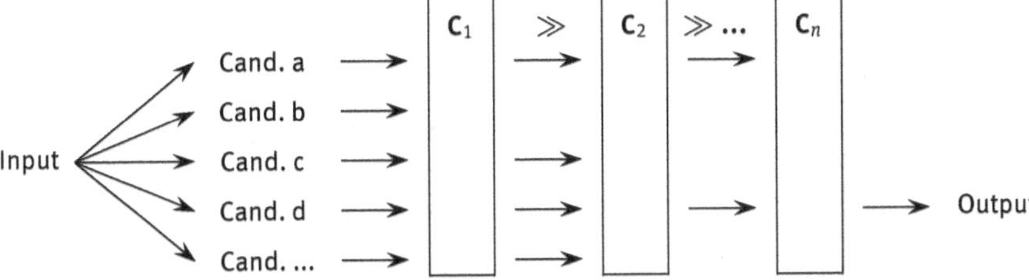

Fig. 1.1: Mapping of input to output in OT grammar (Kager 1999: 8)

component called *Evaluator*, evaluates this set and selects the optimal candidate, which is the actual output (Kager 1999: 8). The actual output incurs less serious violations of the set of relevant constraints in comparison to other candidates. OT grammar thus consists of three components:

(22) *Components of the OT grammar* (Kager 1999: 19)
LEXICON: contains lexical representations (or underlying forms) of morphemes, which form the input to:
GENERATOR: generates output candidates for some input, and submits these to:
EVALUATOR: the set of ranked constraints, which evaluates output candidates as to their harmonic values, and selects the optimal candidate.

These components work as an input-output mechanism as illustrated by the functional notation in (23).

(23) *The grammar as an input-output mechanism* (McCarthy & Prince 1993b: 5)
***Gen*(input)** $\Rightarrow$ {cand_1, cand_2 ... cand_n}
Eval {cand_1, cand_2 ... cand_n} $\Rightarrow$ **output**

The Evaluator reduces the set of candidates step by step. It checks whether the set of candidates conforms to the highest ranked constraint and sorts those out which do not. The surviving candidates are evaluated with respect to the next constraint and so on. The mapping of the input to the output in OT grammar is illustrated in figure 1.1.

Importantly, the Evaluator does not look ahead: the elimination of one candidate by a constraint C_n is not affected by a lower-ranked constraints C_{n+m}. This property is called *strict domination* (e.g. Kager 1999: 22):

(24) **Strict domination:** violation of higher-ranked constraints cannot be compensated for by satisfaction of lower-ranked constraints.

The evaluation of the set of candidates is usually displayed in a tableau. The ordering of the constraints in the header line indicates their ranking, the highest ranked constraint is leftmost, constraints ranking lower are further right. Constraints separated by solid lines differ in their ranking, constraints separated by dashed lines are of equal rank or their rank differences are irrelevant for the current evaluation.

The tableau in tab. 1.3 illustrates an evaluation of two candidates with respect to four relevant constraints. These constraints are ranked in a specific order: C_1 dominates C_2, which in turn dominates C_3 and C_4. Domination is a transitive relation, thus C_1 also dominates C_3 and C_4. C_3 and C_4 do not dominate each other. This ranking is illustrated in (25).

(25) $C_1 \gg C_2 \gg C_3, C_4$

Tab. 1.3: Example of an OT-Tableau

input	C_1	C_2	C_3	C_4
☞ a. candidate a		*	*	*
b. candidate b	*!			

The optimal candidate is indicated by '☞'. Candidate a. is more harmonic than candidate b. although a. violates more constraints than b. Candidate b. violates the highest ranked constraint C_1 while a. does not. At this point candidate b. is filtered out. This fatal violation is indicated by '!'. The performance of the candidate regarding constraints C_2, C_3 and C_4 is irrelevant for the evaluation. Candidate a. is optimal since there are no candidates available performing better than candidate a. The evaluation illustrated in tableau 1.3 is thus a good example of the strict domination principle.

It has to be noted, however, that tableaux serve illustrative purposes and therefore tend to simplify things; this includes:

- The set of candidates is reduced to the most plausible ones, leaving the fact aside that there is an (in principle) infinite set of candidates including ∅.
- The set of constraints is reduced to the most relevant ones.
- The input and candidate set is traditionally presented linearly, although non-linear properties of the candidates are also evaluated.

1.4.1 An OT account of Phonological Feet

In this section, I will demonstrate how OT-analyses work with the help of the analysis of foot assignment in German by Knaus & Domahs (2009).

We begin with the definition of the relative constraints. Let us return to the discussion of the properties of phonological feet in German and English, cf. §1.2.2. The metrical parameters of foot assignment (cf. table 1.2) are the basis for constraints in phonological analyses of foot assignment in German and English.

The first metrical parameter, *foot type*, is usually expressed by a constraint called RHYTHMTYPE=TROCHEE or simply TROCHEE, which states that feet are head-initial (e.g. Prince & Smolensky 1993), and by the constraint FOOT-BINARITY, which states that feet are binary at the moraic or syllabic level of analysis (e.g. Prince & Smolensky 1993). These constraints are either undominated or highly ranked (for German cf. Alber 1997, Féry 1998, Knaus & Domahs 2009; for English cf. Pater 2000).

The parameter *direction* is expressed by certain rankings of alignment constraints. Alignment constraints as proposed by (McCarthy & Prince 1993) demand that one unit is aligned with another unit. In the literature, we can find the constraints ALIGN-FOOT-RIGHT and ALIGN-FOOT-LEFT, which demand that every phonological word ends (ALIGN-FOOT-RIGHT) or begins (ALIGN-FOOT-LEFT) with a foot. The direction right-to-left is established by ranking (ALIGN-FOOT-RIGHT) higher than ALIGN-FOOT-LEFT (cf. Féry 1998 for German, Hammond 1999 for English). A similar result can be archived by employing the constraints ALLFT-LEFT (McCarthy & Prince 1993a) and RIGHTMOST (Prince & Smolensky 1993). The former states that every foot stands in initial position of the prosodic word and the latter states that the right edge of the head-foot coincides with the right edge of the prosodic word. ALLFT-LEFT is a gradient alignment constraint and assesses one constraint violation for every prosodic constituent intervening between the relevant foot edge and the relevant word edge. In order to establish the direction right-to-left, RIGHTMOST dominates ALLFT-LEFT (cf. Knaus & Domahs 2009 for German).

Quantity sensitivity is accounted for by the constraint WSP (Weight-to-Stress Principle, Prince 1990). This constraint requires heavy syllables to be stressed (Prince & Smolensky 1993). In most OT-approaches, this constraint is dominated by the aforementioned ones (cf. Pater 2000 for English, Alber 1997 for German).

The parameter *extrametricality* is expressed by the constraint NONFINALITY, which states that the final syllable is not footed (Prince & Smolensky 1993). This constraint is rather highly ranked in analyses of English (e.g. Hammond 1999) but either very low-ranking or completely ignored in analyses of German word stress (e.g. Alber 1997, Féry 1998).

Additionally to the constraints corresponding to the metrical parameters, the constraint PARSE-σ, which motivates the footing of syllables, is assumed as well. Furthermore, the tendency that adjacent stressed syllables are avoided (cf. Liberman & Prince 1977) is expressed by *CLASH. While grammatical words often display unfooted syllables, *CLASH is rarely violated by grammatical words. This is reflected by a relatively high ranking of *CLASH and a relatively low ranking of PARSE-σ.

The list in (26) gives an overview of the constraints mentioned so far.

(26)
a. TROCHEE: Feet are head-initial (Prince & Smolensky 1993).
b. FOOT-BINARITY: Feet are binary at a syllabic or moraic level of analysis (Prince & Smolensky 1993).
c. ALING-FOOT-RIGHT (ALIGN PRWD, R; FT, R): Every Prosodic Word ends with a foot (McCarthy and Prince 1993).
d. ALING-FOOT-LEFT (ALIGN PRWD, L; FT, L): Every Prosodic Word begins with a foot (McCarthy and Prince 1993).
e. ALLFT-LEFT (ALIGN FT, L; PRWD, L): Every foot stands in initial position in the prosodic word (McCarthy & Prince 1993a).
f. RIGHTMOST (ALING HEAD-FT, R; PRWD, R): The right edge of the head-foot coincides with the right edge of the prosodic word (Prince and Smolensky 1993).
g. WSP (Weight-to-Stress Principle): A heavy syllable is stressed (Prince and Smolensky 1993).
h. NONFINALITY: The final syllable is not footed (Prince & Smolensky 1993).
i. PARSE-σ: Syllables are parsed into feet (Prince & Smolensky 1993).

Consider the following tableaux, which exemplify the footing of the words mentioned in §1.2.2; the first tableau exemplifies the case of a trisyllabic word consisting of light syllables only (Knaus & Domahs 2009: 1400). Note that tableau 1.4 does not list all candidates Knaus & Domahs (2009: 1400) analyse. The candidates presented here shall just give an impression.

Let us briefly discuss the violations the candidates incur in order of the constraints. Candidate e. incurs one violation of TROCHEE since the head is not initial in the first foot (feet are indicated by round brackets, 'ˈ' indicates the main stress of a word).

Two candidates violate *CLASH: in candidate c. there is a secondary stress adjacent to the main stress, in candidate d. all syllable are stressed and thus all stressed syllables are adjacent. Candidate c. therefore incurs one and candidate

Tab. 1.4: cf. Knaus & Domahs (2009: 1400)

/L.L.L/	TROCH.	*CLASH	FOOT-BIN.	RIGHTMOST	PARSE-σ	ALLFT-L
a. (ˈL.L)L				*!	*	
☞ b. L.(ˈL.L)					*	*
c. (ˈL).(L.L)		*!	*	**		*
d. (ˈL).(L).(L)		*!*	***	**		***
e. (L.ˈL).L	*!			*	*	

d. two violations of *CLASH. These two candidates also incur violations of FOOT-BINARITY since in these candidates are feet that are made up of one light syllable only.

All candidates – except for candidate b. – violate RIGHTMOST because only candidate b. has the foot bearing the main stress aligned with the right edge of phonological word. For candidate a., this is a fatal violation.

Candidates a., b., and e. have an unparsed syllable and thus violate PARSE-σ. Finally, candidates b., c., and d. violate ALLFT-LEFT. Candidates b. incurs one violation of that constraint because one syllable intervenes between the only foot in this word and the left word edge. Candidate c. incurs one violation since there is one foot between the second foot and the left word edge. And candidate c. incurs three violations because the first foot intervenes between the second foot and the left word edge and the first and the second foot intervene between the third foot and the left word edge.

Candidate b. is the winner of the evaluation because – compared with the other candidates – candidate b. performs best with respect to the constraint hierarchy.

The analysis presented here is valid for German words like *Bikini, Kasino* and *Mikado* but also for their English cognates. This analysis is consistent with the results of Domahs et al. (2013) presented in §1.2.2: in words with a light ultimate syllable a 1-foot structure is built, stress lies on the penultimate syllable.

Let us turn to the analysis of a word that leads to a two-foot structure according to Domahs et al. (2013): in a trisyllabic word with a heavy ultimate syllable a final monosyllabic foot and a initial bisyllabic trochee is built, stress may fall on the ultimate or antepenultimate syllable.

The violations of candidates a., c., and e. are not very different from the violations of candidates a., c., and e. in tableau 1.4. With a heavy ultimate syllable, candidate e. violates FOOT-BIN only twice and not thrice like candidate e. with a final light syllable in tableau 1.4. More interesting are candidates b., c., and f.

Tab. 1.5: cf. Knaus & Domahs (2009: 1402)

/L.L.H/	TROCH.	*CLASH	FOOT-BIN.	RIGHTMOST	PARSE-σ	ALLFT-L
a. (ˈL.L).H				*!	*	
b. L.(ˈL.H)					*!	*
c. (ˈL).(L.H)		*!	*	**		*
☞ d. (L. L).(ˈH)						**
e. (ˈL).(L).(H)		*!*	**	**		***
f. L. L.(ˈH)					*!*	**

Candidate f. has a final monosyllabic foot and two unparsed syllables. It thus violates PARSE-σ twice; Candidate b. has a final bisyllabic foot with a heavy syllable in weak position. Since its first syllable is not parsed, it violates PARSE-σ once. Candidate d., on the other hand, parses all syllables into feet: the two light syllables built up an initial trochee and the heavy syllable constitutes a monosyllabic foot. This candidate thus does not incur any violation of PARSE-σ and only two violations of the lower ranked constraint ALLFT-L, which are not relevant in this evaluation. Candidate d. is thus the winner of the evaluation.

Interestingly, the OT-analysis of Knaus & Domahs (2009), as presented here, can do without a constraint employing the weight-to-stress principle as constraint; an introduction of the constraint WSP into the evaluation would not change the results of the evaluations. In their analysis, weight influences the foot structure assignment only via FOOT-BINARITY: heavy syllables can constitute monosyllabic feet.

1.4.2 Applying OT to Graphematics

The analysis of the graphematic foot (and the graphematic syllable) is couched within a declarative framework. In that it is similar to the framework employed by Evertz & Primus (2013). For this reason, all generalisations throughout this work should be understood in terms of constraints, even if not explicitly stated so. In comparison with Evertz & Primus (2013), this work will take one step further by implementing generalisations about graphematic feet and syllables into a formal Optimality Theory account. In this section, I will describe why and how OT is employed in this work.

The research of writing systems seems to be predestined for optimality theoretical approaches as Wiese (2004: 305) points out:

> In theoretically oriented research, writing systems [...] and orthographies [...] are often supposed to follow general preferences, though exceptions to these obviously exist, and the principles are often in conflict with each other[...]. Furthermore, there is often an obvious functional motivation for these rules/ preferences.

Wiese shows with this observation that researchers in the field of graphematics are aware that they rather describe conflicting constraints than strict rules even without explicitly employing optimality theoretic models. He summarises the parallels between previous works on preferences in writing systems and the fundamental assumptions in OT as follows (cf. Wiese 2004: 326):

1. Graphematic principles are often in conflict.
2. Such conflicts between principles are what OT is about.
3. Correspondences between levels or components are expressed naturally.
4. There is no commitment to a derivational or autonomous treatment.
5. Applying OT to writing systems allows for seamless integration with current theoretical work in phonology and morphology.

I have already argued for a non-derivational but declarative analysis of writing systems in §1.1, OT is the fitting formal framework for such an analysis. Moreover, since OT can account for differences between languages by reranking the same set of constraints and not by formulating different sets language-specific constraints, OT seems to be an elegant framework for comparing languages.

We will consider two kinds of constraints: 1) graphematic well-formedness constraints and 2) mapping constraints. Graphematic well-formedness constraints in this work pertain to graphematic syllable and foot structure. In analyses where, for instance, the assignment of graphematic foot structure is considered, these constraints apply to graphematic candidates relative to a graphematic input. In analyses in which mapping is considered, the input and the output is dependent on the relative perspective. In a coding direction, the input is a phonological form and the output is a graphematic form; in the decoding direction, a graphematic input maps onto a phonological output.

Mapping constraints may cause problems for an OT analysis. OT states that constraints are universal, i.e. they are present in all languages. Languages differ solely in their ranking of these constraints. The mapping between phonemes and graphemes, however, seems to be language specific. In the (relatively scarce) literature on graphematics within an OT-framework, we can find two ways in which this problem is dealt with. Baroni (2013) formulates bidirectional grapheme-phoneme mapping constraints and states that these are language specific. Wiese (2004) also states that mapping relations between graphemes and phonemes are language specific, but he does not implement them as constraints. Wiese (2004:

312) claims that regular grapheme-phoneme correspondences are part of "the structural description of a specific language, just as the set of phonemes, the set of morphemes (sound-meaning correspondences), etc." Wiese therefore takes the phoneme-grapheme correspondences for granted in his analyses. Irregular correspondences (e.g., *enough*) are explained by lexical specifications provided in the input.

I will follow Wiese's approach for two reasons: 1) his model is more consistent with the basic assumptions of OT and 2) the specific grapheme-phoneme correspondences are of little interest in this work, which is dedicated to supra-segmental graphematics: interesting for this work is, for instance, that <a> in English corresponds to a unary phonological vowel in a closed and strong graphematic syllable and to a binary phonological vowel in an open and strong graphematic syllable; to which vowel specifically, however, is not of interest. I suppose that these *structural* mapping constraints are indeed universal in alphabetic writing systems.[8]

1.5 Outline of this Work

As sketched in §1.3, the outline of this work parallels the graphematic hierarchy (as proposed in the same section).

We will work our way up starting from the bottom of the hierarchy with the discussion of letter features, letters, and graphemes in chapter 2.

Having established the lowest levels of the graphematic hierarchy, we will move on with the graphematic syllable in chapter 3. We will continue the discussion started in chapter 2 and explore which functions graphemes serve as lowest supra-segmental units within a graphematic hierarchy and thus within a syllable. We will also continue the discussion about letter features started in chapter 2 and employ them in order to categorise letters into classes relevant for syllable structure. We will move on with a discussion of subsyllabic constituents, especially the graphematic syllable nucleus. In §3.2.2, I will give a first OT-analysis of vowel quantity mapping that will be resumed in the following chapter.

Chapter 4 is the main part of this work. It is dedicated to the graphematic foot. In the first part of this chapter, I will discuss the two types that can be differentiated in graphematic feet, the canonical and the non-canonical foot (§4.1 and §4.2).

8 For languages that do not exhibit the relevant structural distinction (e.g. unary vs. binary), the constraints apply vacuously. To put it differently, these constraints are still present in the set of constraints but they are simply not relevant.

After that I will present experimental evidence and lexical evidence retrieved from the CELEX database (Baayen et al. 1995) for a theory of graphematic weight (§4.3). With this theory it is possible to offer a formal analysis of the foot. I will give a unidirectional and a bidirectional OT-account of the foot in §4.4.

Chapter 5 concludes this work and addresses some remaining issues and compares briefly the graphematic foot in German and in English.

This work comprises three appendices, two appendices comprise a list of the OT-constraints used in analyses in this work (appendix A) and a list of the experimental items of the study in §4.3.1.3 (appendix B). The third appendix comprises the search results of the various CELEX database studies throughout this word.

2 Features, Letters and Graphemes

The writing systems of English and German use largely the same set of characters. The majority of the character inventories of these writing systems is provided by the Modern Roman Alphabet (MRA), which can be modified by diacritics, such as the acute or umlaut marks. Hindu-arabic digits, punctuation marks and – in the case of German – the language-specific character <ß> are also part of the inventory of the writing systems. Digits and punctuation marks differ from MRA-characters and <ß> in their function: While letters correspond to sounds (or rather phonemes), digits are semasiographic units, and punctuation marks generally cannot be verbalised but mark syntactic structures (cf. Bredel 2008). As we will see in the sections below, these classes differ, not only in their function, but also in their form, i.e. in their features, and their distribution.

(1) Characters of the Modern Roman Alphabet

a. Majuscules:
A, B, C, D, E, F, G, H, I, J, K, L, M, N, O, P, Q, R, S, T, U, V, W, X, Y, Z

b. Minuscules:
a, b, c, d, e, f, g, h, i, j, k, l, m, n, o, p, q, r, s, t, u, v, w, x, y, z

Additionally to the character listed in (1), the German writing system comprises the following characters:

(2) Additional characters of the German writing system

a. Majuscules: Ä, Ö, Ü

b. Minuscules: ä, ö, ü, ß

The characters of the German and English writing system which correspond to phonemes are called letters. Letters can form strings of (in principle) any length. The set of letters is called alphabet (Günther 1988: 67, Rogers 2005: 14). Traditionally, they are regarded as the smallest units of the English and German writing system. We will see in the following sections, however, that letters are complex units, which can be decomposed into smaller segments.

2.1 Letter Features

Several works (Primus 2004, 2006, Fuhrhop & Buchmann 2009; Fuhrhop, Buchmann & Berg 2011) show that the letters of the MRA are not holistic units. They can be decomposed into smaller segments, which carry features. The idea to split

https://doi.org/10.1515/9783110583441-002

letters of the MRA into segments is not new: Eden & Halle (1961), Althaus (1980), Scharnhorst (1988) and Watt (1988), for example, identify elements like hooks, circles and semicircles as distinctive graphematic segments. Psycholinguistic evidence supports a featural analysis of the MRA. Several compelling studies suggest that certain features of the letters help in letter identification (cf. e.g., Pelli et al. 2006).

Before we begin discussing letter decomposition, there are two points that have to be considered in advance: The MRA has two subsets of characters: majuscules (upper-case letters, capitals) and minuscules (lower-case letters), cf. (1). From a historical point of view, majuscules are the basic forms from which the minuscules developed. From a synchronic point of view, however, minuscules are the basic variants (cf. Brekle 1994, 1999, Günther 1988). Majuscules are only used in special circumstances, for example, to mark proper nouns or to mark the beginning of a sentence. Most researchers dealing with letter decomposition therefore focus on the minuscules of the MRA.

Another point that has to be considered prior to a decompositional analysis of the MRA is variation. The shape of letters can vary in handwriting and in print (fonts). The basis of the analysis is a conventional variant of the MRA without serifs (e.g. the font type "Arial"). Primus argues that this qualification is justified because just like in phonology, the linguistic competence enables a hearer/writer "to discriminate linguistically relevant features from features of extra-linguistic relevance" (Primus 2004: 243). Non-distinctive features in this sense are for example serifs. The subject of analysis are therefore letters (nota bene *not* graphemes, see below) as abstract linguistic entities and their linguistically relevant features.

The first feature in discussion is connected to the spatial alignment of the characters of the MRA, cf. (2.1).

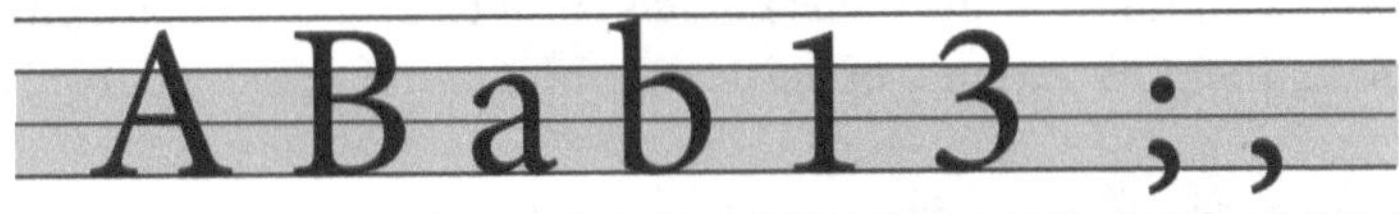

Fig. 2.1: The spatial alignment of MRA-characters (Primus 2004: 244)

Characters of the MRA are aligned to four virtual spaces between five horizontal lines (cf. Althaus 1980, Coueignoux 1981). If we disregard the third line, we can combine the two spaces in the middle into one central space. In (2.1), this space is shaded grey. The first feature, [free], is connected with the central space, cf. (3).

(3) A line is assigned the privative feature [free] if and only if it extends vertically over the central space and at least one outer space. (Primus 2004: 245)

According to this definition, <a> is distinguished from <d> and <q> by the feature [free]. There is no line in <a> that outreaches the central space, the letter <a> thus is not [free]. By contrast, lines in <d> and <q> extend into outer spaces: in <d>, one line extends into the upper outer space; in <q>, one line extends into the lower outer space. The feature [free] is thus connected to the length of lines. Only lines which are long enough to extend to at least one outer space carry the feature [free], short lines cannot reach an outer space and thus do not carry this feature.

The next features describe the vertical or horizontal orientation of lines:

(4) A line is assigned the feature [vertical] if and only if its extension on the up-down dimension is larger than on the left-right dimension. A line is assigned the feature [horizontal] if and only if its extension on the leftright dimension is larger than on the up-down dimension. The dot lacks both features [vertical] and [horizontal] (Primus 2004: 245).

In order to understand (4) better, let us examine the letter <e>. Let us assume that <e> consists of two lines: one semicircle on the left side and one small straight line. The small straight line is clearly extending on the left-right dimension more than on the up-down dimension; or casually speaking, the straight line is not as tall as it is wide. It is thus [horizontal]. The semicircle, on the other hand, extends more into the up-down dimension than into the left-right dimension. The semicircle is therefore [vertical].

A line can be straight or curved. Because Primus assumes that curved lines are more marked than straight ones, she defines a privative feature [curved]. Importantly, Primus (2004: 246) does not recognise diagonal lines as graphematically distinctive. She treats them as variants of vertical or horizontal (mostly curved) lines.

The next features describe vertical contrasts and horizontal orientation (Primus 2004: 246f):

(5) Vertical contrasts
- a. [free down]
  - i. for curved lines: The curved line is open downwards. E.g. <r>
  - ii. for straight heads: The coda is at the top of the head. E.g.<p>
- b. [free up]
  - i. for curved lines: The curved line is open upwards. E.g. <j>
  - ii. for straight heads: The coda is at the bottom of the head. E.g. <b>

(6) Horizontal orientation
  a. [leftwards]
    i. for curved lines: The curved line is open leftwards. E.g. <j>
    ii. for straight heads: The head has the coda to its left. E.g. <d>
  b. [rightwards]
    i. for curved lines: The curved line is open rightwards. E.g. <r>
    ii. straight heads: The head has the coda to its right. E.g. <b>

In the features above, the lines a letter consists of are divided into two classes. A line is either a head or a coda of a letter. Every letter comprises exactly one head but may lack a coda.

Fig. 2.2: Example of a head and a coda

The following inner-graphematic constraints describe the properties of heads and codas within letters (cf. Primus 2004: 248f.).

(7) VERTICALHEAD: A non-vertical segment depends on a vertical line; i.e., there is no horizontal line or a dot without a vertical line.

(8) NOFREECODA: The coda of a character lacks the feature [free].

(9) NOLEFT: The character is not [leftwards].

The constraint VERTICALHEAD is, according to Primus (2004: 248), inviolable for MRA-letters. Therefore, every letter consists of (at least) one vertical line. The second constraint is also high-ranking. The constraint NOFREECODA ensures that heads can be identified by the feature [free], that is, if a line is [free], i.e. it extends in one outer space, it must be a head as no coda may extend into an outer space. The third constraint NOLEFT is ranked higher than its negation NORIGHT for letters. Although NOLEFT is violable (and is actually violated by some letters), NOLEFT describes the unmarked orientation of letters. In other words, letters conforming to NOLEFT are less marked than letters violating NOLEFT.

In order to identify the head, Primus (2004: 250f) formulates the following heuristics based on the constraints presented above:

(10) Head heuristics for letters: If there is only one line, it is the head (obligativity). Among two lines with a different axial orientation, the vertical one is the head (VERTICALHEAD). Among two vertical lines distinguished by [free], the [free] one is the head (NOFREECODA). Among two lines of approximately equal length, the initial, i.e. left, one is the head (NOLEFT).

At this point at the latest, one further problem becomes apparent: for several letters, there is more than one segmentation option possible. Why, for instance, should <e> consist of one horizontal line and a vertical semicircle? After all, there is more than one alternative to this segmentation: <e> could also be segmented into one horizontal straight line and two small horizontal semicircles, or into a horizontal line, a hook and a semicircle.

Primus formulates a maxim to deal with this problem:

(11) Analyse a letter in such a way as to obtain the smallest number of segments and constraint violations (Primus 2004: 245).

Let us examine the alternative segmentation options for <e> in light of the maxim in (11). The first of the mentioned alternatives produces two segments, the other options result in three segments. According to the quantitative segment-based criterion of the maxim, the option resulting in two segments is preferred over the options resulting in three segments. Moreover, the second and third alternative each violate VERTICALHEAD because there are no vertical segments qualifying as head in these options.

Primus (2004: 251) summarises the basic properties of MRA-letters: Letters must include a vertical segment. Canonical letters have a rightwards orientation and are properly closed, i.e. the segments letters consist of are connected and enclose the space between them. For canonical and non-canonical letters alike, the following constraints apply: i) The head of a letter is the only obligatory element on which codas depend on and ii) the role of a character within the extended MRA-system is determined by the properties of its parts and the way they are concatenated.

2.2 Letters

The features and constraints discussed in the last section concern segments and the way they can be combined. Segments form complex units called letters. As mentioned above, there are other units within the writing system of German and English apart from letters, such as digits and punctuation marks.

There are several ways to distinguish letters from other units within the writing systems of English and German. One way was mentioned at the beginning of this chapter. Only letters systematically correspond to single phonemes. Digits are semasiographic units and punctuation marks do not correspond to phonemes or strings of phonemes (morphemes). Thus, letters differ from other units within the writing system in their function.

Letters can also be distinguished from other units by their distribution. Günther (1988: 67) defines letters by their distribution as characters which may form strings of, in principle, any length. This definition excludes punctuation marks but includes digits. In order to differentiate digits and letters, Günther (1988: 67) points to the complementary distribution of letters and digits: digits and letters cannot occur arbitrarily alternately in normal text between two spaces.

Berg et al. (2016) use features as introduced above to distinguish letters from other characters. As mentioned briefly above, canonical letters form closed geometrical figures, i.e. the segments letters consist of are connected and enclose the space between them. Berg et al. (2016) state that <k> is open since its coda turns from the head. The other property of canonical letters is being rightwards, cf. (6).

Digits tend to be closed and leftward oriented (cf. 1, 2, 3, 4, 7, 9)[1] and punctuation marks tend to be neither closed nor oriented in any direction[2] (Berg et al. 2016).

Tab. 2.1: Classification of units of the writing systems of English and German on formal basis (Berg et al. 2016, my translation)

	closed	**not leftwards**
Letters	+	+
Digits	+	–
Punctuation marks	–	no left/right orientation

2.3 Graphemes

The notion grapheme is a multifaceted term. In the psychological, but also in the linguistic literature, there are at least three definitions as, e.g., Henderson (1985) or Kohrt (1985) point out. In some psychological or psycholinguistic publications, the term grapheme is identical with what we have called the letter as abstract

1 But cf. 6, which is leftwards oriented, and 8, which is symmetrical.

2 But cf. comma and semicolon, which can be seen as leftwards oriented.

unit (see §2.1 above). In this context, 'abstract' means indifferent to variations in typeface, handwriting, etc. I will disregard this definition since it is covered by the notion of abstract letters as introduced above. The two other definitions are sketched in i) and ii):

i) Graphemes can be defined by their correspondence to phonological units (e.g. Wiese 1987). Thus, a grapheme is a written unit that corresponds to exactly one phoneme. This definition reflects the basic idea of the dependency theory (cf. chapter 1) that written language derivates from spoken language with no or only minor regularities of its own. By this definition, e.g. <h> and <ch> are graphemes in English and German: <h> corresponds to the phoneme /h/ in *house* and its German cognate *Haus* and <ch> corresponds to /ʃ/ in *chef* and *Chef* 'boss'.

ii) Graphemes can be defined autonomously as the smallest contrastive units within the writing system. This definition parallels the definition of the phonological counterpart of the grapheme, the phoneme, and entails that the set of graphemes of a written language can be determined by the same means as the set of phonemes of a spoken language, by minimal pairs (e.g. Henderson 1985, Kohrt 1985, Zifonun et al. 1997, Eisenberg 2006). According to this definition and method, <h> and <ch> are graphemes of English and German: <h> and e.g. <m> contrast in *house* - *mouse*, *Haus* - *Maus* and <ch> and e.g. <m> contrast in *chess* - *mess*, *Rauch* - *Raum* 'smoke - room'.

In the case of <h> and <ch>, the models do not come to different results, however, the total set of graphemes obtained by the methods of the autonomous and derivational model are not identical. Let us consider the case <qu> like in *quest*. Does <qu> comprise one or two graphemes? Henderson (1985: 144) points out that this question is not strictly answerable with a definition relying only on the correspondence to phonology. <qu> corresponds to two phonemes, /kw/, but what is the graphematic correspondent of /k/ and what is the graphematic correspondent of /w/? Considering that the definition in i) states that a grapheme corresponds to exactly one phoneme, the question cannot be answered without making decisions which are not based on the definition in i). The definition in ii), however, can answer the question: <qu> is an inseparable unit and contrasts with other graphemes as, e.g., *quest* - *best*. <qu> is thus a complex grapheme consisting of two letters.

There are also differences between grapheme sets within different approaches within the autonomous model. Eisenberg (2006: 306f.), for instance, does not count <c, v, x, y> as graphemes of German. He argues that those letters are not used productively in the German writing system and hence are not graphemes. Zifonun et al. (1997: 257), on the other hand, do include them in the grapheme inventory of German since minimal pairs with the letters in question can be found (e.g. *vage* 'vague' - *sage* 'say') although they acknowledge that <c, y> mark non-native words.

For this work I assume that all MRA-characters are elements of the writing systems of German and English, although <c> marks non-native words in German and English. <y> also marks non-native words in German, in English, it marks non-nativeness only when it occurs word-medially. Thus, the greek origin of words like *abyss* or *rhythm* are marked with <y>. In other cases, <y> marks the border of a word, e.g. *activity* - *activities*, *fly* - *flies* - *lady* - *ladies*, cf. §3.1.2.

Berg et al. (2016) point to the fact that different approaches within the autonomous model also lead to different inventories of complex graphemes. The sequence <ie> in German, for example, comprises according to the distributional criterion two graphemes since both letters of <ie> can be substituted (e.g. *Tier* – *Teer* 'animal – tar'; *Stiel* – *still* 'handle – silent'). In word division, however, <ie> behaves like a unit; in words like *frie-ren* '(to) be cold,' <ie> remains as whole with the first syllable and is not split, cf. **fri-eren* vs. *Kat-ze* 'cat.'

These seemingly contradicting observations can be accounted for by adopting a supra-segmental definition of the grapheme, cf. the definition in (12).

(12) Graphemes are the smallest supra-segmental units within a graphematic hierarchy (cf. Berg et al. 2016).

The relationship between letters and graphemes in a non-linear approach is straightforward: structural positions dominate letters. We regard those structural positions as graphemes. In the illustrations, the grapheme tier consists of nodes denoted 'C' or 'V' based on their status within the graphematic syllables. §3.1 will elaborate on the CV-tier in graphematic syllables.

(13)

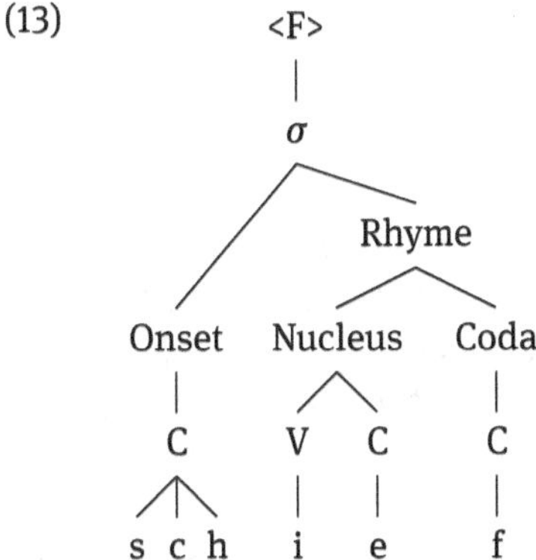

In (13) above, the structural graphematic positions of the word *schief* 'crooked' are displayed in a supra-segmental structure of the graphematic foot the word comprises, cf. §1.3. Such an analysis can explain the seemingly inconsistent behaviour of <ie>: on the one hand, <ie> is dominated by two structural positions (this explains why the letters are substitutable), on the other hand, the structural positions dominating <ie> are dominated by the nucleus of a graphematic syllable. The fact that nuclei cannot be hyphenated in word division (cf. Evertz & Primus 2013: 2-3, §3.3) leads to the indivisibility of <ie> (Berg et al. 2016). Combinations of <a, e, i, o, u> that are dominated by the same nucleus will be called *graphematic diphthong* henceforth. For a featural definition the class of letters forming graphematic diphthongs, the v-letters, cf. §3.1.1.2.

Let us now compare the graphematic diphthong <ie> with <sch> as analysed in (13). <sch> is dominated by one structural position, while <i> and <e> are dominated by one structural position each (cf. Primus 2010).

The analysis of <sch> resembles, in part, the non-linear analysis of affricates in phonological syllables. In fact, affricates and complex graphemes can be compared: on a segmental level, affricates are two different consonants (a stop followed by a fricative), but phonotactically they behave like one unit. These properties can be captured by a model with a structural position dominating the two segments (cf. e.g. Wiese 2000).

In contrast to the analysis in (13), Fuhrhop & Peters (2013: 204-206) assume that <sch> actually consists of two graphemes, <s> and <ch>. Like in the discussion about the grapheme-status of <ie>, they base their assumption on distributional facts:

(14) a. *Masche – manche – Maske, Maste*
('stitch – some – mask, mast (Dat.)')
b. *Esche – Elche – Espe*
('ash [tree] – elks – aspen')
c. *Lusche – Lurche; luschig – lustig*
('weakling – amphibian, weak – funny')

The examples in (14) show that graphematic minimal pairs can be found in which <s> and <ch> respectively can be substituted by single letters. This contrasts with Eisenberg's (2006: 306) observation that <s> cannot be substituted when <sch> is syllable-initial: e.g. *Schaum* 'foam' – *Baum* 'tree', *Raum* 'space', *Saum* 'hem', but **Xchaum* (where X is any other letter than <s>). He thus regards <sch> as one grapheme.

Word division provides further evidence for the analysis in (13): <sch> is indivisible in word division, e.g. *wa-schen* – **was-chen* '(to) wash'. Similar cases like <tz> or <ss>, however are divided, cf. *Kat-ze* 'cat', *As-se* 'aces.'

In a supra-segmental approach, we can regard word division as a phenomenon related to the skeletal tier of the graphematic syllable and state that in word division in German, the graphematic syllable after the hyphen starts with exactly one filled structural position (if there is at least one filled structural position and if there are no intervening morphological reasons, cf. §3.3 for a discussion on hyphenation. Note that in loanwords, words with a hiatus and in proper names, phonological syllable boundaries may determine hyphenation, e.g. <Man-fred>).[3]

Letters with diacritics, such as umlaut marks, <ä, ö, ü> can be counted as complex graphemes; <ä>, for instance, consists of the letter <a> and umlaut marks (e.g. Gallmann 1985). The dots in <i, j> can be called diacritics as well, but in contrast to other diacritics, they do not bear any function. The diaeresis, for example, marks a syllable nucleus (e.g., *naïve*, [naˈiːv]), and the umlaut mark indicates vowel fronting (e.g. *Gast* - *Gäste* 'guest - guests', [gast] - [gɛstə]). By contrast, the dots in <i, j> do not even distinguish letters from each other in the writing systems under consideration.[4] Thus, I count letters with diaeresis or umlaut marks as complex graphemes, while <i, j> are not complex graphemes (cf. Primus 2003).

The letter <ß> also belongs to the set of complex graphemes of German. While the complexity of other complex graphemes is obvious, the complexity of <ß> is not visible at first sight. The elements other complex graphemes consist of are easily distinguishable: complex graphemes consist of more than one letter, e.g. <sh> ,<ch>, <qu>, or feature umlaut marks or other diacritics, <ä>, <ü>, <ö>. The grapheme <ß> consists – at least diachronically – of two elements, <ʃ> and <s>[5], but the internal make up is obscured by the continuous line that makes <ß> look like one element. Another evidence for the complexity of <ß> is capitalization: before the introduction of capital <ß> into the "Amtliche Regelungen" in June 2017, <ß> was written <SS> as in <GROSS> 'great' in words which are written in capital letters only (for instance in passports).

Importantly, the unit grapheme does not render the unit letter obsolete. Some regularities apply to the letter and not to the grapheme. Capitalization, e.g., applies to initial letters and not to initial graphemes.(*Show* vs. **SHow*).

---

3 Fuhrhop & Peters (2013: 206) acknowledge that word division is in fact an argument against their interpretation of <sch> as two graphemes, they, however, are unsure how heavy this arguments weighs. Cf. chapter 5 for a discussion addressing this issue.

4 In contrast to the writing systems of English and German, there is a dotless and a dotted <i> in the writing system of Turkish. These are two different letters corresponding to two different phonemes (<ı> - /ɯ/, <i> - /i/).

5 Respectivly <ʒ>. Hence the name "*Eszet*" (Brekle 2001, cf. Bollwage 2010 for a discussion).

2.4 Summary of this chapter

In this chapter, the lowest levels of a graphematic hierarchy were introduced: features, letters and graphemes. Letters are complex units consisting of segments like hooks, semicircles and lines. These segments, which can be described by features, are in a hierarchical relationship with each other: when there are two segments, one is the head, the other is the coda of the letter; when there is only one segment, this segment is the head (but cf. the case of <c>, see above).

Letters can be distinguished from other units of the writing system by features. Three classes, letters, digits and punctuation marks, can be established on featural grounds.

The next higher level in the graphematic hierarchy are the graphemes. Contrary to the traditional views that graphemes are defined by their correspondence to phonemes or by their distribution in minimal pairs, graphemes are viewed in this work as the lowest supra-segmental units within the graphematic hierarchy. This supra-segmental view captures the fact that some processes, like hyphenation at the end of line, consider graphemes and that other processes, like capitalisation, apply to letters.

3 The Graphematic Syllable

The unit syllable is not confined to spoken language. There is growing evidence that the syllable is also a relevant unit in graphematics (Butt & Eisenberg 1990, Prinz & Wiese 1990, Günther 1992, Maas 1992, Primus 2000, 2003, Rollings 2004, Fuhrhop & Buchmann 2009, Fuhrhop et al. 2011 etc.), which is reinforced by psycholinguistic evidence (cf. e.g. Caramazza & Micelli 1990, Badecker 1996, Domahs et al. 2001, Weingarten 2004, Weingarten et al. 2004, Nottbusch et al. 2005).

If the syllable is a cross-modally available unit, there must be a basic trait of the syllable common in spoken and written language. Primus' (2003) basic observation is that syllabic units (and with them all prosodic units above the syllable within the prosodic or graphematic hierarchy) are constituted by alternating structures. In phonetics and phonology, such alternations are manifested by articulatory openings and closings, by increasing and decreasing amplitude of the acoustic signal and by increasing and decreasing sonority (Tillmann 1980, Vennemann 1982, Pompino-Marschall 1993, 1995, Neef 2002). These alternations are called *rhythm* in spoken language (Primus 2003).

Of course, not every alternating structure qualifies as syllabic unit. Primus (2003) gives two defining constraints: First, the wavelength of the alternation must have a certain value in order to be perceivable as oscillation (cf. Tillmann 1980). If the wavelength is too long, only the alternating feature (for instance tone, amplitude) is noticed (e.g. intonation on sentence level). If the wavelength is too short, the alternating structure will be perceived as another feature (e.g. certain vibrations of the tip of the tongue are perceived as one segment, [r]). Second, one element of the alternating structure must be more salient than other elements. This element is constitutive of the syllable, which makes it its obligatory constituent. This unit is usually called the syllable peak or *nucleus*.

Based on the second condition, we may define the nucleus as the most sonorous element of a syllable. *Sonority* is a concept designed for spoken language. It is noteworthy, however, that there is an ongoing debate about whether sonority has phonetic correlates or not. There are some findings from articulatory (e.g. Dogil 1989, Clements 1990, Hume & Odden 1996, Eisenberg 2006) and acoustic (e.g. Price 1980, Pompino-Marshall 1995, Hurch & Maas 1998, Lavoie 2001) phonetics that partly justify sonority hierarchies but no phonetic model is able to explain the effects of sonority satisfactorily (Neef 2002). Clements (1990) concludes that "there is reason to question whether a uniform, independent phonetic parameter corresponding to sonority can be found, even in principle" (cf. section 1.2).

https://doi.org/10.1515/9783110583441-003

Since no clear phonetic correlate of sonority can be found, researchers turn to more general cognitive concepts. A concept of sonority in this sense, which could be employed in all media of language, is *perspicuity*, *prominence* or *salience*. Clements (1990) employs this notion for phonological syllables, Perlmutter (1992) and Brentari (2012) for syllables in sign language and Primus (2003), Domahs & Primus (2015) for syllables in writing systems.

In the following section I will present the skeletal structure of the graphematic syllable. The length hierarchy that will be discussed within this section is the graphematic realisation of salience in graphematic syllables. Then I will present the subsyllabic constituents of the graphematic syllable and explain their relevance. The next section of this chapter is devoted to word division at the end of a line and its relation to graphematic syllables. Finally, this chapter concludes with a brief summary.

As we have seen in the discussion so far, the names of some graphematic units, e.g. the syllable, are the same as the names of the phonological units they correspond to. In order to avoid cumbersome names, I will use "g" as a prefix referring to a graphematic unit and "p" as a prefix for a phonological element in case of doubt.

3.1 The CV-tier

Like in phonology, a graphematic syllable has a skeletal tier with obligatory and non-obligatory positions. The skeletal tier of German and English phonological syllables consists of an obligatory V-position with optional C-positions before and after the V-position (cf. Clements & Keyser 1983). The V-position of the p-syllable is defined as the sonority peak of the syllable and is the constituting element of the nucleus. The sonority rises monotonically towards the peak and decreases monotonically from it (e.g. Selkirk 1984). Hence, the V-position is also called the *syllable peak* (cf. §1.2).

The CV-positions illustrated by the example *blank*[1] in (1) (repeated from §1.2) make up the phonological core syllable.

1 This example is valid for English and German. The only difference is the vowel quality in German which is [a] instead of [æ].

(1) *Syllable template for English and German p- and g-syllables* (cf. Wiese 2000: 38, Giegerich 1992: 144, 149-150)

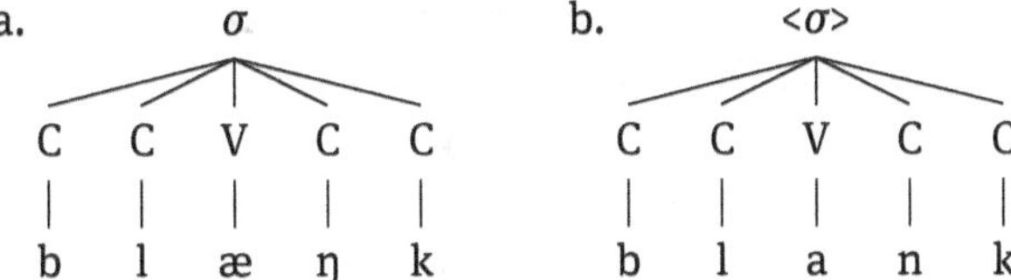

Let us now turn to the graphematic syllable. Graphematic syllables do also have a skeletal tier as illustrated in (1b). Every g-syllable has exactly one V-position with optional C-positions. The V-position of a graphematic syllable is also called its *peak*.

While in phonological syllables vowels and sonorants are licensed in the V-position, the V-position of graphematic syllables is restricted to a certain kind of letter, the *vowel letters* or shorter, *v-letters* (see §3.1.1).

(2) Every g-syllable has a v-letter in its peak (Maas 1999: 265, Primus 2003: 31, Evertz & Primus 2013: 5).

According to the constraint in (2), there is no g-syllable without a v-letter. In order to understand the constraint in (2), we have to introduce the notion of v-letters.

3.1.1 Definition of v-letters

3.1.1.1 Definitions of v-letters in previous works

Many graphematic approaches define v-letters by correspondence rules. Venezky (1970, 1999), for instance, states in his grapheme-phoneme correspondence rules that a v-letter corresponds to a phonological vowel, either a *free* or a *checked* one; e.g. <a> corresponds to the free vowel /e/, like in *sane* or to the checked vowel /æ/, like in *sanity* (Venezky 1999: 174). Rollings (2004) is concerned with spelling, i.e. phoneme-grapheme correspondences. He does not define v-letters explicitly but notes regular correspondences. Leaving the direction of the correspondences aside, these two approaches have in common that they define v-letters by regular correspondences to phonological vowels. The following definition subsumes these approaches:

(3) V-letters are letters that regularly correspond to phonological vowels.

This definition is problematic for two reasons. One is a technical issue, the other one concerns the definition as whole. The first and easier problem lies within the notion *regularly*. When is a correspondence regular and when not? For instance, is <y> a v-letter? <y> corresponds to /j/ in words such as *yet, beyond, lawyer* but also to /aɪ̯/ as in *cycle, sky* and also to /ɪ/ as in *rhythm* or /i/ as in *lady*. All these correspondences can be called regular. Venezky (1999) solves this problem pragmatically, he places <y> in the class of v-letters but also in the class of c-letters. Indeed, the definition above does not rule out a v-letter also being a c-letter.

The theoretical problem with a v-letter definition by regular correspondences to sounds is that this definition relies on the phonological level. The aim of this work, however, is to show that writing systems are parallel to phonological systems and that they are (although interdependent) partly independent of each other (cf. chapter 1). Let us therefore examine further possibilities to define v-letters on independent and, at best, graphematic grounds.

Another possible solution to the problem of defining v- and c-letters is to argue that the distinction between v-letters and c-letters is a matter of rote memorisation. At one point, a learner has to memorise which letters belong to the class of v-letters and which ones belong to the class of c-letters. If that is true, an extensional definition like the one Evertz & Primus (2013) propose would be appropriate:

(4) The inventory of v-letters in English and German comprises <a, e, i, o, u, y> (these letters may be modified by diacritics). There is one additional v-letter in English, <w> (cf. Evertz & Primus 2013: 5).

An extensional definition is probably the simplest one. Cases like <y> and <w> still need consideration, though. The definition above divides letters into two classes, it does not rule out, however, that a letter belonging to the inventory of v-letters is also part of the inventory of c-letters (only the set of v-letters but not the set of c-letters is defined in (4)). The letters <y> and <w> thus have a dual membership: In words like *yield* or *well* they act as c-letters, in words like *day* and *show* they act as v-letters. In other words, <y> and <w> are either v- or c-letters depending on the context (which is in fact the same solution that Venezky (1999) proposes, see above). If we employ the definition in (4), we have to define the situation in which <y> and <w> can act as v-letters. In other words, extensional definitions like the one in (4) need further constraints.

To sum the discussion about extensional definitions up: the good thing about the definition in (4) is its simplicity. The bad thing, however, is that the definition is axiomatic and thereby arbitrary. An arbitrary stipulation does not explain, for instance, when <y> and <w> are used as v-letters and when as c-letters. Although this definition does not rely on the phonological level, it is still not graphematically motivated.

A promising way to define letter classes in purely graphematic terms is the distributional method proposed by Berg (2012). Berg searched for graphematic minimal pairs in the CELEX database (Baayen et al. 1995) and studied which letters are substitutable in the same position within these minimal pairs (e.g. in the graphematic minimal pair *kit* - *fit*, <k> can be replaced by <f>). He counted how often one letter could be substituted with another letter. For example, if there were 25 pairs involving the letters <k> and <f> (like in *kit* - *fit*), the value for <k> – <f> would be 25. The values were systematised in a contingency table. With the help of multidimensional scaling plots, Berg visualised the relations between the variables in his contingency table. The more often a letter can be substituted by another letter, the closer these two letters appear in the plot, cf. figure 3.1.

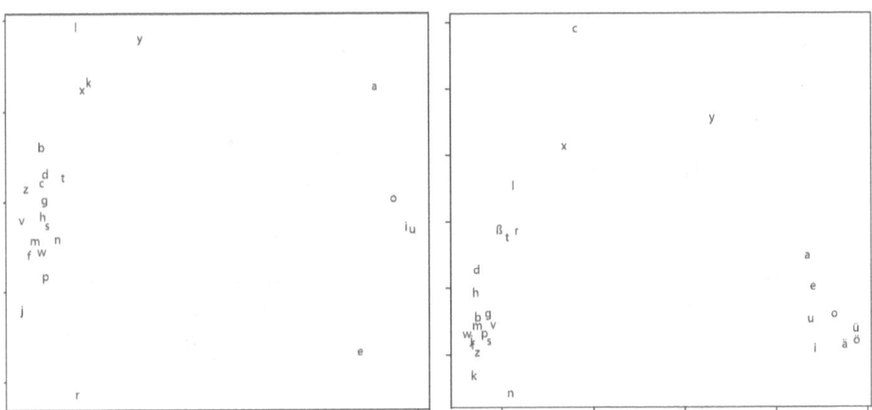

Fig. 3.1: Multi-dimensional scaling plot for English (left) and German (right) (Berg 2012: 34-35)

The plots reveal that there are two distinct sets of letters in German and English[2], there is a larger set of letters (on the left side of the plots) and a smaller set of letters. "Vowel letters can thus be defined as the members of the smaller of two groups of elements in an MDS [multi-dimensional scaling] plot or a cluster analysis of their substitutability" (Berg 2012: 37). Interestingly, <y> is quite similar to consonant-letters in English while it is between the two groups in German. This reflects the

2 There were very similar results for Dutch, but since this work is not concerned with the writing system of Dutch, I will leave the report of the results for Dutch out.

different distribution of this letter in German and English. For example, in English, a word-final <y> does not form minimal pairs with <i>; on the contrary, these two letters are distributed complementarily, which leads Berg to the conclusion that these letters seem to be allographs (Berg 2012: 34). In German, <y> can replace a vowel or a consonant letter. According to Berg (2012: 35), a non-hierarchical cluster analysis groups <y> with the vowel letters in German. The letter <w> is clearly part of the larger set in both languages and thus according to Berg's definition, a c-letter in English and German.

Berg's analysis is quite convincing for it defines the two sets of letters by their distribution and not by reference to phonology. I would therefore prefer his method to the two previous definitions. It has to be noted, however, that the distributional analysis does not help to identify the set of v-letters by a distributional criterion. Berg only uses a quantitative criterion: v-letters constitute the smaller of the two sets.

I will, therefore, present the analysis of Fuhrhop & Buchmann (2016), who define v-letters in terms of their graphematic features. The featural definition will show that all and only the letters Berg's study unquestionably revealed to cluster as v-letters are also v-letters in featural terms.

3.1.1.2 A featural definition of v-letters

It is possible to define v- and c-letters by their letter features (cf. §2.1 for an overview of letter features). Fuhrhop & Buchmann (2016) demonstrate that the letter groups identified by Berg (2012) also form two distinct classes, if the features of the letters that form these groups are taken into account. Their analysis is based on the works of Primus (2004, 2006), Fuhrhop & Buchmann (2009) and Fuhrhop et al. (2011)

A first approximation to a featural definition of v-letters based on the features of Primus (2004, 2006) is given below:

(5) *First approximation to a featural definition of v-letters:*
A v-letter is a letter with a ¬[free] head which is either [curved] or [free up]:
- ¬[free] and [curved]: <a, e, o>
- ¬[free] and [free up]: <i, u>.

In this context, the negation sign ¬ symbolises the absence of a privative feature. The lengths of the head lines of <a, e, o> do not exceed the middle space (cf. (7)), and the head line itself is not straight but [curved]. The v-letters <i, u> share the feature [non-long]. Instead of having a [curved] head, they are [free up], which means that they have an opening upwards. Note that <y> is not included here. I will discuss this letter further below.

The definition in (5) does, however, define <v, w> as v-letters since both are [free up] and not [free]. Let us discuss whether such an inclusion is desirable. <w> occurs in the nuclei of g-syllables in English (cf. *show, vowel, new, shawl*). This leads Evertz & Primus (2013) to include <w> in their extensional definition of v-letters. They are, however, aware that <w> is not like every other v-letter. Unlike to other v-letters, <w> cannot constitute a syllable on its own. Fuhrhop et al. (2011) also discuss the status of <w>. They argue that <w> is a positional variant of <u>. This argument is based on two observations: first, in English, <w> and <u> are almost complementarily distributed in the second nuclear position and second, in a sequence <Vu> (V being a variable for any v-letter), <u> can be substituted by <w> without changing the phonological value of the corresponding vowel: e.g. *caution, law*; *feud, stew*; *foul, now*; *soul, follow* (cf. also Evertz & Primus 2013). These observations show that <w> is not licensed in the V-position of English g-syllables. Another argument against the inclusion of <v, w> in the class of v-letters are the results of the distributional analysis of Berg (2012) which show that <v, w> do not cluster with the letters <a, e, i, o, u> listed in (5).

The definition in (5) is therefore not restrictive enough and needs some refinement. To be precise, we need to be able to distinguish <v, w> from <i, u> on featural grounds: The heads of <v, w> and <i, u> are similar in the respect that they do not exceed into an outer space and thus are [free], but while the heads of <i, u> are straight, the heads of <v, w> are slant. This is one of the observations that leads Fuhrhop & Buchmann (2009) and Fuhrhop et al. (2011) to regard length not as a privative feature, like [free], but as a scalar criterion. They distinguish four types of heads:

(6) *Types of heads* (Fuhrhop et al. 2011: 280-282, Fuhrhop & Buchmann 2016)
- a. Long heads: f, t, j, h, p, b, k, g, d
- b. Slant heads: z, v, w, s, x
- c. Short straight heads: m, n, r, l, i, u
- d. Short bent heads: e, o, a

The figure in (7) exemplifies some of the head types mentioned above.

(7) Letters with long vs. short heads (Fuhrhop et al. 2011: 276)

p b d t k (q) g vs. a e i u o

Long heads cross the central space, while slant heads and short straight heads do not cross the central space. The difference between slant and short straight heads is the way in which they connect the lines which border the central space. Short straight heads connect these lines in the shortest way, slant heads, by contrast, are longer.

<m, n, r, l> and <i, u> have the same type of heads, i.e. short straight heads. The classification of <l> seems odd at first sight. Fuhrhop et al. (2011) and Berg et al. (2016) argue that <l> is composed of a short straight head with a coda on top. Their argument is based primarily on the strong tendency of letters to consist of at least two elements (but cf. <c> and <i, j>, see below, as possible exceptions).

<m, n, r, l> and <i, u> differ in their connection of the head and the coda. The coda connects at the top of the head in <m, n, r, l>, they are [free down]. The coda of <u> is connected at the bottom of the head. <i> has no coda at all since the dot of <i> is a non-distinctive diacritic in German and English (Primus 2004, 2006, Berg et al. 2014; for an alternate view cf. e.g. Fuhrhop & Buchmann 2016). <i, u> are therefore [free up]. Fuhrhop et al. (2011) and Fuhrhop & Buchmann (2016) call <a, e, o> and <i, u> compact letters. Table 3.1 gives an overview of all of the groups of letters that emerge when letter length is considered.

Tab. 3.1: Graphematic length hierarchy (cf. Domahs & Primus, 2015)

long	**slant**	**short straight**		**short curved**
		free down	**free up**	
			compact	
b,p,q,d,g,k, h,t,ß,j,f	v,w,x,z,s	m,n,l,r	i,u	a,e,o

The groups in the two rightmost columns are the shortest letters or, using the notion of Fuhrhop & Buchmann (2016), the compact letters. The length increases from the right to the left.

In the introduction of this chapter, we discussed salience as inter-medial foundation of the syllable. Now we can continue this discussion. Coueignoux (1981) shows that the middle space is most salient for letter recognition. A short letter, which is fully comprised within the boundaries of the middle space, is thus more salient than a long letter, which is partially outside the middle space.

We can modify the insufficient definition in (5) by adopting the length features in (6). The definition in (5) defines the most salient class of letters, the compact letters, cf. table 3.1, as v-letters.

(8) A v-letter is a letter with a [short bent] head or a letter with a [short straight] head which is [free up] (cf. Fuhrhop & Buchmann 2016).
- [short bent]: <a, e, o>
- [short straight] and [free up]: <i, u>.

The definition in (8) refines (5) by replacing the privative feature [free] with letter length. Letter length can be understood as features ordered on a scale. The single features on this scale were introduced in (6). By adopting letter length we can distinguish letters featuring a [slant] head, e.g. <v,w>, and letters featuring a [short straight] head, e.g. <i, u>. This is exactly the distinction the definition in (5) could not make.

C-letters may be defined complementarily as being letters that are not v-letters. But it is also possible to define them independently: c-letters are featurally defined by having a [long] or [slant] head or by being [free down]. According to this definition, <b, d, f, g, h, j, k, p, q, t, s, v, w, x, z> have [long] or [slant] heads, i.e. their heads surpass the middle space or are slant. The letters <l, m, n, r> are [free down], in other words, they are not closed upwards by their coda. Fuhrhop & Buchmann (2009) analyse <l> as bisegmental. The long line of <l> is divided into a short head at the bottom and a short coda on top. Under this analysis, <l> is [free down]. At first glance, <c> appears to be a v-letter since it only consists of a curved line. Fuhrhop et al. (2011) argue that <c> is an allograph of <k> with a missing head.

A rather problematic letter is <y>. If the head of this letter is the long line on the right, <y> is a c-letter which is exceptionally licensed in g-syllable peaks. If the head is on the left, it combines a slant head with a long coda. A long coda, however, violates the constraint NoFreeCoda (8), the letter would thus be highly marked. Moreover, a slant head would also indicate that <y> is a c-letter.

Let us have a closer look at <y>. In English and German, <y> is attest in the nucleus and in the margins of graphematic syllables, cf. table 3.2.

Tab. 3.2: Occurrences of <y> in German and English (cf. Fuhrhop & Buchmann 2016: 365)

	German	English
Onset	Yoga, Yacht	yard, year
1. nuclear position	System	shy
2. nuclear position		boy
syllable boundary	loyal	royal

Furhop & Buchmann (2016: 365) argue that word-medially, <y> only occurs in loanwords and proper names in English and German. These loanwords, however, can be quite well integrated and frequent in use, e.g. *type* and *Typ* 'type' or 'guy [colloquial]'. Thus, <y> can even be seen as a "loanword marker" (Furhop & Buchmann 2016: 365). Moreover, in German word onsets there is a tendency to substitute <y>, cf. *Jacht, Joga, Joghurt* (Fuhrhop 2005: 35). To this end, some linguists challenge the status of <y> as a grapheme in German (cf. Eisenberg 2006: 306).

In English, <y> can occupy the first or the second nuclear position and can occur in the syllable margins. However, <y> cannot form complex onsets (Furhop & Buchmann 2016: 365). Interestingly, in words in which <y> occupies the first nuclear position, e.g. *lady*, <y> is replaced by <ie> when <y> is not at the end of the word, e.g. *ladies*. When <y> is in the second nuclear position, e.g. *boy*, this change does not occur.

In section 3.1.2 I will argue in accordance with Fuhrhop & Buchmann (2009), Fuhrhop et al. (2011) and Fuhrhop & Buchmann (2016) that <y> functions as a word boundary marker (cf. *lady* vs. *ladies*) or morpheme boundary marker (*boy+s*, *lady+like*) and is acceptable word-medially only in marked domains of the lexicon like in proper names or loanwords, such as *rhythm* or German *Rhythmus*. The exceptionality of <y> is thus functionalised: <y> marks word or morpheme boundaries or the non-nativity of words (Berg et al. 2014, Furhop & Buchmann 2016: 365).

Summarising, the great advantage of a featural definition of v- and c-letters is that it offers a graphematic visual criterion to identify the letter classes established by Berg's (2012) distributional analysis (see above). The featural definition proposed here establishes <a,e,i,o,u> as v-letters, <y> as an exceptional v-letter in both languages, and the rest as c-letters. This is exactly the clustering established by the distributional analysis of Berg (2012). As to <w>, both the featural definition and the distributional analysis yield a c-letter. That conforms to the observation that <w> cannot appear in the peak (V-position) of a graphematic syllable.

Returning to the constraint formulated in (2) that every g-syllable must contain a v-letter in its peak (V-position), both graphematic definitions, the featural and the distributional one, appropriately isolate the class of letters that are needed in peak position (leaving only <y> as an exceptional v-letter that is restricted to marked g-syllable peaks). The featural definition is also in line with the letter sequencing principle by Fuhrhop & Buchmann (2009) and Fuhrhop et al. (2011) who developed on basis of Primus' work a graphematic counterpart to the sonority sequencing principle.

3.1.2 Length sequencing principle

The length sequencing principle is based on the observation that letters with long heads and letters with short heads occur in a certain order within a graphematic syllable (Naumann 1989, Eisenberg 1989). Fuhrhop & Buchmann (2009) and Fuhrhop et al. (2011) observe that in canonical graphematic syllables the length of letter heads decreases towards the V-position and increases towards the syllables edges.

The graphematic salience hierarchy presented in the section above is the graphematic counterpart of the sonority hierarchy, however, the graphematic salience hierarchy is not established by phonological correspondences, but by purely graphematic considerations. Likewise, the length sequencing principle by Fuhrhop & Buchmann (2009) and Fuhrhop et al. (2011) forms the graphematic counterpart of the sonority sequencing principle (cf. §1.2.1). Just as the length hierarchy, the length sequencing principle is motivated solely graphematically.

(9) *Length sequencing principle* (LSP) (Fuhrhop et al. 2011: 283)
The graphematic syllable core [i.e., the V-position] is occupied by the most compact grapheme. The length of the segments increases monotonously toward both syllable edges.

There are some cases, however, that do not comply with the LSP. Fuhrhop & Buchmann (2016) list the following exceptions to the LSP in German and English.[3]

Tab. 3.3: Exceptions to the LSP (cf. Fuhrhop & Buchmann 2016)

	German	English
<s> in onset	<sp, st, sch>	<sp, st, sh>
<s> in coda	after nearly all long letters in English and German	
<h>	lengthening-h	<sh>
<c>	only in combination with <h, k>	
	<ck> as allography to <k>	<ck> as allography to <k>
<y>	only in loanwords	word-initially or word-final (word-medial in loanwords)
Peculiarities	<tz, ß>	<wn, wl> word-final, <wh> word-initial

3 They also list exceptions to the LSP in the French writing systems. I will omit these findings here.

According to Fuhrhop et al. (2011), <s> has a slant head. The element which fills the central space is slant in the sense that a line departs from top left to down right. The head is bent on both sides, i.e. at the beginning and at the end of the head. <s> has thus a shorter head than letters with a long head (e.g. <p, t, k, h>) but a longer head than letter with a short straight head (e.g. <m, n, r>).

In German and English, <s> can appear in syllable onsets together with <p> and <t>, e.g., in *space*, *Spaß* 'fun'; *stern*, *Stern* 'star'. These occurrences are violations of the LSP since the length does not decrease towards the V-position: <p> and <t> are long, <s>, however is slant and thus shorter.

In the coda, <s> can appear with nearly all long letters, e.g. *legs*, *singst* '(you) sing'. These occurrences also pose violations of the LSP.

These violations of the LSP can be explained morphologically (Fuhrhop & Buchmann 2016). The violations mark morphological complexity, such as plural or genitive (in English further marked with apostrophe). Fuhrhop & Buchmann (2016) thus conclude that the LSP-violations of <s> function as cues to morphological complexity.

Other violations are caused by <h>. <h> has a long head and is thus at the bottom end of the length hierarchy. In German, <h> appears syllable-initially, after a v-letter as so-called lengthening-<h> and in combination with other letters, such as <c> or <ch>. The syllable-initial <h> marks the beginning of a g-syllable as in *gehen* 'to go'. In cases like *gehen*, <h> conforms to the LSP, but syllable-initial <h> can also appear (due to morphological reasons) syllable-medially as in *gehst* 'you go'. In cases like *gehst*, <h> marks the end of the stem, <st> violates the LSP. The lengthening-<h> in words like *wahr* 'true', *Wahn* 'delusion', *Ohr* 'ear' causes violations of the LSP. The letters after <h> are shorter than <h> without being part of a new syllable. Fuhrhop & Buchmann (2016) argue that in some cases, e.g., *fährst* '(you) drive', <h> marks morphological complexity, but the other examples provided here indicate that this is not always the case.

<h> is also an element in complex graphemes, like <ch>, <sh> and <sch>. In syllable onsets, e.g. Engl. *chase*, *shut*, Ger. *schau* 'look' , <h> leads to a violation of the LSP.

<y> is a generally a problem for the length hierarchy, the featural definition of v-letters and the peak restriction in (2), which states that only v-letters are licensed in the V-position of a graphematic syllable. As mentioned in §3.1.1.2 above, <y> has either a long head (if the head is on the right side of the letter), or a slant head with a long coda. In both cases, <y> must be classified as c-letter. Indeed, in words like *yacht, yield, yard* and *Yacht, Yoga* (German), <y> is in a graphematic C-position. Words like these conform to the LSP. In words like *rhythm, physics, psychology* and their German cognates *Rhythmus, Physik, Psychologie*, however, <y> is in the V-position of the syllable. Words like these do not conform to (2) and fur-

thermore violate the LSP. This non-conformity may be licensed by the fact that these words are non-native (in both languages). In German, <y> occurs in marked domains of the lexicon (such as loanwords, words of dialectal origin or proper names) exclusively. This fact leads Eisenberg (2006: 306) to the conclusion that <y> is not a grapheme of the native vocabulary of German. This might be exaggerated, but as pointed out in the former section, <y> can be seen as a "loanword marker" in German (Furhhop & Buchmann 2016: 365).

In English, <y> marks the end of a word, cf. e.g. *lady - ladies*, *fly - flies* or morpheme, e.g. *ladylike*. This change is not observable in combination with other v-letters (e.g. *boy - boys*, **bois*) but there is another system: in g-diphthongs, <i> and <y> are distributed complementarily depending on the word border., cf. *paint, point, weight* vs. *say, joy, grey*. Word-finally <y> appears, word-medially <i>. Although <y> generally violates LSP, its exceptional length is functionalised in the writing system of English: <y> indicates word and morpheme boundaries, word-medially it indicates non-native words (cf. Fuhrhop & Buchmann 2016: 365-366).

Summarising, we can say that the letter sequencing principle is – much like the sonority sequencing principle – violable. Importantly, in many cases it is violated systematically in order to mark the morphological structure of words. The graphematic hierarchy and the letter sequencing principle are the graphematic counterparts of the sonority hierarchy and of the sonority sequencing principle, but the LSP and the graphematic length hierarchy do not derive from their phonological counterparts, they are deduced independently on graphematic grounds.

3.2 Subsyllabic Constituents

In phonology, most syllable models have constituents between the level of the syllable node and the skeletal tier (CV-tier). These constituents are the onset and the rhyme, which dominates the nucleus and the coda, they have been introduced in §1.2.1.

I assume that the same constituents exist in graphematic syllables (cf. for the same view Primus 2010, Evertz & Primus 2013):

(10) *Subsyllabic constituents of the graphematic syllable*

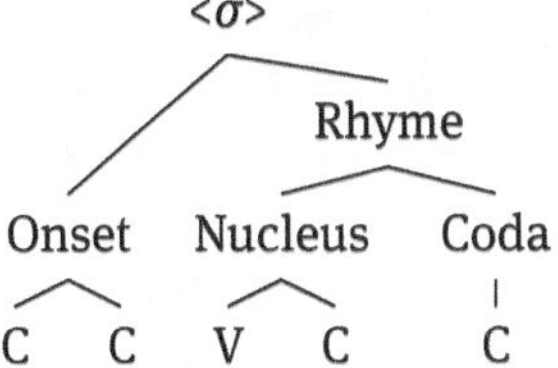

The subsyllabic constituents are abbreviated in figures as *On*, *Rh*, *Nu* and *Co* throughout this work.

In the following section I will discuss the constituents nucleus and coda and their relevance for syllable types in the writing systems of German and English.

3.2.1 Nucleus, Coda & Syllable Type

As in phonology, there are generally two kinds of graphematic syllables (which may have subtypes): full and reduced syllables. The differences between these syllable types are – like in phonology – a result of their differences in nucleus structure:

(11) BRANCHING-GN

a. The nucleus of a full g-syllable in a prosodically strong position is branching.

b. All other nuclei do not branch.

Table 3.4 summarises the most important traits of the syllables types.

Tab. 3.4: Graphematic syllable types

Type	Nucleus	V-position
full	± branching	any g-vowel
reduced	– branching	only <e>

As mentioned in the table above, the status of a syllable determines which letters are licensed in its V-position:

(12) a. Only v-letters are licensed in the V-position of a graphematic syllable (cf. Maas 1999: 265, Primus 2003: 31, Evertz & Primus 2013).

b. Among v-letters only <e> is licensed in the V-position of a reduced g-syllable (Evertz & Primus 2013).

According to (12), the occurrence of <e> as sole letter within a syllable is a necessary condition for a reduced g-syllable, however, it is not a sufficient condition. On the other hand, the occurrence of any other letter than <e> is a sufficient condition for a full syllable, however, it is not a necessary condition. Consider the examples *face* and *fence*. In the first graphematic syllable of *face*, <fa>, there is only one v-letter, <a>, therefore, this g-syllable satisfies the sufficient condition for a full g-syllable. The first syllable of *fence*, <fe>, satisfies the necessary condition for a reduced g-syllable, and does not satisfy the sufficient condition for full g-syllables. We will see however, that <fe> in *fence* is indeed a full syllable (cf. §4).

It follows from the peak restriction in (12) requiring that each graphematic syllable contains at least one v-letter that words like *Dirndl* 'dirndl dress' or *Stubn* 'inn' are graphematically monosyllabic, although the sonorants [l] or [n] in [dɪʀn.dl̩] and [ʃtuː.bn̩] constitute a second syllable in the phonological representation of each word. These words are thus phonologically bisyllabic but graphematically monosyllabic. This analysis is supported by the fact that words like <Dirndl> or <Stubn> are not separable, even though the hyphenation of segments consisting of only two letters is possible, e.g. <Wes-te> 'waistcoat' (Evertz & Primus 2013: 6). The words <Dirndl> and <Stubn> are of dialectal origin, the standard German spellings of words with syllabic sonorants, however, contain v-letters, such as in <Trottel> 'idiot', <Beutel> 'bag' and <Feudel> 'floorcloth' (Fuhrhop & Peters 2013: 230). It is the same restriction that causes the occurrence of mute <e> in words like <tickle> or <handle>. In English as well as in German, there is no g-syllable without a v-letter.

3.2.1.1 Full Syllables

There are basically two types of graphematic full syllables; they can be strong or weak (i.e. they can be the head of a foot or not). Weak full g-syllables have a non-branching nucleus, while strong full g-syllables have a branching nucleus.

Let us begin our discussion with strong graphematic syllables. Strong graphematic syllables have an obligatory branching nucleus, i.e. the nucleus of a strong g-syllable dominates two structural positions. This property is expressed in the constraint BRANCHING-GN in (11). This constraint can be satisfied in three ways:

(13)

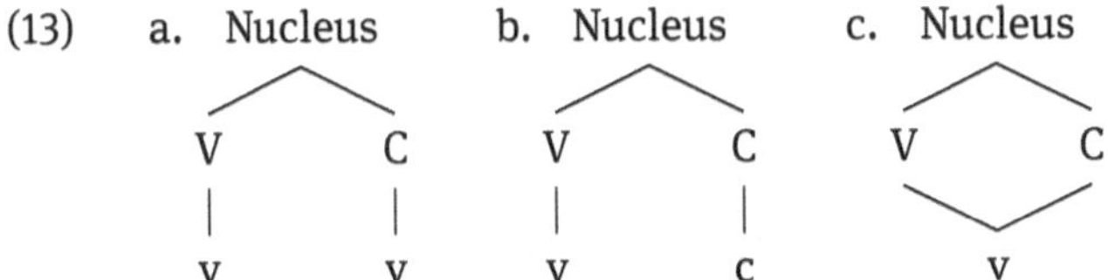

The structure in (13a) is probably the most intuitive one. The nucleus dominates two structural positions, which in turn dominate two v-letters. This is the case in the first syllables of the following examples: *Auge* 'eye', *augment*, *Schnee* 'snow', *fear*, *lee*. In the structure in (13b), the V-position dominates a v-letter and the nuclear C-position dominates a c-letter. Examples for this structure are the nuclei of the first graphematic syllables of the following words: *Tinte* 'ink', *man*, *in*. In the third structure, the two nuclear positions dominate one v-letter. I assume that this is the case in the first g-syllables of the following examples: <la.dy>, <pi.lot>, <Na.se> 'nose', <Buch> 'book', <Kuh> 'cow'.

Note that the structures in (13) closely resemble phonological structures: (13a) resembles the nuclear structure of a diphthong, (13b) resembles the nuclear structure of a phonological syllable with a lax vowel and (13c) resembles a phonological nucleus with a tense vowel.

Let us have a closer look at the structures in (13). In §2.3 we introduced the notion *graphematic diphthong* for structures like in (13a). Graphematic diphthongs can be defined as follows, cf. Berg et al. (2016):

(14) A graphematic diphthong consists of two v-letters dominated by the nucleus of the same graphematic syllable.

The notion of graphematic diphthong does not entail that graphematic diphthongs only correspond to phonological diphthongs. The definition in (14) is purely graphematic and does not state anything regarding correspondences to phonological units. In fact, although there are graphematic diphthongs that correspond to phonological ones, there are also graphematic diphthongs corresponding to phonological monophthongs. Table 3.5 gives an overview of German graphematic diphthongs and phonological correspondents.

Tab. 3.5: Graphematic diphthongs in German and their phonological correspondents (cf. Berg et al., 2016)

2nd position without correspondent			2nd position with correspondent		
<aa>	/a/	*Haar* 'hair'	<ai>	/ai̯/	*Hai* 'shark'
<ee>	/e/	*Heer* 'army'	<au>	/au̯/	*Haut* 'skin'
<oo>	/o/	*Moor* 'marshland'	<ei>	/ai̯/	*Leid* 'harm'
<ie>	/i/	*Lied* 'song'	<eu>	/ɔi̯/	*neu* 'new'

Primus (2010) notes that the phonological function of v-letters in the second position of a g-diphthongs in German can be captured by letter features: v-letters with a bent head, <a, e, o>, do not correspond to a sound within a phonological diphthong, v-letters with straight head, <i, u>, do. Regarding vowel quantity, graphematic diphthongs in German always correspond to either long vowels or diphthongs.

Let us now turn to graphematic diphthongs in English. Table 3.6 is based on Berg & Fuhrhop (2011) and Berg et al. (2016). The data in this table are based on the most frequent correspondences and leave out diphthongs which are followed by

<r> since <r> influences the phonological correspondences of graphematic diphthongs (Rollings 2004: 93ff., Berg & Fuhrhop 2011: 453). Furthermore, only correspondences of prosodically strong syllables are considered in this table because the phonological form and thus (de)coding partly depends on stress (Berg et al. 2016).

Tab. 3.6: Graphematic diphthongs in English and their correspondences (cf. Berg & Fuhrhop 2011)

2nd position without correspondent			2nd position with correspondent		
<au>	/ɔ/	*fraud, haul*	<ai>	/eɪ̯/	*plain, pain, fail*
<ea>	/i/	*bean, meat*	<ei>	/eɪ̯/	*veil, vein*
<ee>	/i/	*meet, seed*	<oi>	/ɔɪ̯/	*point, toil*
<oa>	/əʊ̯/	*groan, loan*	<eu>	/(j)u/	*feud, neuter*
<oo>	/(u)/	*tool, moon*	<ou>	/aʊ̯/	*loud, house*
<ie>	/i/	*field, fiend*			

Like in German, all graphematic diphthongs correspond to 'free' vowels (cf. e.g. Venezky 1970, 1999), i.e. either long monophthongs or diphthongs. Berg et al. (2016) note that in second position, <i> corresponds to /ɪ/, and <u> corresponds to /ʊ/ or /(j)ʊ/; the only exception is <au>, which corresponds to the monophthong /ɔ/. This means that only in <au>, <u> has no phonological correspondent in the second position in a g-diphthong. The v-letters <a, e, o> do not have a phonological correspondent in the second position of a graphematic diphthong. However, there are exceptions to these regularities. Berg et al. (2016) call the correspondences in table 3.6 'primary correspondences'; there are also secondary correspondences, which differ from primary correspondences.

In §1.2 above, we have introduced the notions *binary* for phonological monophthongs and diphthongs dominated by two structural positions and *unary* for monophthongs dominated by only one structural position. Analogously to the phonological notion of unary and binary, we can call the structures in (13a) and (13c) binary graphematic vowels. With a notion like this we can formulate the structural mapping constraint in (15) which captures the correspondences we have seen in tables 3.5 and 3.6:

(15) i. A binary g-vowel maps onto a binary p-vowel and vice versa.
ii. A unary g-vowel maps onto a unary p-vowel and vice versa.

The bidirectional mapping constraints in (15) state that the structural dominance relation between the CV-tier and the vowel must be identical in both representations. These mapping constraints are violable. In English, for instance, there is a number of words with g-diphthong that correspond to unary phonological vowels, e.g. *dead, threat, cook, blood, wood.*

Till now we have only seen evidence for the mapping of structures like (13a) onto binary p-vowels. I will now present evidence that this mapping constraint is also valid for structures like in (13c).

We can see from the set of graphematic diphthongs in German and English that not every thinkable combination is actually used in the writing systems. In English, there is no graphematic diphthong that starts with <i, u>, except for <ie>. A sequence of v-letters starting with either <i> or <u> corresponds usually to two heterosyllabic vowels as in *fluid* and *liar* (cf. Berg et al. 2016).

In German there is no graphematic diphthong in which the second letter displays umlaut marks, cf. <Baum> 'tree' – <Bäume> 'trees' and not *<Baüme>. According to Wiese (2000: 159-162), the underlying representation of the diphthong in <Bäume> is /aʏ/. The process of umlauting thus changes the second component of the diphthong: /au/ – /aʏ/, the first part remains unaffected.[4] Since umlaut is indicated by umlaut marks, the ungrammatical form *<Baüme> would be closer to the actual phonological representation (Primus 2003: 42).

Moreover, g-diphthongs consisting of two identical v-letters do not feature umlaut marks, cf. <Boot> 'boat' – *Bötchen* 'boat (diminutive)', but not **Böötchen*, cf. Primus (2003: 40).

Thus we see that <a, o, u> may appear in the second nuclear position, but <ä, ö, ü> may not. What differentiates these letters? The letters <ä, ö, ü> are complex graphemes; each consist of a v-letter and diacritics. <a, o, u>, on the other hand, are not complex, cf. §2.3. This observation leads Primus (2003, 2010) to the conclusion that complex graphemes are barred from the second nuclear position.

(16) *COMPL-C_{gN}: The second nuclear position of a g-syllable is barred for complex graphemes (Primus 2003: 40, my translation).

4 The surface form of the diphthong in *Bäume* is often transcribed as /ɔʏ/. Wiese (2000: 187) demonstrates that the change from /a/ to /ɔ/ in the umlauted diphthong is the result of an assimilation of /a/ to the second component of the diphthong, /ʏ/. The change from /a/ to /ɔ/ cannot be the result of umlauting, since umlauting /a/ results in /ɛ/ as in *Ball* 'ball' – *Bälle* 'balls' (Wiese 2000: 182).

The fact that the C-position of the nucleus is barred for complex graphemes is a cue to the identification of other positions within the syllable. V-letters with umlaut marks or other diacritics indicate the V-position of a syllable since they are in the nucleus but barred from its C-position; and complex graphemes after the V-position indicate the coda since they are barred from the nuclear C-position.

I will illustrate the interaction of the nucleus constraint in (11) and the constraint barring complex graphemes from the nuclear C-position in (16) with the help of the word <Maß> 'measure'.

As we have seen in §2.3, <ß> is a complex grapheme. According to (16) it may not appear in the second nuclear position of a graphematic syllable. The graphematic structures of <Maß> is displayed in (17).

(17)

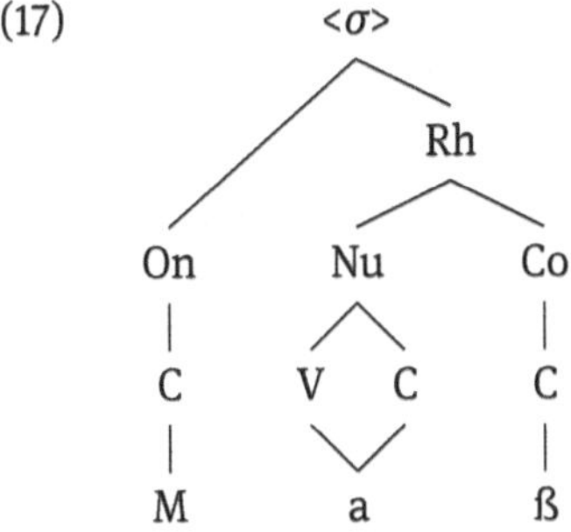

In (17), the complex grapheme <ß> is dominated by the coda and not by the nucleus in compliance with *COMPL-C_{gN}. The v-letter <a> is dominated by both positions of the branching nucleus, conforming to BRANCHING-GN.

The constraints *COMPL-C_{gN} and BRANCHING-GN thus explain very straightforwardly the structures of syllables with <ß>. The following tableau illustrates the evaluation for <Maß> as sketched above:

Tab. 3.7

<Maß>	*COMPL-C_{gN}	BRANCHING-GN
☞ a. $[\text{M}]_{On}$ $[\text{a}]_{Nu}$ $[\text{ß}]_{Co}$		
b. $[\text{M}]_{On}$ $[\text{a -}]_{Nu}$ $[\text{ß}]_{Co}$		*!
c. $[\text{M}]_{On}$ $[\text{a ß}]_{Nu}$	*!	

Let us have a closer look at the tableau above. The brackets in the candidate column indicate subsyllabic constituents. *On*, *Nu* and *Co* in subscript indicate onsets, nuclei and codas. All candidates have identical onsets, <M>. The nuclei and codas vary. The single <a> in the nucleus of the first candidate is associated with both structural positions of the nucleus, as opposed to the second candidate, whose <a> is dominated by only one structural position. The second structural position is empty as indicated by '-'. This results in a violation of BRANCHING-GN, indicated by a star in the row of the second candidate. While <ß> forms the coda of the two first candidates, the third candidate has no coda. The <ß> of the third candidate is dominated by the second nuclear position, resulting in a violation of *COMPL-C_{gN}. Since the first candidate satisfies both constraints, the violations of the second and third candidate are fatal. Candidate a. thus wins the evaluation and is the optimal output.

Note that the graphematic structure in (17) corresponds exactly to its phonological counterpart (18), although the graphematic structure is motivated independently by graphematic constraints. The analysis of <Maß> is thus an example of the structural mapping constraint presented in (15) with respect to binary g-vowels as presented in (13c).

(18)

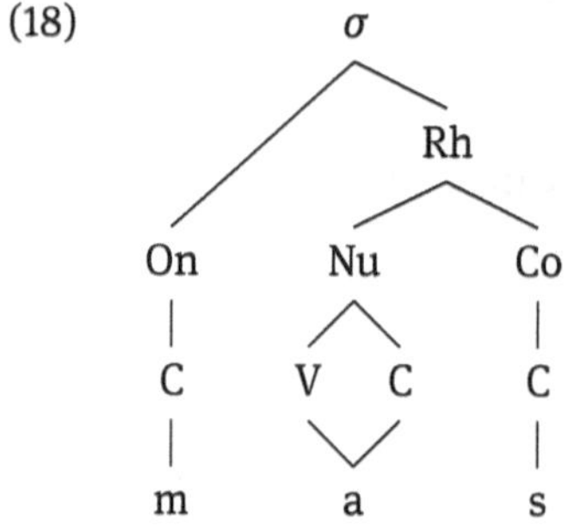

In German, <h> shares with <ß> the property that it is barred from the nucleus (but unlike <ß>, <h> may appear in the onset of a g-syllable). Primus (2000) formulates the following supra-segmental distributional constraint for <h>: "<h> may only appear in a post-nuclear C-position of a graphematic syllable that immediately follows a nuclear C-position occupied by a vocalic element" (Primus 2000: 23, my translation). The following examples from Primus (2000: 24)[5] illustrate the effect of the distributional constraint, cf. (19).[6]

(19) a. b. c.

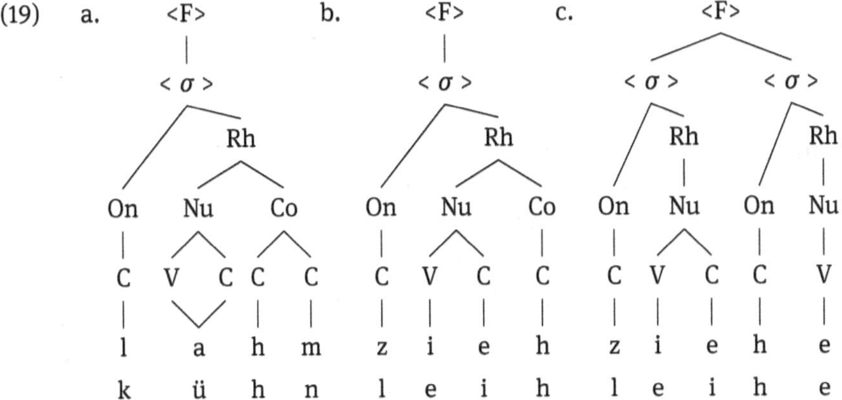

In (19b), the nucleus is occupied by two v-letters; <h> therefore constitutes the coda. The structure in (19c) illustrates the case in which <h> opens a second g-syllable. The evaluation of the syllable structure in (19a) is almost identical to the evaluation in (17). The only difference is that *COMPL-C_{gN} does not apply to <h>, therefore, *COMPL-C_{gN} is replaced by the distributional constraint *NUCLEAR-<h> barring <h> from the nuclear C-position. Consider tableau 3.8 for <lahm> 'lame'.

Tab. 3.8

<lahm>	*NUCLEAR-<h>	BRANCHING-GN
☞ a. $[l]_{On}$ $[a]_{Nu}$ $[hm]_{Co}$		
b. $[l]_{On}$ $[a\ \text{-}]_{Nu}$ $[hm]_{Co}$		*!
c. $[l]_{On}$ $[a\ h]_{Nu}$ $[m]_{Co}$	*!	

5 I changed the original illustration in two points by adding the subsyllabic constituent rhyme and by changing the highest node in the tree structures from <ω> indicating a graphematic word to <F> indicating a graphematic foot.

6 Translations: *lahm* 'lame', *kühn* 'brave', *zieh* 'pull', *leih* 'borrow', *ziehe* '(I) pull', *leihe* '(I) borrow'.

Tab. 3.9

<fish>	*COMPL-C_{gN}	BRANCHING-GN
☞ a. $[f]_{On}$ $[i]_{Nu}$ $[sh]_{Co}$		*
b. $[f]_{On}$ $[i\ sh]_{Nu}$	*!	

The candidates in tableau 3.8 differ with respect to their nucleus and their coda. Both nuclear positions of candidate a. are associated with <a>. <h> and <m> are dominated by the coda. The coda of candidate b. has the same structure, but the <a> in candidate b.'s nucleus is associated with one structural position only. Thus, the nucleus of candidate b. is not branching, which poses a violation of BRANCHING-GN. In candidate c., <a> and <h> are dominated by the nucleus, <m> is the only segment dominated by the coda. Since <h> is dominated by the nuclear C-position of the nucleus, candidate c. violates *NUCLEAR-<h>. Candidate a. does not violate any constraint, the violations of the other candidates are thus fatal and candidate a. is the winner of the evaluation.

An obvious problem for the analysis so far are syllables such as *fish, cash, Tisch* 'table', *Bach* 'brook.' Since (16) bars complex graphemes from the second nuclear position and full g-syllables have a branching nucleus (11), the v-letters of these words would have to occupy two structural positions within the nucleus. However, a v-letter that occupies two positions (in other words, a binary g-vowel) maps onto a binary p-vowel. This is not the case in the previous mentioned words: *fish, cash, Tisch, Bach* only contain a unary vowel in their phonological representation. Primus (2003) solves that problem by introducing a ranking of the constraints. She assumes that BRANCHING-GN ranks lower than *COMPL-C_{gN} (cf. Primus 2003). This ranking is illustrated in (20).

(20) *COMPL-C_{gN} $\gg$BRANCHING-GN

Let us have a look at the word *fish*. The phonological form [fɪʃ] contains a unary vowel and thus should map onto a graphematic word with a unary g-vowel, i.e. a v-letter that is dominated by only one structural position. The question is whether the complex grapheme <sh> is dominated by the nucleus or the coda. The constraint BRANCHING-GN requires that the nucleus of <fish> is branching, the constraint *COMPL-C_{gN} however prevents <sh> from occupying the second nuclear position, cf. tableau 3.9.

The result of the evaluation illustrated in tableau 3.9 is the structure in (21). According to Primus (2003: 45) it is plausible to assume that the nuclear C-position is not associated in cases like *la.chen* 'to laugh' or – in our case – *fish*. The superfluous C-position is eliminated, in other words, the nucleus is not branching. The brackets in tableau 3.9b. correspond to the constituents in (21).

(21)

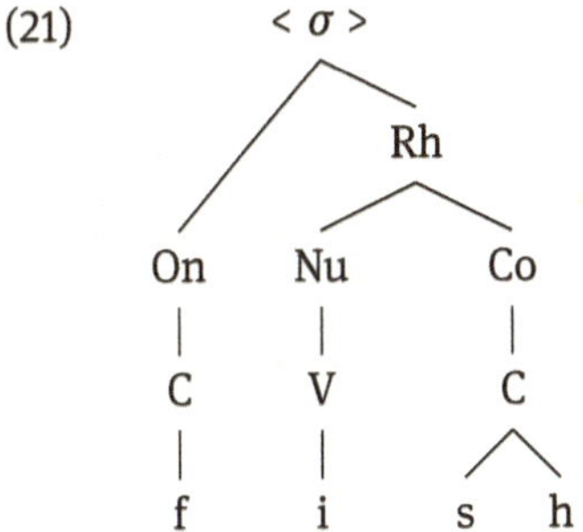

For a writer, both cases of complex c-graphemes are rather unproblematic. The undominated constraint *COMPL-C_{gN} causes the complex grapheme to be dominated by the coda. For a reader however it seems to be more complicated. Why are v-letters of syllables ending with complex graphemes of the type <sh>, <sch> connected with only one structural position while v-letters of syllables ending with <ß> or <h> are connected with two positions?

In order to be able to answer this question, let us have a closer look at te two types of graphemes under discussion. The difference between <ß> and other complex c-graphemes is their sub-graphemic make-up. As mentioned above, although <ß> is complex, it looks like one element – like <h>, a grapheme consisting of only one letter and also barred from the nucleus. A possible explanation for the difference between <h> and <ß> on the one side, and complex graphemes consisting of more than one letter on the other side could be the following hypothesis: the more letters a syllable-final, post-vocalic complex grapheme consists of, the likelier is the preceding v-letter decoded as unary p-vowel.

A search in the CELEX database (Baayen et al. 1995) confirms this hypothesis. There are 455 monosyllabic[7] items in the database of English lemmas which end in either <ch>, <sh>, <ph> or <th>. Out of these lemmas, 158 items decode a binary p-vowel. A very high percentage of these 158 items with binary p-vowels are coded with two v-letters (e.g. *tooth*). If we subtract them, 71 items (e.g. *march, graph, growth, bath*) remain. Two of these words had <w> following the v-letter

7 I chose to take monosyllabic words as a sample to avoid duplicate results stemming from compounds, such as *path* - *footpath*.

Tab. 3.10: Monosyllabic words ending in complex graphemes in English and German

	Results for English	
	# of words	**examples**
total	455	
unary p-vowel	297	*blush, cash, with*
binary p-vowel	158	*branch, growth*
two v-letters	87	*breech, couch, tooth*
<r>	48	*birth, north, starch*
remaining	23	*both, ninth, graph*
	Results for German	
	# of words	**examples**
total	222	
unary p-vowel	175	*Blick* 'look', *Loch* 'hole'
binary p-vowel	47	*Fleisch* 'meat', *Fluch* 'curse'
two v-letters	32	*Brauch* 'custom', *deutsch* 'German'
Umlaut	1	*ätsch* 'ha-ha' (interjection)
remaining	14	*Schmach* 'humiliation', *Tuch* 'cloth'

(*growth, strewth*). In the preceding section, we discussed v-letter definitions including <w>. As we have seen, <w> is a positional variant of <u>. The occurrence of <w> in this context is thus well motivated. A further 48 items had <r> following the v-letter. According to Rollings (2004: 93-95), a v-letter followed immediately by <r> encodes "heavy vowels": /aː, ɛː, ɔː/ as in *cart, fern, word* and *fort, warm* (with <r> being silent in non-rhotic dialects such as Received Pronunciation).

For German, the following results were found: There are 222 monosyllabic items in the database of German lemmas ending with either <ch>, <sch> or <ck>. 47 of these items decode a binary p-vowel. After subtracting the items with two v-letters corresponding to the binary p-vowel, only 15 items remain. One word contains an umlaut (*ätsch* 'ha-ha'(interjection)), which can be seen as a form of marking device (but consider *hübsch* 'pretty', [hʏpʃ] and *Kölsch* 'Cologne-style beer', [kœlʃ] without binary p-vowel). Interestingly, of these 14 items only 3 ended in <sch> (*Barsch* 'perch', *Drasch* 'hurry' (regional), *Tratsch* 'gossip'), the rest ended in <ch>. Table (3.10) summarises the findings for German and English.

We can summarise these findings as follows: The generalisation that the number of letters a syllable-final complex grapheme consists of has an influence on the status of the vowel as binary or unary holds for English and German data. The number of segments has an influence on the decoding of vowels. A binary p-vowel is coded, in general, with more than one letter if a complex grapheme is present in the syllable coda.

Figures 3.2 and 3.3 illustrate that the generalisation above covers ca. 95% of cases. There are only 5.1% of monosyllabic words in English and 6.3% of monosyllabic words in German with a complex grapheme consisting of more than one segment that decode a binary vowel without a special graphematic marker, such as doubled v-letters or <r> after a v-letter.

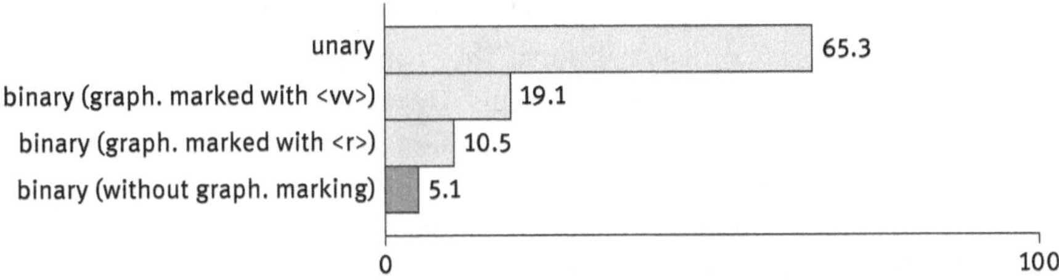

Fig. 3.2: Decoding of g-vowels in monosyllabic words ending in complex graphemes in percent (English data)

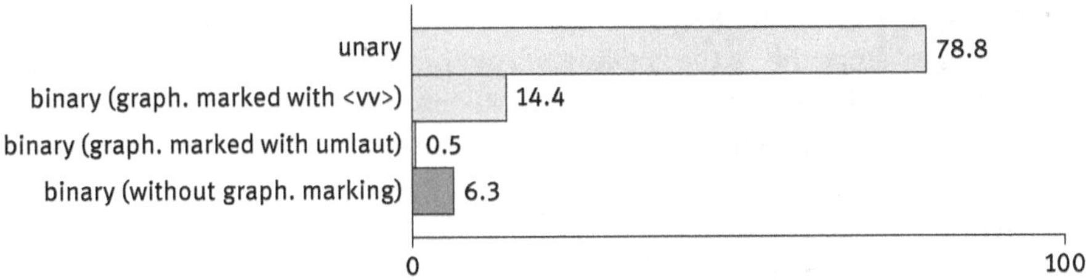

Fig. 3.3: Decoding of g-vowels in monosyllabic words ending in complex graphemes in percent (German data)

The findings of the CELEX search allow two interpretations. First, the analysis so far is correct and all complex graphemes (plus <h>) are barred from the nucleus. The presence of complex graphemes consisting of more than one letter in the coda of a graphematic syllable causes the nuclear C-position of the same syllable to be deleted. The second interpretation is contrary to the analysis so far: complex graphemes consisting of more than one letter are licensed in the nuclear C-position; in other words, instead of *COMPL-C_{gN} there is a constraint barring letters featuring umlaut marks and <ß> from the nuclear C-position. A constraint like this is quite similar to the one proposed for the banning of <h> from the nuclear C-position.

At this moment it is not possible to ultimately decide between these two interpretations of the results. Both interpretation can account for the data. The decisive argument of Primus (2003, 2010) is that the constraint *COMPL-C_{gN} can account for ambisyllabicity coding. However, I will show in §4.1 that this argument needs to be reconsidered in light of English data. For now we will leave this question open.

Let us turn to another aspect of graphematic nuclei. The constraints we have discussed so far are structural constraints. They concern the internal make-up of the graphematic syllable; they are not explicitly concerned with mapping relations. Implicitly, they contribute to mapping due to the structural mapping constraint in (15), which states that the nucleus structure of both representations, the phonological representation and the graphematic representation of a word, map onto each other. The structural constraints determine the structural make-up of the syllable, correspondence constraints map that structure onto the phonological structure.

Rollings (2004: 32-34) notes that graphematic syllable structure is used to code vowel quantity. Consider the pair /pleɪ̯n/ and /plæn/. These two words are potential homographs because the main correspondences of <a> in English are /eɪ̯/ and /æ/. "[...] /pleɪ̯n/ is a closed syllable although the vowel is tense. It is not spelled 'plan' since this is the spelling of /plæn/ in which the vowel, in a closed syllable, is lax. The spelling strategy here is to make the syllable orthographically open, by adding a 'dummy' silent vowel letter after the 'n', namely 'e"' (Rollings 2004: 33).

In accordance with Rollings' observation, Evertz & Primus (2013: 7) suggest the violable syllable structure mapping constraints in (22).

(22) In English, graphematic v-monophthongs in a strong g-syllable map
  a. onto a binary vowel if the g-syllable is open, and
  b. onto a unary vowel if the g-syllable is closed.

This constraint may be overridden by certain higher ranking constraints which may obfuscate the correspondence described by the mapping constraint. We will explore some of these constraints in this section. For a further analysis of the constraint in (22) cf. chapter 4, where its foot-sensitivity is discussed.

The constraints in (22) capture the decoding, i.e., reading, perspective. Evertz & Primus (2013) show that the mapping direction can be reversed by logical contrapositon in a non-derivational, constraint-based model, as defended here. The constraint (22a), for example, is equivalent to the statement that a non-unary (=

binary) vowel is mapped onto a v-letter in a non-closed (= open) g-syllable. The two mapping perspectives thus lead to two bidirectional regular correspondences (cf. table 3.11).

Tab. 3.11: Bidirectional correspondences of quantity coding and decoding (Evertz & Primus 2013)

v-letter in open strong g-syllable ↔ binary vowel	v-letter in closed strong g-syllable ↔ unary vowel
late, mate, mane, lane, sane, shake, lake, later, saner; table	*lad, mat, man, van, fan, sack, lack*
mete, gene, scene; meter, Peter	*met, bed, bet, fed, gem, pen, hen*
bite, dine, site, ride, ripe, white, shine; biter, diner, riper, hider, finer; rifle, title	*bit, din, sit, rid, rip, wit, hid, thin, sin*
dope, hope, tone, node, cone, rope, smoke; doper, hoper, choker	*drop, hop, ton, nod, con, hock, smog*
cute, nude, rude, tune, fume	*cut, mud, nut, fun*

Let us take a closer look at the two subconstraints in (22). (22a) combines the constraint militating for branching nuclei in strong full g-syllables, BRANCHING-GN (11), and the structural mapping constraint in (15): If a g-syllable is open, i.e., if there are no c-letters after the v-letter, the v-letter must be dominated by two structural positions in order to comply to BRANCHING-GN. This means that the v-letter is binary in structural terms. The structural mapping constraint in (15) states that binary g-vowels map onto binary p-vowels. The first g-syllables in words like *late, mete, bite, hope, cute* therefore correspond to binary p-vowels.

The correspondences shown in table 3.11 are obscured in some cases. Evertz & Primus (2013: 9) list some irregular patterns:

i. <o+Nasal+e> for a unary vowel: *done, one, come, some*
ii. <e> after <s> distinguishing stem final from inflectional <s>: *goose, mouse, cheese, dense, tense*. This kind of <e> does not disambiguate the phonological value of the first vowel.
iii. idiosyncratic cases, like *camel*
iv. <r> closing a syllable with an irregularly binary vowel (vowels in closed syllables are regularly unary): *scar, for, fur, fir*
v. <ight> and sonorant+c-clusters closing a syllable with a binary vowel: *sigh, night, find, ball, palm, cold*

Other instances of opaque patterns are explicable by their etymology (cf. Venezky 1999: 86). The superfluous <e> in *belle* or *tulle*, for example, can be explained by their Modern French origin. Another irregular pattern are words written with <v>. Words like *give* and *dive* are opaque with respect to their vowel quantity.[8] We will see in chapter 4 that <v> also behaves exceptionally in ambisyllabicity (de)coding.

We will examine the word *late* a bit closer in order to understand the mapping constraint in (22) better. (23a) illustrates the graphematic structure of *late*, (23b) illustrates its phonological structure.

(23) a. b.

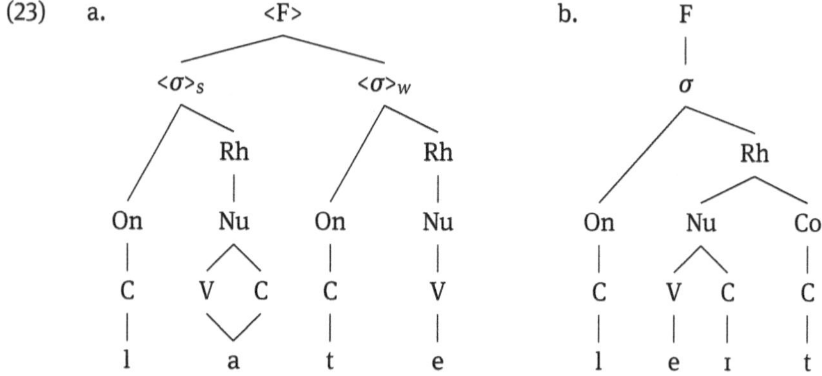

As we can see, there is a mismatch between the graphematic (a) and the phonological (b) structure in (23). The phonological representation of *late*, [leɪt], is phonologically monosyllabic, the graphematic representation, <la.te>, is graphematically bisyllabic. Note, however, that there are binary vowels in both structures: a diphthong in the phonological structure and a v-letter dominated by two structural positions in the graphematic structure. As in the cases of <h> and <ß> discussed above, the structural parallelism in (23a,b) results from an independent graphematic constraint.

The second subconstraint in (22) states that a graphematic v-monophthong, i.e. a single v-letter non-adjacent to another v-letter in the same g-syllable, maps onto a unary vowel if the g-syllable is closed. This is the case in words like: *man, leg, bin, dog, mud*. Let us have a look at the graphematic and phonological structure of *man*.

8 Interestingly, the non-standardised spelling of <love>, <luv>, is perfectly transparent.

(24) a. b.

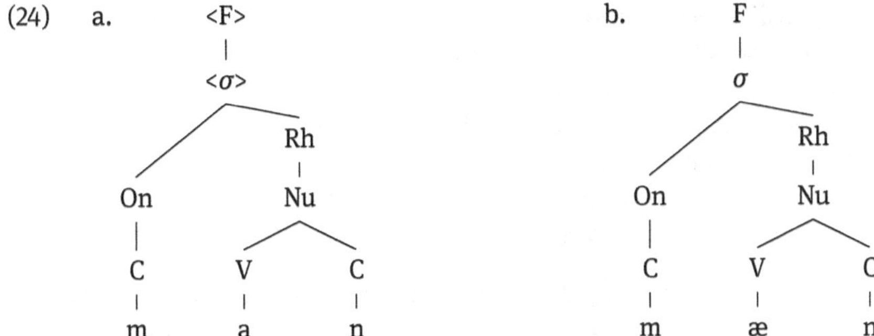

The structures in (24) are identical: The g-syllable <man> contains a v-monophthong in a closed and strong g-syllable which maps onto a unary p-vowel (also in a closed syllable).

The situation in German is different. The first part of the constraint in (22), which states that open g-syllables map onto binary p-vowels, seems to be valid in German. Let us consider the examples *Tag* 'day' and *Tage* 'days':

(25) a. b.

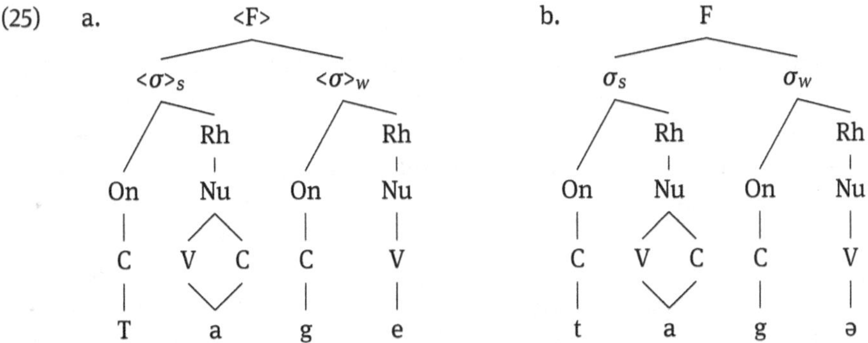

The structures of the word *Tage* are identical in both representations: The v-letter in the open first syllable of <Ta-ge> maps onto the binary vowel of /taːgə/.

Words like <platt> - [plat] 'flat' in which a closed g-syllable corresponds to a unary p-vowel conform to (22). Consider the example from above, but this time in singular. The singular form of *Tage* is <Tag> - [taːk]. The graphematic syllable <Tag> is closed but does not correspond to a binary p-vowel. Even worse, there are closed g-syllables with v-monophthongs with ambiguous phonological correspondences, e.g. <weg> - /wɛk/ 'away'; <Weg> - /weːk/ 'way'.

Examples like *weg* - *Weg* lead Neef (2005) to the conclusion that v-letters in German are generally underspecified regarding their correspondence to unary or binary p-vowels, but as we have seen above, this is not true for v-letters in open g-syllables. They always map onto binary p-vowels. Only v-letters in closed g-syllables seem to be underspecified in German.

The difference between English and German regarding the constraint (22b) may stem from *paradigmatic leveling* (cf. Kiparsky 1982, Kenstowicz 1996):

(26) Paradigmatic Levelling: Morphologically related variants of a lexical unit have identical representations.

As stated in (26), there is a strong tendency to level the morphological variation of a lexical unit. Let us look at the historical vowel shift that is responsible for the phonological vocalic contrast under discussion. In both languages, it turned unary vowels in stressed open syllables into binary vowels. In Early Modern German, for example, the plural form /tatən/ 'deeds' turned into /taːtən/, while the singular form /tat/ was unaffected by this rule. The phonological difference between these morphologically related forms has been leveled in favour of the binary variant, e.g., /taːt/. This phonological leveling is not coded graphematically and is responsible for many cases of graphematic ambiguity in monosyllabic words in German. Instead, leveling affected graphematic c-gemination to a considerable extent, such as in *Ritter* 'knight' and *Ritt* 'ride'. As a consequence of this leveling, it is the c-geminate pattern that is the reliable indicator of a unary vowel in monosyllabic words (as well as in bisyllabic words, cf. chapter 4 below). A monosyllabic word with a closed syllable and no c-gemination is ambiguous, cf. *weg* 'away' with a unary vowel and *Weg* 'way' with a binary vowel as well as the regional variation in the pronunciation of *Bad* 'bath' and *Gas* 'gas'. In addition, there are words with a binary vowel ending in a consonant cluster, e.g. *Arzt* 'doctor', *Obst* 'fruit', *Mond* 'moon'.

The situation is different in English. The effects of the vowel shift are not leveled phonologically, cf. the variant pronunciation of the stem of *final* and *finality*, *bathe* and *bath*, *provoke* and *provocative*. As to graphematic leveling, many variants, such as *jobber* and *job*, *hotter* and *hot*, *sinner* and *sin*, are exempt from leveling.

I will elaborate on how paradigmatic leveling interacts with the other constraints discussed in this section in §3.2.2. Graphematic c-gemination will be discussed in greater detail in the following chapter.

3.2.1.2 Reduced Syllables

Reduced syllables have non-branching nuclei. This means that the nucleus of a reduced syllable dominates exactly one position. This is the constituting property of reduced syllables. Readers, of course, cannot see the structure itself, they have to infer it by analysing cues. In this section, I will discuss the structure of reduced syllables and explain how readers can infer this structure.

In phonology, the identification of reduced syllables is straightforward: If the sonority peak of a syllable is schwa or a consonantal sonorant, it is a reduced syllable[9].

For a reader, the task of identifying a reduced g-syllable is harder because an identification on segmental grounds alone is insufficient. As mentioned above, only <e> is licensed in the nucleus of reduced g-syllables (Evertz & Primus 2013); however, <e> may also appear in nuclei of non-reduced g-syllables. In <fence>, for instance, <e> is the peak of two syllables: The first g-syllable is a full g-syllable, the second g-syllable is reduced. The occurrence of <e> is therefore a necessary, but not a sufficient, condition for the identification of reduced g-syllables. Clearly, reduced graphematic syllables cannot be defined only by specifying which segments are licensed in the nucleus, there must be more conditions:

(27) A graphematic syllable is called reduced
  i. if its nucleus is not branching,
  ii. if its peak is <e>,
  iii. if it is situated in a prosodically weak position within a foot,
  iv. and if it is light.

In order to understand the conditions in (27) better, let us return for a moment to reduced phonological syllables. The foot structure and the nucleus structure are closely connected (Wiese 2000: 280). The head of a foot is stressed. According to Wiese (2000) only branching nuclei are capable of bearing stress, non-branching nuclei can therefore be seen as defective. Wiese (2000: 108, 280) even claims that reduced syllables underlyingly do not have a nucleus at all. He argues that reduced syllables are therefore skipped in stress rules. In other models (e.g. Giegerich 1992), reduced syllables have a non-branching nucleus (but are also irrelevant for stress rules). Being unable to carry stress equals being unable to be in a prosodically strong position. Thus, a reduced syllable cannot be the head of a foot.

9 In English, also [ɪ] is licensed in nuclei of reduced syllables.

The segmental restriction confining the nuclei of reduced p-syllables to sonorants or schwa (or [ɪ] in English) is an epiphenomenon of the connection of the nucleus and the foot structure. They are the only elements that are licensed in the V-position of a non-branching nucleus and thus the only elements licensed in the peak of a reduced p-syllable (cf. section 1.2.1 for a broader discussion). Full vowels which, due to stress shift, end in a weak foot position are therefore reduced to schwa: *atom* [ˈætəm] - *atomic* [əˈtɒmɪk] (cf. chapter 4), *compost* [ˈkɒmˈˈpɒst] - *compost heap* [ˈkɒmpəstˈˈhip] (Giegerich 1992: 285). Reduction is thus not only a segmental process but also a supra-segmental one: a nucleus is reduced to only one structural position.

Let us now consider the conditions in (27): The connection between foot and nucleus structure also exists in graphematics. Only syllables with a branching nucleus can be the head of a foot. Reduced g-syllables have non-branching nuclei (27i) and thus cannot be heads of feet.

Unlike in phonology, the segmental nucleus restriction in graphematics is not directly connected to nucleus and foot structure. <e> is the regular correspondent of schwa, but this letter can also appear in a branching nucleus (e.g. the first syllable of *fence*, see below). As mentioned above, the occurrence of <e> is a necessary but not sufficient condition for reduced g-syllables (27ii).

We can see, however, the connection of nucleus and foot structure in the following observation: A reduced g-syllable cannot appear in isolation (just like a reduced p-syllable cannot appear isolated). It needs the presence of a strong syllable within the same foot domain. There is no foot consisting of a reduced syllable only since every foot must contain exactly one head (which is strong by definition, cf. chapter 4 below). There is only one strong position within a foot: Every foot (regardless whether g or p) is head-initial. All other positions in the foot domain are prosodically weak. A reader has therefore to identify the head of a foot in order to identify a reduced g-syllable within this foot (27iii). I will elaborate on graphematic feet in chapter 4. For now we can say that the first and third conditions in (27) are applicable to both p- and g-syllables and that the status of a syllable (head or non-head of a foot) is closely connected to the properties of its nucleus.

The fourth condition (27iv) refers to the weight of the g-syllable. The more segments, i.e. letters, the rhyme of a g-syllable dominates, the heavier it is (cf. §4.3 for a broader discussion). The nucleus of a reduced syllable contains exactly one segment, that is <e>. In order to be light, there can only be one more segment in the rhyme. If there are more segments, the syllable is heavy, and by that, not only a full syllable, but also likely to be head of a foot (cf. *lament*, *confess*, *Kompliment* 'compliment' etc.).

The lightest reduced g-syllable is an open g-syllable with <e> as peak. I call this type of syllable *minimal syllable*. In the writing system of English, minimal syllables have one property which distinguishes them from other reduced syllables. The nucleus of a minimal syllable does not map onto a phonological nucleus. Put differently, the nucleus of a minimal syllable is – with few exceptions (see below) – mute. This type of syllable can be used to code prosodic properties of a word without adding phonological material or even changing the phonological syllable structure of the preceding syllable in the decoding process. The function of minimal syllables will be described in more detail in chapter 4.

Minimal syllables in German, on the other hand, are not mute. This difference between the writing system of English and German can be accounted for in an optimality theoretic framework. But before turning to the optimality theoretic account in the next section, let us have a look at the data.

A CELEX (Baayen et al. 1995) search aided by a JAVA-script confirmed the existence and relevance of the minimal syllable in English. There are 52.447 items in the CELEX database of English lemmas. 9450 items end with <e>. 8870 items end with an <e> not adjacent to another v-letter. 97 items that match the latter criterion actually end with a phonological vowel. Most of these items are not native or proper nouns, e.g. *adobe, agave, apostrophe, catastrophe, Chile, coyote, facsimile, sesame, Zimbabwe*. Statistically speaking, only 1.1 % of words ending in a single <e> not adjacent to another v-letter actually end with a vowel. In other words, for 98,8% of the items with a final <e>, this <e> is mute.

In the next step I refined the search in order to be able to check whether words ending in a minimal syllable ended with a corresponding reduced syllable that does not necessarily end with a vowel (like, for instance <fire> - [faɪ̯ər] and <tickle> - [tɪkl̩]). Of all 52.447 items there are only 720 items ending in a corresponding reduced phonological syllable. This means only 7.6% of words ending in <e> also have a corresponding reduced p-syllable. In total, 92.4% of minimal g-syllables do not correspond to a phonological syllable nucleus.

If we subtract words with more than one letter between the final <e> and the next v-letter, there are only 70 (0.7%) items with a corresponding reduced syllable. All of these items show the pattern <-ire> or <-yre>, e.g. *fire, tyre*.[10]

The last step was taken in order to eliminate a side effect: if there is more than one intermediate letter between the final <e> and the next v-letter (of the preceding syllable), the onset of the <e>-syllable corresponds to a syllabic consonantal sonorant, e.g. <acceptable> - [əkˈseptəbl̩]. I will discuss this behaviour in the next section. The following table summarises these findings:

10 Two items, the loanwords *krone, vivace* deviate from this pattern.

Tab. 3.12: Lexical exceptions to the minimal syllable constraint in English

lemmas ending in	total	percentage	examples
<C*e>	8.870	100	*fence, mace, fire, Chile*
/reduced syllable/	720	7.6	*fire, tickle, sizzle*
/V/	97	1.1	*catastrophe, Chile, Zimbabwe*
<Ce> & /red. syll/	70	0.7	*fire, tyre*

Now that we have established the main properties of reduced graphematic syllables we may return to the critical example *fence* from the beginning of the section. At first glance, both syllables of this word qualify as reduced graphematic syllables since both syllables contain <e> as the sole v-letter. The default assumption is that a foot is trochaic (cf. chapter 4). This means that a reader assumes that the first syllable of a sequence of two syllables is the head of a foot, if there is no evidence to the contrary. In the case of *fence*, there is no evidence against the default assumption. On the contrary, the fact that the second syllable satisfies the necessary condition for a reduced g-syllable reinforces it.

A reader must therefore assume that the first graphematic syllable <fen> is in a prosodically strong position, whereas the second syllable <ce> is prosodically weak:

(28)

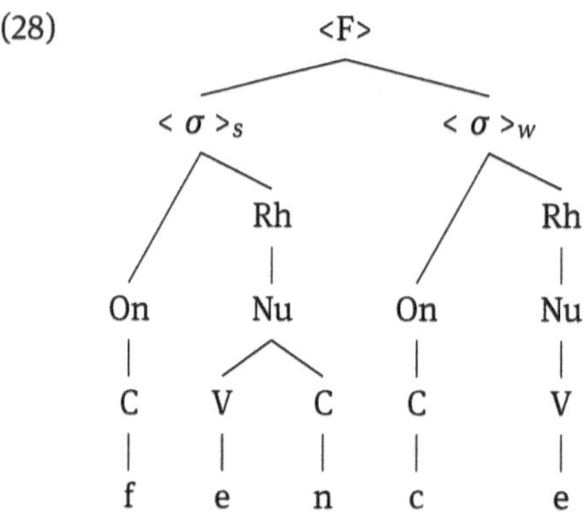

The second syllable is light: it is an open syllable with a simple onset, the sole v-letter is <e>. As we have seen in the quantitative analysis above, there is a very strong tendency that the nucleus of a g-syllable like this does not map onto a phonological nucleus. In other words, it is very likely that a g-syllable like the last g-syllable in <fence> is a minimal syllable, so, there is a very strong preference to map <fence> onto the following phonological structure:

(29)

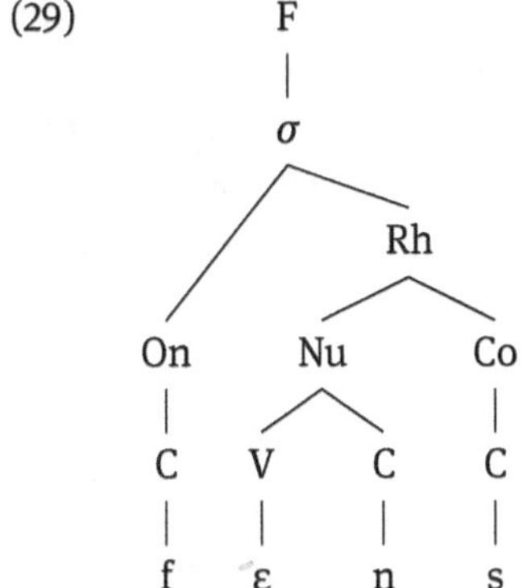

For now we can summarise the following points: First, the only v-letter that is licensed in the peak of a reduced graphematic syllable is <e>. Second, the nucleus of a reduced g-syllable does not branch. Third, because only syllables with branching nuclei can be heads of feet, reduced syllables are always in prosodically weak positions, i.e., non-head positions. This property is shared by phonological and graphematic syllables alike. And fourth, reduced graphematic syllables are light: next to <e> only one more c-letter can appear in a reduced g-syllable.

In English, there is a subclass of reduced g-syllables, the minimal syllable. This kind of syllable does not have a coda at all. The nucleus of a minimal g-syllable does not map onto a phonological nucleus. A CELEX-search revealed that there are very few lexical exceptions to this constraint, most of them are proper nouns or non-native words. In German, however, minimal syllables do map onto a phonological nuclei. In the following section, this difference will be discussed within an optimality theoretic approach.

3.2.2 A first OT-analysis of vowel quantity correspondences

In the previous sections we explored the make-up of the subsyllabic constituents of the graphematic syllables in English and German. I will now present an optimality theoretic analysis that will reveal how vowel quantity corresponds to graphematic syllable structures. The necessary constraints for this analysis were presented and explained in the previous sections. I will repeat them for convenience in a form which is better applicable for an OT-analysis.

As I have sketched in the introduction, there are different kinds of constraints. We need three types of constraints for this analysis: *markedness* or *well-formedness constrains*, *faithfulness constraints* and *mapping* or *correspondence constraints*. Markedness or well-formedness constraints militate for unmarked and well-formed outputs. Faithfulness constraints are violated when there are differences between input and output or, in the case of OO-faithfulness constraints, when there are differences between outputs. These constraints generally conflict with markedness constraints. Finally, there are mapping or correspondence constraints. Since the input and the output in OT analyses of the correspondence of phonological and graphematic syllable structures are mapping relations, these constraints belong in this case to the faithfulness constraints.

Two basic faithfulness constraints in OT are constraints militating against deletions and epentheses:

(30) *Constraints militating against deletion and epenthesis* (e.g. Kager 1999: 67f.)
   i. MAX:
      Input segments must have output correspondents. ('No deletion')
   ii. DEP:
      Output segments must have input correspondents. ('No insertion')

The next input-output correspondence map unary p-vowels onto closed g-syllables and binary p-vowels on open g-syllables. These constraints were introduced in (22). I will repeat them here for convenience in a shortened fashion, cf. (31).

(31) *Vowel quantity mapping constraints* (cf. Evertz & Primus 2013)
   i. UNARY:
      A unary p-vowel bidirectionally corresponds to a v-letter in a closed and strong g-syllable
   ii. BINARY:
      A binary p-vowel bidirectionally corresponds to a v-letter in an open and strong g-syllable

UNARY and BINARY are bidirectional constraints. The conditions within the constraint have two values, (unary/ binary) and (closed/ open). One value is the negation of the other value: a non-closed syllable is open and a non-unary vowel is binary.

If a candidate violates one constraint, it also incurs a violation of the other constraint. Consider the phonological form [leɪ̯t], which has a binary vowel, as an input. If this form was coded <lat>, the binary p-vowel would map onto a single v-letter within a strong and closed g-syllable. A candidate <lat> therefore violates BINARY since this constraint demands that a binary p-vowel maps onto an open and strong g-syllable. But <lat> also violates UNARY because UNARY states that a v-letter in a closed and strong g-syllable maps onto a unary p-vowel. In the input, however, there is a binary p-vowel. This consideration is also valid when we turn the perspective: consider the graphematic form <la.te> with an open and strong first syllable as input. A phonological candidate [læt] with a unary p-vowel violates BINARY because this constraints states that an open and strong g-syllable maps unto a binary p-vowel. This candidate also violates BINARY because the unary p-vowel of the candidate does not correspond to a v-letter in a closed and strong g-syllable.

These considerations show that a violation of one constraint leads to a simultaneous violation of the other constraint. Thus, every violation of BINARY is also a violation of UNARY and vice versa. This means that UNARY and BINARY are tied (i.e. they are on the same level in a constraint hierarchy), it also rather suggests that they are, in fact, not two, but one constraint. I will therefore subsume these constraints under the label UNARYBINARY.

As we have seen in the consideration above, another plausible candidate regarding the input [leɪ̯t] is <la.te>. Due to the constraint in (2), which states that every g-syllable has a v-letter in its peak, we can conclude that <la.te> is bisyllabic. Its first syllable is graphematically open because <e> constitutes an own g-syllable with <t> as onset. The graphematic form thus satisfies UNARYBINARY, which demands a correspondence of binary p-vowels and open and strong g-syllables. The price for this conformity is a violation of DEP since in <la.te> there is an additional segment, <e>, that does not correspond to any segment in the input.

A third plausible candidate is <la>. This candidate consists of the open first syllable of the second candidate only. As we have seen above, the open g-syllable does not violate UNARYBINARY, however, there is one segment in the input, [t], that has no correspondent in the output. The candidate thus violates MAX.

Only the second candidate, <late>, is optimal. This means that in order to conform to UNARYBINARY, elements can be added but not deleted. The ranking in (32) summarises the discussion so far:

(32) UNARYBINARY ≫MAX ≫DEP

3.2.2.1 English Cases, p → g

We begin our analysis of the correspondence of phonological and graphematic syllable structures of English words with a phonological input and a graphematic output. We examine the examples <late> - /leɪt/ and <lad> - /læd/ The first word, *late* is phonologically monosyllabic and contains a binary vowel, to be more precise, the diphthong /eɪ̯/, but it is graphematically bisyllabic <la.te>. The second word is graphematically and phonologically monosyllabic. Its p-syllable contains a unary vowel. Tableau 3.13 illustrates the evaluation of *late*.

Tab. 3.13

/leɪ̯t/	UNARYBINARY	MAX	DEP
☞ a. la.te			*
b. lat.te	*!		**
c. lat	*!		
d. la		*!	

The input in tableau 3.13 contains a binary vowel. UNARYBINARY can therefore only be satisfied if the corresponding vowel of a candidate is housed by an open and strong syllable. This is the case in candidate a. and d., but not in b. and c. The corresponding vowels in candidates b. and c. are in a closed and strong syllable. Candidate b. furthermore violates DEP twice because the segments <te> appear in the input but not in the output. The v-letter of candidate d. is housed by an open and strong syllable, but this syllable is open because there is no correspondent to [t], which is present in the input. Therefore, candidate d. violates MAX. The winning candidate satisfies all constraints except for DEP. The additional segment <e> constitutes an own syllable which takes <t> as an onset and thereby opens the first syllable.

But why is <e> and not another v-letter inserted? After all, a candidate *<la.to> satisfies UNARYBINARY as well as <la.te>. In the previous section, I introduced the minimal syllable, a graphematic syllable whose nucleus has no phonological correspondent. A minimal syllable requires as a necessary (but not sufficient) condition <e> as the sole v-letter. All other g-syllables with any other v-letter are not minimal syllables and thus correspond to phonological nuclei. The input /leɪ̯t/ is monosyllabic. A candidate *<la.to> thus does not match the input, as it would probably be decoded /leɪ̯.toʊ̯/. I propose the following special case of DEP, which is able to rule out candidates like *<la.to>:

(33) DEPNUC: Every nucleus in the output corresponds to a nucleus in the input.

In order to understand the constraint DEPNUC better, let us examine when the constraint can be violated and when not. The constraint is not violated, when there is a nucleus in the output and there is a corresponding nucleus in the input. It is violated, however, when there is a nucleus in the output but not in the input. Let us apply these considerations to the case at hand. The input is /leɪ̯t/. This input is monosyllabic, this means there is only one nucleus. There are two candidates that have not been ruled out yet, *<la.to> and <la.te>. In both candidates, the nucleus of the first g-syllable corresponds to the nucleus in the input. There is, however, no nucleus in the input for the graphematic syllable <to> in *<la.to>. *<la.to> therefore violates DEPNUC. <te> in <la.te> is a minimal syllable. Nuclei of minimal syllables do not correspond to phonological nuclei. A minimal syllable like <te> in <la.te> thus cannot violate DEPNUC.

DEPNUC therefore rules out candidates whose second syllable is opened by any other v-letter than <e>. For the forthcoming evaluation it does not matter how this constraint is ranked relatively to the other relevant constraints. With any constraint ranking comprising DEPNUC, words like *<la.to> are ruled out.[11]

Let us turn now to monosyllabic p-syllables with unary p-vowels.

Tab. 3.14

/læd/	UNARYBINARY	MAX	DEP
☞ a. lad			
b. la.de	*!		*
c. lad.de			*!*
d. la	*!	*	

The case of the monosyllabic word *lad* is quite simple. The winning candidate <lad> violates no constraints. Every other candidate adds or deletes segments compared to the input and violates thus DEP or MAX. Candidates d. and b. furthermore violate UNARYBINARY since their first syllables are open, while in the input there is a closed syllable.

3.2.2.2 English Cases, g → p

Let us now turn to the analysis of the correspondence of syllable structures in Eglish. This time, the input is graphematic and the output is phonological. We begin with *lad*, cf. table 3.15.

11 In §4.4.3.2 I will present a bidirectional optimality theoretical approach which can do without this constraint.

Tab. 3.15

<lad>	UNARYBINARY	MAX	DEP
☞ a. læd			
b. leɪ̯.tə	*!		*
c. lædə			*!
d. læ		*!	

Once again, the evaluation is quite simple. The winning candidate a. violates no constraint. Every other candidate adds or deletes segments and thus violates DEP or MAX. Candidate b. additionally violates UNARYBINARY since there is a mismatch between the syllable structure in the input and the p-vowel of the output.[12]

The next evaluation shows that our set of constraints is not complete. Evaluating *late* with a graphematic input and only the three constraints discussed so far yields an incorrect output, cf. tableau 3.16. Candidates b. and d. violate UNARYBINARY: the first syllables of b. and. d. each contain a unary p-vowel, whereas the first g-syllable of the input is open and strong. Candidate a. violates MAX because the <e> in the input does not have a correspondent in a.; in c., on the other hand, there is a correspondent to <e>. In conclusion, although candidate a. is the desired output, it performs worse than candidate c. in the evaluation.

Tab. 3.16

<la.te>	UNARYBINARY	MAX	DEP
(☞) a. leɪ̯t		*!	
b. læt	*!	*	
☹ c. leɪ̯.tə			
d. lætə	*!		

12 Candidate d. is not only suboptimal because of its violation of MAX; candidate d. is also phonologically ill-formed. I have excluded phonological well-formedness constraints in this analysis in order to keep the focus on the correspondence constraints.

As I have shown in the previous section on reduced graphematic syllables, the nucleus of a minimal g-syllable does not have a phonological correspondent; and <te> in <la.te> is a minimal g-syllable. This property of the minimal g-syllable is expressed in (34):

(34) MINSYLL: The nucleus of a minimal g-syllable does not correspond to a phonological nucleus.

Because /leɪt/ and not /leɪ.tə/ corresponds to <la.te>, MINSYLL must rank higher than MAX. MINSYLL does not conflict with UNARYBINARY, I therefore assume that they belong to the same stratum. Tableau 3.17 illustrates the evaluation of <la.te> with a graphematic input and the new constraint.

Tab. 3.17

<la.te>	UNARYBINARY	MINSYLL	MAX	DEP
☞ a. leɪt			*	
b. læt	*!		*	
c. leɪ.tə		!*		
d. lætə̩	*!	*		

Candidates a. and b. display the same violations as in the evaluation illustrated in tableau 3.16. In addition to the violations discussed above, candidates c. and d. each violate MINSYLL because both of them have a phonological correspondent to the minimal syllable in the input.[13]

3.2.2.3 German Cases, p → g

Let us now turn to German. At first sight, German data are confusing. As mentioned above, binary p-vowels may correspond to graphematically closed and open syllables in German (cf. <Weg> 'way' – [veːk] vs. <weg> 'away' – [vɛk]). Another property that differentiates German from English is that in German, nuclei of minimal g-syllables do have phonological correspondents, therefore, there must be a different constraint ranking in German.

13 A candidate like *[leɪ̯.t] would not violate any of the constraints displayed in tableau 3.16, however, this candidate would be phonologically ill-formed (cf. the previous footnote).

Since the nuclei of minimal g-syllables have phonological correspondents in German, MAX must be ranked higher than MINSYLL. I assume that MAX also dominates UNARYBINARY because it is not possible in German – like in English – to open a g-syllable by deleting segments of the input. Since no epentheses, like, for example, minimal syllables, are used to open g-syllables in German, DEP must rank higher than UNARYBINARY. This constraint hierarchy is illustrated in (35):

(35) MAX, DEP ≫UNARYBINARY

As we have seen earlier, the evaluation of the correspondent of a closed phonological syllable containing a unary vowel is trivial since the optimal candidate does not violate any of the relevant constraints. I will thus skip those analyses. I will concentrate on binary p-vowels corresponding to single v-letters in closed and open g-syllables. Let us examine the examples <Tag> - [ta:k] 'day' and <Ta.ge> - [ta:.gə] 'days'. We begin with the evaluation of the graphematic correspondent of /ta:g/, cf. tableau 3.18.

Tab. 3.18

/ta:g/	MAX	DEP	UNARYBINARY
☞ a. Tag			*
b. Ta.ge		*!	
c. Ta	*!		
d. Taag		*!	
e. Tahg		*!	

The first (and only) syllable of the winning candidate a. is strong and closed, but the input contains a binary vowel. Candidate a. therefore violates UNARYBINARY. All other candidates, however, either add (candidates b., d., e.) or delete (c.) segments of the input, while they conform to UNARYBINARY. The segmental faithfulness to the input outranks the vowel mapping constraints. Thus, there is no better alternative to the input /ta:g/ than candidate a.

The evaluation of the correspondent of an open p-syllable with a binary vowel is quite simple, cf. table 3.19. The winning candidate a. does not violate any constraint. All other candidates are unfaithful to the input with regard to the segments (b., c. and d.) or do not comply to the bidirectional constraint UNARYBINARY (b. and c.).

Tab. 3.19

/taː.gə/	MAX	DEP	UNARYBINARY
☞ a. Ta.ge			
b. Tag.ge		*!	*
c. Tag	*!		*
d. Ta	*!*		

3.2.2.4 German Cases, g → p

As opposed to the situation in English, nuclei of minimal syllables in German have a phonological correspondent. The constraint MINSYLL militating for a zero correspondence of nuclei of minimal syllables must therefore rank lower than MAX. The ranking of MINSYLL relative to UNARYBINARY is irrelevant, both possible rankings yield the same result.

(36) MAX, DEP ≫UNARYBINARY, MINSYLL

Tableau 3.20 illustrates an evaluation applying this ranking. The input is comparable to the earlier discussed example <la.te> in English: there is a strong and open first g-syllable and a minimal g-syllable. In English, candidate b. would be the optimal output, however, since MINSYLL is ranked lower than MAX, candidate b. and c.[14] perform worse than a. and d. In addition to its violation of MAX, candidate c. does not conform to UNARYBINARY. Candidate d. violates UNARYBINARY and the equally high ranking constraint MINSYLL. Candidate a. violates only MINSYLL and is thus the optimal output.
The next example, <Tag> - [taːk], needs some consideration before we begin with the evaluation. <Tag> is a strong g-syllable ending in a single c-letter. With the current ranking and the current constraints, the optimal correspondent of <Tag> would be *[tak] with a unary vowel.

As we have discussed earlier, the reason why the nucleus of <Tag> corresponds to a binary vowel can be explained by morpheme constancy. Morpheme constancy denotes the tendency that morphologically related variants of a lexical unit have identical representation, cf. (26) above. A lexical unit in this sense is

14 Neef (2005) and Geilfuß-Wolfgang (2007) argue that final devoicing in German works as a sort of "phonological corrective" (Geilfuß-Wolfgang 2007: 145) making sure that a reader pronounces all obstruents in the rhyme of a syllable voiceless. This phenomenon is purely phonological and needs no discussion here.

Tab. 3.20

<Ta.ge>	MAX	DEP	UNARYBINARY	MINSYLL
☞ a. taː.gə				*
b. taːk	*!			
c. tak	*!		*	
d. tagə			*!	*

the stem. The principle of morpheme constancy is hence also known as *stem constancy* (e.g. Wiese 2004, Geilfuss-Wolfgang 2007). Let us have a look at the written and spoken paradigm of *Tag* (cf. table 3.21).

Tab. 3.21: The phonological and graphemtatic representation of the paradigm of the German noun *Tag* 'day'

	Phonological		Graphematic	
	Sg.	**Pl.**	**Sg.**	**Pl.**
Nominative	taːk	taː.gə	Tag	Ta-ge
Genitive	taːks/taː.gəs	taː.gə	Tags/Ta-ges	Ta-ge
Dative	taːk/taː.gə	taː.gən	Tag/Ta-ge	Ta-gen
Accusative	taːk	taː.gə	Tag	Ta-ge

As we can see in the phonological representation of the paradigm of *Tag* in table 3.21, there is a single consonant following the first p-vowel. In the plural forms (optional in genitive and dative singular), this single consonant forms the onset of the syllabic suffix due to onset maximation (cf. §1.2). Since no phonological syllable may end in a unary p-vowel, the p-vowel in the first syllable is binary in forms with a syllabic suffix. Due to stem constancy, all p-vowels in the singular forms, even those with a closed first syllable, are also binary.

If these considerations are valid for *Tag*, why is the decoding of a graphematic form like <Weg> ambiguous? This is because the word *Weg* is ambiguous: there is a noun *Weg* 'way' and an adverb *weg* 'away'. While the noun *Weg* is inflected like *Tag* in table 3.21, the adverb *weg* is not inflected at all, therefore, the noun *Weg* is subject to stem constancy and has a binary vowel whereas the adverb *weg* is not part of a paradigm that could be the cause for stem constancy. It has thus a unary vowel (in compliance to UNARYBINARY).

How can we describe stem constancy in an OT-model? Regarding the input and the output, I assume that the matter of whether or not a word has syllabic suffixes in its paradigm is part of the input. For example, input <Tag> is enhanced to <Tag> + <e>. The output thus does not only consist of one form, but of (at least) two forms.

Stem constancy can be understood as a faithfulness relation between outputs (OO-faithfulness, cf. e.g. Kager 1999, Burzio 2005 for an overview). OO-faithfulness constraints are instances of identity constraints (McCarthy & Prince 1995a):

(37) IDENTITY(γF): Let α be a segment in S_1 and β be its correspondent in S_2. If α is [γF], then β is [γF].

The general identity constraint in (37) states that the value γ of a feature F must be identical in corresponding segments. At the moment, we are not interested in features and segments, but in supra-segmental structures and their properties. We will thus employ the IDENT-constraint on supra-segmental units. The units S_1 and S_2 can be the input or the output of an evaluation. Identity constraints can hence be used to describe input-output-faithfulness (IDENT-IO), but also to describe output-output-faithfulness (IDENT-OO).

For the question at hand we are interested in vowels. I therefore propose the constraint IDENT-OO[UnBin] demanding that vowels of an output are identical regarding being unary or binary.

Let us now consider the ranking. In German, phonological stem constancy is obviously higher ranked than UNARYBINARY because the nucleus of <Tag> related to <Ta.ge> corresponds to a binary vowel at the expense of UNARYBINARY, cf. the ranking in (38):

(38) MAX, DEP, IDENT-OO[UnBin] $\gg$UNARYBINARY, MINSYLL

The evaluation in tableau 3.22 illustrates the application of the ranking in (38)[15]. Note that the input contains two forms according to the considerations above.
In contrast to this evaluation, where the paradigm played a role, we will now examine the evaluation of correspondents of the adverb *weg*.
This evaluation strongly resembles the evaluation of *lad* or other words with a closed g-syllable and a unary p-vowel: the optimal candidate does not violate any relevant constraint since it satisfies UNARYBINARY. IDENT-OO[UnBin] is irrelevant in this evaluation because there is only one output.

15 MAX and DEP are irrelevant in this evaluation, they are therefore left out of tableau 3.22

Tab. 3.22

<Tag>, <Ta.ge>	IDENT-OO[UnBin]	UNARYBINARY
☞ a. taːk, taː.ge		*
b. tak, taː.ge	*!	

Tab. 3.23

<weg>	IDENT-OO[UnBin]	UNARYBINARY
a. veːk		*
☞ b. vɛk		

It has to be noted, however, that there are a number of exceptions to stem constancy. There are, for instance, some words that have regional variants that cannot be explained with this analysis, e.g. *Gas* 'gas' or *Bad* 'bath' are attested with unary and binary vowel although they have syllabic suffixes in their paradigm.[16] *Gas* and *Bad* with unary vowels thus violate IDENT-OO[UnBin] but conform to UNARYBINARY.

One way to treat cases like these in Optimality Theory is to assume that the input of exceptional cases is enriched with additional information. In the case of, *Gas*, for example, the input is enriched with the additional information that the v-letter in the singular form of the word maps onto a unary vowel. I propose an input-output faithfulness constraint, IDENT-IO[UnBin], that is satisfied when the specifications in the input and the status of phonological vowel in the output regarding being unary or binary are identical. IDENT-IO[UnBin] ranks at least as highly as IDENT-OO[UnBin]; if it ranked lower, the result would be as for <Tag> (cf. Wiese 2004: 324 for a similar analysis of exceptional spelling in German); cf. tableau 3.24.

This short first analysis of vowel quantity correspondences illustrates how the most relevant constraints interact. The main difference between German and English in this regard is the different ranking of the faithfulness constraints MAX and DEP relative to UNARYBINARY and MINSYLL. UNARYBINARY and MINSYLL are ranked highest in English. These constraints are often satisfied by violating MAX

16 The Duden phonetic dictionary (2000) lists them with a binary vowel, which is in line with the analysis presented here. The variants with unary vowel are mainly spoken in the northern half of Germany. In these varieties of German, paradigmatic leveling did not take place or only partially took place.

Tab. 3.24

<Gas> /UN/ ; <Gas>+<e>	I-IO[UnBin]	I-OO[UnBin]	UnaryBinary
a. gaːs, gaː.sə	*		*!
☞ b. gas, gaː.sə		*	

and Dep. In German, on the other hand, the faithfulness constraints Max and Dep are among the highest ranked constraints. Another difference is the ranking of the stem constancy constraint Ident-OO[UnBin]. While it is among the highest ranked constraints in German, in English, it is the lowest ranked constraint. (39) illustrates the different rankings in German and English.

(39) i. German:
Max, Dep, Ident-OO[UnBin] ≫UnaryBinary, MinSyll
ii. English:
UnaryBinary, MinSyll ≫Max ≫Dep ≫Ident-OO[UnBin]

The OT-analysis proposed here has the advantage that it explains the similarities between German and English with the same set of constraints and the differences between these two systems by a different constraint ranking.

In this section we have neglected foot structure. In chapter 4, I will continue the analysis and show what influence foot structures have on the analysis. Also, I will introduce a bidirectional OT-model, which will turn out to be even simpler than the unidirectional analysis presented here. I will revisit and amend the discussion so far there.

3.3 Hyphenation and Resyllabification

If a graphematic word is hyphenated at the end of a line, it is separated into parts that – in many instances – correspond to graphematic syllables. The segments that emerge from hyphenation, however, do not necessarily conform to graphematic syllables. In this section, I will discuss the relation of graphematic syllables and hyphenations that occur at line breaks.

The empirical basis for hyphenations in English and German in this chapter and the remainder of this book are “Webster’s Third New International Dictionary of the English Language” (Gove 2002) and the “Duden – Deutsches Universalwörterbuch” (Duden 2015).

In German, there are three hierarchically ordered constraints according to which words are hyphenated at the end of the line (cf. Primus 2010 for German). The highest priority has the division according to morphological boundaries formed by roots in compounds (e.g. <Tier-art> vs. *<Tie-rat> 'animal species') and by prefixes (e.g. <ver-armt> vs. *<ve-rarmt> 'impoverished'). Secondly, if there is no such morphological boundary, the hyphenation is grapheme-based (Günther 1992): the last grapheme between two v-letters belongs to the syllable of the second v-letter (e.g. <wid-rig> 'adverse', <Ra-che> 'revenge', <dunk-le> 'dark'). If the morphological boundaries in compounds or prefixed words are unclear, the application of the first principle is optional and word division according to the grapheme-based constraint is also possible (e.g. <hin-auf> or <hi-nauf> 'up'). Thirdly, words with hiatus are divided according to their phonological syllable boundaries (e.g. <na-iv> 'naïve'). Non-native words such as <Februar> 'February' can be hyphenated according to the grapheme-based constraint, <Feb-ruar>, but also according to phonological syllable boundaries, <Fe-bruar> (cf. Günther 1992; Primus 2003).

Word division in English is different. Additionally to morphological boundaries formed by roots in compounds, also boundaries formed by suffixes are relevant in English word division, cf. e.g. <sing-er> (Zenker 2011). In monomorphemic words, word division is mainly guided by UNARYBINARY, cf. e.g. <fin-ger>. Consider the following examples:

(40) Internal word division after a strong syllable in English (cf. Gove 2002):
  a. Binary vowel: *de-viant, fu-ture, lu-minous, lu-bricate*
  b. Unary vowel: *gov-ern, mod-ern, cam-era, prop-erly, fab-ricate*

(41) Internal word division after a strong syllable in German (cf. Duden 2015):
  a. Binary vowel: *Fu-tur* 'future tense', *Er-de* 'earth', *wid-rig* 'adverse'
  b. Unary vowel: *Ker-le* 'guys', *wid-men* 'dedicate', *Li-mit* 'limit', *Ka-mera* 'camera'

Let us examine some examples further. Consider the words *govern* and German *Limit* 'limit'. The two words have in common the fact that their first phonological syllable is the head of a foot, and that the p-vowel of the first syllable is unary. Regarding their word division, however, they differ. The German word is hyphenated after the v-letter, <Li-mit> and the English word is hyphenated after the c-letter <gov-ern>.

The hyphenation of Ger. <Li-mit> conforms to the hierarchy for German word division as sketched above. The highest ranking constraint, hyphenation according to morphological boundaries formed by prefixes and roots, does not apply since *Limit* is a morphologically simple word. The next constraint is the grapheme-based one, which states that the last grapheme between two v-letters belongs to the syllable of the second v-letter. <Li-mit> is hyphenated according to this constraint. The third principle, hyphenation according to phonological syllable boundaries does not apply because it is lower in the hierarchy than the second principle, which is applicable to <Limit>. Moreover, [lɪṃɪt] has an ambisyllabic consonant. Strictly speaking, the phonological principle cannot be applied because the phonological boundary is ambiguous.

The hyphenation of <gov-ern> is not explicable with the hierarchy for German word division. If we apply the German hierarchy, <govern> would be hyphenated incorrectly as *<go-vern>. As hinted above, the constraint UnaryBinary guides word division in English. Thus, let us have a look at the graphematic syllable structure of <gov> and <go>.

(42) a. b.

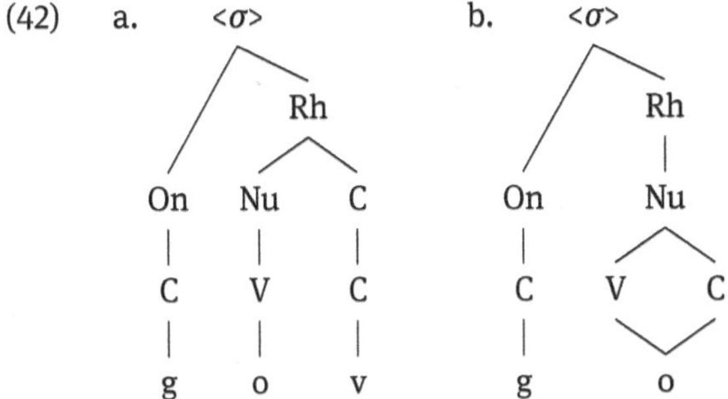

The syllable <go> is open while the syllable <gov> is closed. According to UnaryBinary, the v-letter in <go> corresponds to a binary p-vowel, while the v-letter in <gov> corresponds to a unary p-vowel. If <govern> were hyphenated as *<go-vern>, it would be decoded incorrectly as [goʊ̯.və˞n]. The correct word division <gov-ern> with a closed strong g-syllable, however, maps onto the correct phonological form [gʌvə˞n]. The constraint UnaryBinary must thus rank higher than the one-grapheme-rule.

While in German word division, UnaryBinary does not play a role, it is one of the most important constraints in English word division. One constraint which can override UnaryBinary in word division is a morphological constraint stating that a word is divided according to morphological boundaries. In contrast to German, this also includes suffixes in English. Consider the example <mover>. We would expect that this word to be hyphenated in such a way that the first syllable is open, *<mo-ver>. In that way, there would be no violation of UnaryBinary, however, the correct hyphenation is <mov-er>. The hyphen separates the suffix in compliance to the morphological constraints but it thereby creates a strong syllable that violates UNARYBINARY. I will readdress the issue of the relationship of graphematic syllables and the syllables that emerge in word division in chapter 5.

Let us now turn to the resyllabification of reduced g-syllables. As we have seen earlier, nuclei of minimal syllables do not correspond to phonological nuclei. In a word like <cute>, <e> does not correspond to a phonological vowel. The onset of the second g-syllable, <t>, however, has a correspondent. This correspondent belongs to the coda of the first p-syllable, [kju:t].

This is not possible in a word like <table>. A syllable like *[teɪ̯bl] is ill-formed due to its violation of the sonority sequencing principle, cf. §1.2. This violation can be avoided, if the sonorant [l] constitutes the nucleus of a second p-syllable, as in [teɪ̯bl̩], cf. (43).

(43)

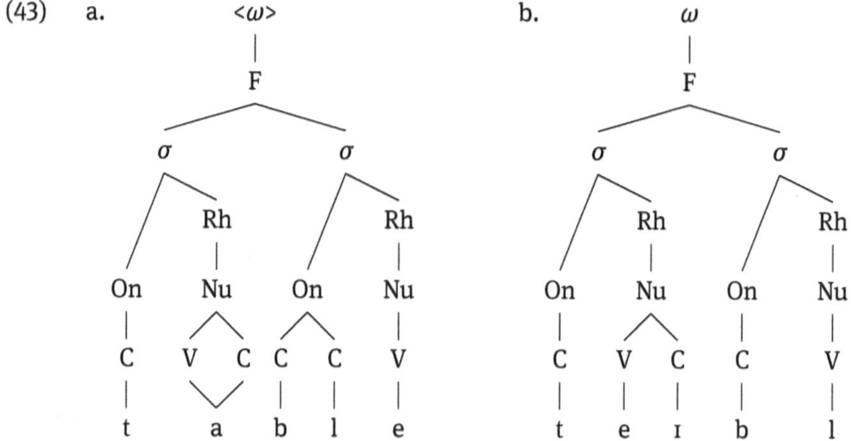

The example in (43) shows again that UNARYBINARY guides word division in English. In order to code the binary vowel of *table*, the first g-syllable must be open. Thus, the hyphenation at the end of the line of <table> is <ta-ble> and not *<tab-le> (cf. Gove 2002).

3.4 Summary of this Chapter

In this chapter, I introduced the basic concepts of the graphematic syllable. Like in the phonological syllable, there are structural positions that make up the skeletal tier of a syllable. The most salient position is called V-position, all other positions are called C-position. Every g-syllable has exactly one V-position.

Letter features can be used to establish a graphematic length hierarchy. The letters at the top end of the length hierarchy are called compact letters or v-letters. These are letters which have a [short bent] head or which have a [short straight] head and are [free up]. Only v-letters are licensed in the V-position of a graphematic syllable. Note however that v-letters are defined independently from phonological vowels on the basis of the length hierarchy of letters.

Based on the observation that letters with long heads and letters with short heads occur in a certain order within a graphematic syllable, Fuhrhop & Buchmann (2009) and Fuhrhop et al. (2011) postulate the length sequencing principle (LSP). The LSP states that the V-position of a graphematic syllable is occupied by a v-letter and that the length of letter decreases towards the V-position and increases from it. The LSP is thus the graphematic counterpart to the sonority sequencing principle (SSP) and the length hierarchy of letters can be seen as the graphematic counterpart of the sonority hierarchy. Again, the length hierarchy of letters and the LSP were established independently of their phonological counterparts.

After having established these most fundamental elements of a syllable structure, we examined subsyllabic constituents of the graphematic syllable.

The nucleus is the constituting subsyllabic constituent of the graphematic syllable. There is a distinction between full and reduced graphematic syllables. Full g-syllables have branching nuclei, whereas nuclei of reduced g-syllables do not branch. This property is crucial for (de)coding vowel quantity as was shown in an analysis within the optimality theory framework.

Finally, we examined the relation of word division and graphematic syllables. We found that there is a difference between German and English word division. The highest constraint in morphologically simple words is the one-grapheme-rule in German and UNARYBINARY, a bidirectional constraint that maps phonological vowels onto graphematic syllable structures, in English. The OT-treatment proposed here has revealed that syllable-structure related phenomena in English and German can be captured by a small number of constraints that are ranked differently in these two languages.

4 The Graphematic Foot

Graphematic units are defined parallel to their phonological counterparts, therefore we may define the graphematic foot as a sequence of at least one and at most two graphematic syllables. Exactly one g-syllable of this sequence is the head of the foot. The notion *head* refers to the hierarchically highest element within a unit. This means that the head is the only obligatory element and determines basic properties of other elements within the same unit (sisters in a tree diagram) and of the unit as a whole. Graphematic feet are – like feet in phonology – head-initial in English and German.

In phonology, the head of a foot is the (only) stressed syllable within this foot. This syllable is also called *strong*. All other syllables of the foot are unstressed and called *weak*. Since stress is a phonological category, I will employ the notions *strong* vs. *weak* for graphematic feet and their subordinated units.

In this chapter I will give an outline of the graphematic foot as a unit in the writing systems of English and German. In the first two sections, I will discuss properties of the canonical and non-canonical graphematic foot. Hereafter I will present experimental and lexical evidence for the relevance of graphematic foot structures and the role of graphematic weight. Finally, I will provide an analysis of the graphematic foot within the framework of optimality theory (OT).

4.1 The Canonical Foot

In §1.2, we established that there is a distinction between canonical and non-canonical phonological structures in English and German. The definition of canonical and non-canonical structures is also valid for the writing system of German and English. I repeat the definition for canonical structures in (1).

(1) The canonical foot in German and English is a trochee. If it is bisyllabic, it ends in a reduced syllable. The canonical phonological word in German and English ends in a trochee with a reduced syllable.

The figures in (2) are examples of canonical graphematic structures in English and German.

https://doi.org/10.1515/9783110583441-004

(2) a. b.

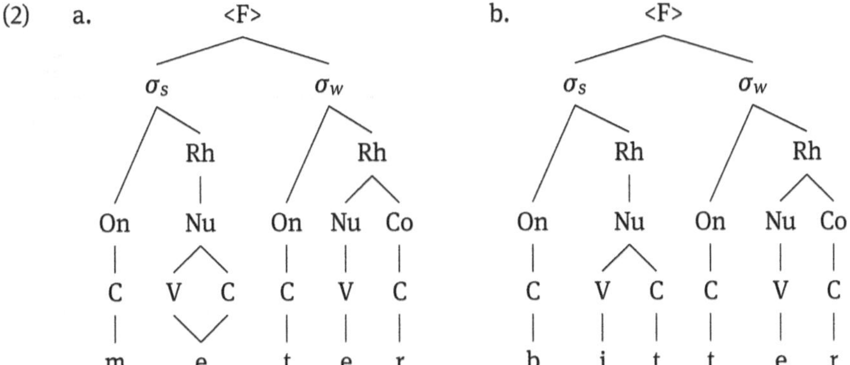

4.1.1 Identification of Canonical Feet

How can readers identify canonical structures like in (2)? In the previous chapter we learned that every graphematic syllable has a v-letter in its peak, i.e. V-position, cf. (2), and that among v-letters only <e> is licensed in the peak of a reduced graphematic syllable cf. (27).

Let us have a look at two English examples, <rude> and <gene>. In both words, there are two letters that qualify as v-letters: <u> has a [short straight] head and is [free up] and <e> has a [short bent] head. All other letters are c-letters: <r, n> are [free down] and <d, g> have [long] heads, cf. §3.1.1. The v-letters in both words are not adjacent, thus we can identify two syllable peaks per word due to (2). Having a v-letter other than <e> as a peak is a sufficient condition for full syllables; thus, the first syllable of <rude> must be a full syllable since its peak is <u>. The second syllables of both words fulfil two necessary conditions for reduced syllables: their peak is <e> and they are light. The canonicity of trochaic structures (1) leads to the default assumption that the two words are trochees, both graphematically and phonologically. A default assumption is an assumption that is regarded true if there is no reason to reject this assumption. In our examples, there is no reason to discard the default assumption, on the contrary, the fact that the second syllable satisfies two necessary conditions for a reduced syllable, strengthens the default assumption. Thus, readers will most likely conclude that the first syllables of the words <rude> and <gene> are the heads of their graphematic feet and that their second syllables are in a weak position and therefore reduced. Table 4.1 summarises the cues to the foot structure of <rude> (cf. Evertz & Primus 2013: 6).

The first line of table 4.1 lists the letters the word is composed of. The next two lines list the relevant features needed to identify v- and c-letters. The letter class can be inferred by letter features. Since the v-letters are not adjacent, they make up

Tab. 4.1: Visual cues to the foot structure of <rude>

letters	**r**	**u**	**d**	**e**
head length	[short straight]	[short straight]	[long]	[short bent]
vertical contrast	[free down]	[free up]		
letter class	c-letter	v-letter	c-letter	v-letter
syllable peak	–	+	–	+
syllable type	full		reduced	
prominence	strong		weak	

the graphematic syllables peaks. Finally, the syllable types and the prominence relations are listed in the bottom lines. Note that the contents of lower strata of the table are deduced from the contents of higher strata. With the help of the cues in table 4.1, readers can deduce the foot structure in (3):

(3)

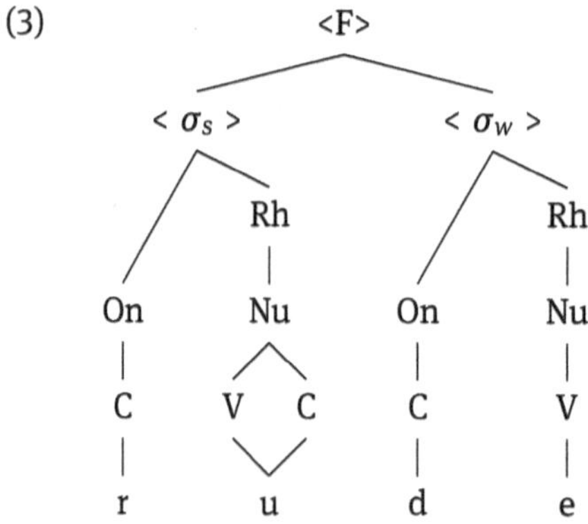

The g-syllable <de> in <rude> is an example of a particular type of reduced g-syllables. I introduced this type of g-syllables as *minimal syllable* in §3.2.1.2. The nucleus of a minimal g-syllable has no phonological counterpart. Put differently, the <e> of a minimal g-syllable is mute. With the help of minimal syllables, prosodic properties of a word can be coded in a minimally invasive way: a minimal g-syllable neither changes the phonological syllable structure nor does it add phonological material.

Let us examine which prosodic properties are coded with reduced graphematic syllables. First, reduced graphematic syllables indicate foot structure by marking a preceding syllable as head of a foot. Second, by marking heads of feet, they also mark if a nucleus branches or not (only and all strong syllables have branching nuclei, cf. §3.2.1).

Consider the example [dɪˈvaɪ̯n]. This word is phonologically non-canonical since its first syllable is not parsed into a foot and its last syllable forms a monosyllabic foot. The ultimate syllable (ult) therefore carries the word stress as indicated by [ˈ] in the linear transcription. The graphematic representation of [dɪˈvaɪ̯n] is <divine>. In this word, there is one reduced g-syllable. Because of its occurrence, we can deduce that the syllable immediately preceding the reduced g-syllable is the head of a foot. We may conclude this because of several facts we know about feet: First, every g-foot contains exactly one head and heads are strong by definition. Second, reduced g-syllables are weak by definition and occur preferably inside of feet; because reduced g-syllables are weak, they are never heads of g-feet. Third, g-feet comprise minimally one syllable and maximally two syllables. Finally, g-feet are head-initial. From these facts, it follows that reduced g-syllables immediately follow heads of g-feet, i.e., strong syllables (for possible exceptions see below).

The g-syllable <vi> immediately precedes a reduced g-syllable and is thus the head of a foot and thereby strong. As a strong g-syllable, <vi> has a branching nucleus, cf. §3.2.1. The first g-syllable <di> is also a full syllable because it fulfils the sufficient condition for full syllables; it has a v-letter other than <e> in its peak. However, as feet are maximally bisyllabic (and also head-initial), it cannot be part of the foot <(vine)$_F$>. Thus, <di> is either a monosyllabic foot or it is an unparsed syllable. For now we will assume that it is an unparsed syllable. This assumption is primarily based on the fact that a reduced g-syllable immediately follows a strong graphematic syllable and that strong syllables tend to avoid being adjacent (at least in phonology, cf. e.g. Liberman & Prince 1977). Furthermore, I will argue in §4.3 that monosyllabic feet have the strong tendency to have a certain minimum weight. <di>, however, is nearly as light as a g-syllable can be: it consists of only one letter dominated by the onset and one letter dominated by the rhyme.

If we accept that <di> is not parsed into a foot, we can assume that <di> has a non-branching nucleus, cf.(11).[1] This is because extrametrical elements are weak by definition and by the fact that only strong graphematic syllables have a branching nucleus (cf. §3.4). The structure in (4) illustrates the graphematic structure we have deduced.

1 Words such as *diverse* also form a final bisyllabic g-trochee. However, the first syllable, <di> can be read with a diphthong (BE) or a unary vowel (AE), cf. Jones (2006). The BE variant might be a lexical exception.

(4)

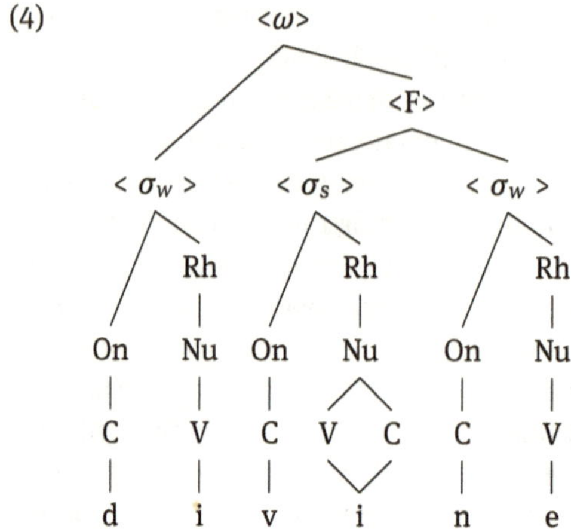

Comparing the graphematic structure with the phonological structure, we can see that although there are differences on the syllabic level (the graphematic representation consists of three, the phonological representation consists of two syllables), the foot level is identical in structural terms: There is one word-final foot and an unparsed syllable preceding this foot, cf. (5).

(5)

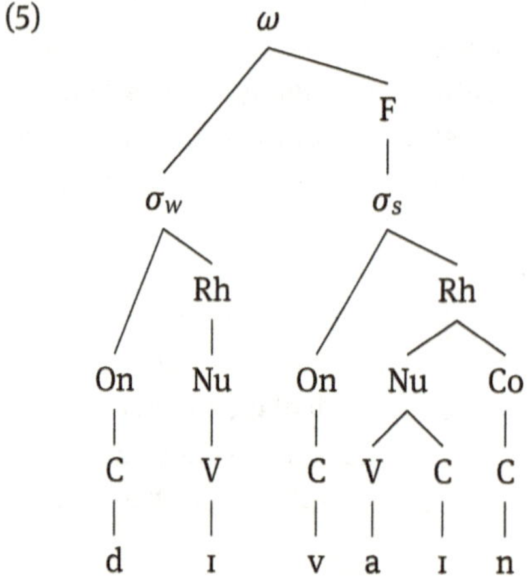

Let us have a look at words consisting of three phonological syllables like [tɛːr.pən.taɪ̯n] or [kæl.kjə.leɪ̯t] where the last p-syllable contains a binary p-vowel. The graphematic representations of these words are <turpentine> and <calculate>. The minimal g-syllables of these graphematic words indicate – like in <divine> – a final bisyllabic g-foot. Unlike the structures we have discussed so far, two g-feet, a strong initial g-foot and a weak second g-foot, emerge, cf. (6).

(6)

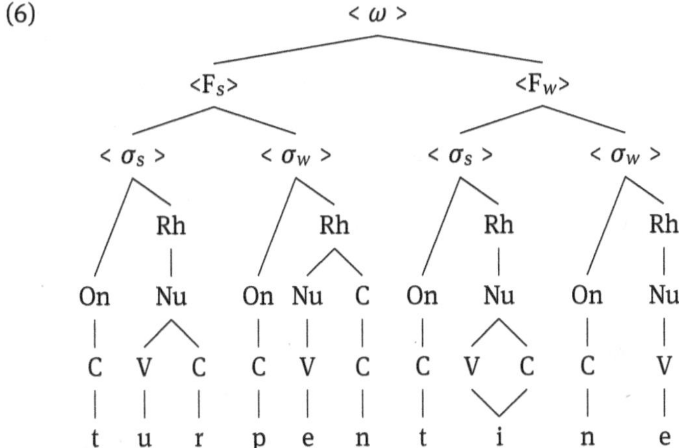

A reduced g-syllable and its preceding g-syllable constitute a final bisyllabic g-foot in all cases discussed so far. A reduced g-syllable thus marks its preceding g-syllable unambiguously as a strong graphematic syllable.[2] Note that due to the final bisyllabic trochee, the graphematic representations of words such as <divine> and <turpentine> are canonical graphematic structures, while the phonological representations of these words are non-canonical.

The identification of graphematic foot structures in German is very similar to the identification of graphematic foot structures in English as presented above. One difference concerns the mapping of minimal graphematic syllables. As we have noted in the preceding chapter, the nuclei of minimal graphematic syllables correspond to phonological nuclei in German as opposed to the nuclei of minimal graphematic syllables in English. Thus, a final <e> as, e.g., in <gu.te> 'good' is not mute. This results in an even closer correspondence of graphematic and phonological structures: In English, there are mismatches in the number of syllables if minimal g-syllables are involved but in German this is not the case.

As in English, there are graphematic words in German that have an unpedified word-inital g-syllable but end in a canonical trochee; (7) lists some of them:

(7) *Antenne* 'antenna', *Forelle* 'trout', *Schimpanse* 'chimpanzee', *Oktober* 'October', *Charakter* 'character', *Lavendel* 'lavender'

---

2 There are some affixes in English, e.g. *-age*, *-able*, that resemble the form of a canonical graphematic trochee with a minimal graphematic syllable. However, these affixes are exceptions to the mapping model presented below.

In the examples above, the reduced graphematic syllables indicate preceding strong g-syllables; and by that the foot structure of the words in (7). The first graphematic syllables are not parsed, cf. the analysis of <di(vi.ne)>, above.

Fuhrhop & Peters (2013) argue for an additional foot type they call graphematic dactyl. As examples of words comprising a graphematic dactyl, they present trisyllabic German words in which the first g-syllable is a strong full g-syllable and the two following syllables are reduced g-syllables, cf. (8a). It is possible to find examples of these kinds of words in English as well, cf. (8b).

(8) a. *Ebene* 'surface', *gebende* 'giving', *muntere* 'bright', *singende* 'singing', *Wanderer* 'hiker', *Zauberer* 'sorcerer'
b. *bitterer, caterer, launderer, murderer, slenderer, sorcerer, wanderer*

The generalisation that a reduced g-syllable indicates a strong immediately preceding g-syllable is not true in these examples. All words in (8) comprise an initial bisyllabic graphematic foot as in <(wan.de).rer>. The last g-syllable thus immediately follows a reduced graphematic syllable contrary to the observations we have made before. In order to be able to explain this deviance, let us have a look at the morphological and phonological properties of the words in (8).

All of the words in (8a) display a phonologically unstressable word-final suffix. In German, stress normally falls invariably on the last syllable before an unstressable suffix,[3] cf. e.g. *ˈJapan* 'Japan' – *Jaˈpan+er* 'Japanese', *Aˈme.ri.ka* 'America' – *A.me.riˈka+ner* 'American'. There is one exception, however: if the suffixed stem already ends in a reduced syllable, e.g. *wander* [ˈvan.dɐ] '(to) hike', stress cannot shift because reduced syllables are not stressable. This means that in a configuration where two reduced syllables follow one full syllable, the full syllable is the head of one foot in which the immediately following reduced syllable is parsed into, while the last reduced syllable is not parsed, e.g. (ˈ*Wan.de*)$_F$*rer* (Wiese 2000: 288).

The English words in (8b) end in a stress-neutral suffix. Stress-neutral suffixes have two properties setting them apart from stress-shifting suffixes (such as *atom+ic, solemn+ity, employ+ee*, etc.). Firstly, they never make any difference to the stress pattern of the stem they are attached to; secondly, such suffixes are always unstressed (Giegerich 1992: 190). The stress-neutral suffix *+en* tends to attach to stress-final stems. If a stress-neutral suffix is attached to a stem ending in a strong syllable, the suffix is parsed into the foot of the strong syllable and thus constitutes a bisyllabic trochee with it, e.g. (*wood*)$_F$ – (*wood+en*)$_F$. An exception

3 Like *+er*, *+isch* is an unstressable suffix in German. Wiese (2000), however, points to the exception *ˈNorwegen* 'norway' – *ˈnorweg+isch* in which the foot structure remains unaffected.

is *+er*; this suffix tends to attach to words whose ultimate *or* penultimate syllable is strong, although the latter is less common than the former. If the latter happens, that is, if a stress-neutral affix is attached to a stem ending in a syllable in weak position, it cannot be parsed into the foot and the suffix remains unparsed, e.g. (*ˈslen.der*)$_F$*+er* (cf. Burzio 1994: 258).

As for the decoding of the foot structure of these rather exceptional words, I believe it is sensible to assume that unstressable suffixes can be identified by the readers and that their prosodic status is lexically specified. A reader can thus ignore such a suffix in assigning the graphematic foot structure in a constellation <σ σ_e af$_e$>, where <σ> is a variable for any graphematic syllable, <σ_e> is a variable for any reduced graphematic syllable, and af$_e$ is a variable for any unstressable suffix. A reader will thus most likely assign the following foot structure: <(σ σ_e)$_F$ af$_e$>.

The words in (8) are thus examples of words that display final syllables which are both phonologically and graphematically extrametrical. Although the notion 'graphematic dactyl' is not wrong on a descriptive level, I refrain from adopting a new type of foot since the prosodic structure of these words can be captured by the foot type we already introduced, i.e. by a bisyllabic trochee (plus an extrametrical syllable).

4.1.2 Vowel Quantity and Ambisyllabicity

Let us now turn to the function of canonical feet. Why is it important that a g-syllable is marked as strong? In §3.2.2, we analysed the correspondences of nucleus structures. Let us recall the relevant constraints (cf. (31) repeated here as (9) for convenience):

(9) *Vowel quantity mapping constraints* (cf. Evertz & Primus 2013)

i. UNARY:
A unary p-vowel bidirectionally corresponds to a v-letter in a closed and strong g-syllable

ii. BINARY:
A binary p-vowel bidirectionally corresponds to a v-letter in an open and strong g-syllable

In §3.2.2 we have seen that these two constraints behave as one single constraint. We thus labelled them as UNARYBINARY.

Up until now we have only focused on whether a g-syllable is open or closed and ignored the first condition of the graphematic side of these bidirectional constraints. The first condition of the graphematic side states that UNARYBINARY is only applicable to *strong* g-syllables. In other words, these constraints only apply to heads of graphematic feet. This is because only g-syllables with branching nuclei are able to map onto binary p-vowels; weak g-syllables have non-branching nuclei and thus can only map onto unary p-vowels.

The minimal g-syllables in words like <divine> and <turpentine> therefore do not only open the preceding syllables graphematically, they also mark them as heads of feet and thereby ensure that the constraints in (9) are applicable to the penultimate g-syllables. The final bisyllabic g-foot that emerges thank to the minimal g-syllables thus provides that the penultimate g-syllable maps onto a strong phonological syllable with a binary vowel. The first graphematic syllable in <divine> is also open, but it does not map onto a binary p-vowel because BINARY does not apply to this syllable as <di> is not strong, cf. (4).

The vowel contrast as described by the constraints above correlates with ambisyllabicity. Strong phonological syllables have an obligatory branching nucleus in English and German. The structural positions of a branching nucleus may be associated with a binary p-vowel or with a unary p-vowel followed by a consonant. If a bisyllabic foot has only one consonant between a first unary p-vowel and a second p-vowel, this consonant is dominated by the nucleus of the first and by the onset of the second syllable due to the branching nucleus of the first syllable and the onset maximation of the second syllable, cf. §1.2. In other words, the intervocalic consonant closes the first and opens the following syllable: the consonant is *ambisyllabic*. The structure in (10) illustrates the phonological representation of *mitten* (and the German homophone *mitten* '(in the) middle'), which comprises an ambisyllabic consonant.

(10)

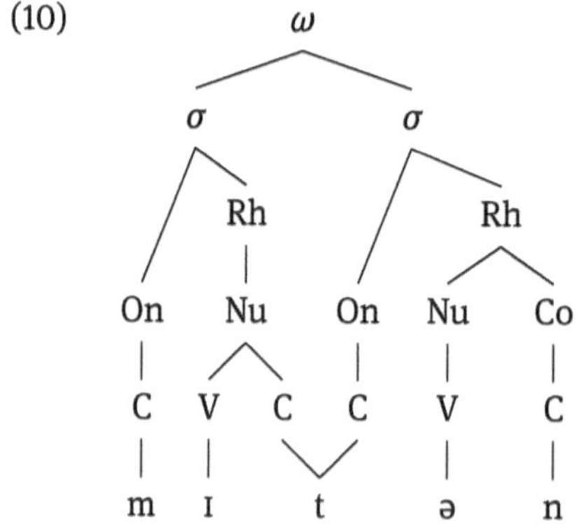

Eisenberg (2006) observes that the *Schärfungsschreibung* in German, i.e. the gemination of c-letters in German, can be attributed to ambisyllabicity.[4]

In the phonological representation, real ambisyllabicity occurs: one segment can belong to two syllables simultaneously. In the writing systems of English and German, syllable boundaries are drawn unambiguously. The gemination of the c-letter that is the regular correspondent of the ambisyllabic consonant results in two single segments which belong to one syllable each. The first of the geminated c-letters is dominated by the nuclear C-position of the first syllable. The second of the geminated c-letters is dominated by the onset of the second syllable. Primus (2003: 34) summarises this observation by stating that there are no ambisyllabic elements in graphematic representations. This fact can be captured by the constraint in (11).

(11) *GRAPHAMBI: Every graphematic element is exhaustively contained in the superordinate unit of which it is a part.

The formulation of *GRAPHAMBI is based on one principle of the strict layer hypothesis presented in §1.2 as (7b.). While this principle is violable in phonological structures, the constraint in (11) is undominated in graphematic representations.

The structure in (12) is the corresponding written representation of the phonological representation of *mitten* in (10).

(12)

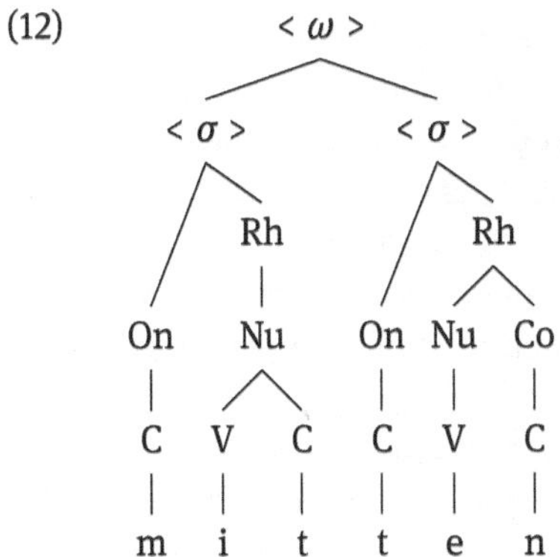

The following constraints capture the facts of the discussion so far. They apply in the German and English writing systems:

4 Eisenberg's model is an alternative to the accent based model, which states that the shortness of a stressed vowel is indicated by the gemination of the following (single) c-letter. For a discussion of the two models, cf. the dispute of Eisenberg and Ramers in *Linguistische Berichte*: Ramers (1999a), Eisenberg (1999) and Ramers (1999b).

(13) Ambisyllabicity (de-)coding in English and German for single intervocalic consonants and c-letters
a. An ambisyllabic consonant is coded by gemination of the c-letter that is the regular correspondent of this consonant (cf. Eisenberg 2006 for German, Rollings 2004 for English).
b. The absence of graphematic c-gemination decodes the absence of ambisyllabicity, and hence an open p-syllable with a binary vowel (Evertz & Primus 2003, cf. also Rollings 2004: 67).

Note that (13b) is logically equivalent to (13a) since (13b) is its logical contraposition. (13) thus captures the coding and the decoding perspective. However, we may *not* enrich the decoding perspective to 'the presence of a c-gemination decodes an ambisyllabic consonant'. Let us restate (13) as an OT-constraint with a syllable structural precision of the notion of c-letter geminate, cf. (14).

(14) GEMINATE
An ambisyllabic consonant is coded by gemination of the c-letter that is the regular correspondent of this consonant. The first letter of the geminate is dominated by the nuclear C-position of the first g-syllable; the second letter is dominated by the onset of the immediately following g-syllable.

The second sentence in (14) is a structural constraint for c-letter geminates. As we have seen in the example in (10), /t/ in /mɪt̩ən/ is ambisyllabic. The corresponding letter <t> in <mit.ten> appears two times, the first letter is dominated by the nuclear C-position of the first g-syllable, the second letter is dominated by the onset of the second g-syllable. The letter in the nucleus of the first g-syllable thus closes the first g-syllable graphematically. Due to the mapping constraint UNARY-BINARY, the first v-letter in a word like <mit.ten> maps unto a unary phonological vowel. Hypothetical words like <mitt.en> or <mi.tten> do not feature a geminate according to this definition.

A peculiarity is the coding of ambisyllabic consonants regularly corresponding to <k> in English and German. Words corresponding to an ambisyllabic [k] display <ck> as in Ger. <Zucker> 'sugar', <Bäcker> 'baker' and Engl. <checker>, <kicker>, <shocker>. According to Venezky (1999: 150), <kk> was replaced in the 15th century by <ck> in the English writing system. But is <ck> a geminate? In order to answer this question we must check whether the second sentence of GEM-

INATE, i.e. the structural restriction for geminates, is true for <ck>. The following short list gives some examples with indicated line breaks (cf. Gove 2002, Duden 2015),[5] cf. (15).

(15) a. *back-er, bick-er, block-er, buck-et, check-er, kick-er, nick-el, shock-er, stack-er*
b. *Bä-cker* 'baker', *De-cke* 'ceiling', *Fa-ckel* 'torch', *Po-cken* 'smallpox', *Wi-ckel* 'compress', *Zu-cker* 'sugar'

If the indicated line breaks exactly correspond to the graphematic syllable boundaries, <ck> is a c-letter geminate in the sense of GEMINATE neither in German nor in English. We noted in §3.3 that in English, suffixes such as *+er* are hyphenated; however, the word division of monomorphemic words such as <buck-et> and <nick-el> cannot support the assumption of a syllabic structure in which <c> is dominated by the nuclear C-position of the nucleus and <k> is dominated by the onset of the following syllable. Yet it has to be noted that <ck> is part of the first syllable in all instances in English.

In German words, on the other hand, <ck> is always part of the second element that emerges in word division. Interestingly, in German, words such as <Zucker> were hyphenated like <Zuk-ker> at the end of the line prior to the spelling reform of 1996 and although <ck> is never part of the first hyphenation element, v-letters followed by <ck> in canonical foot structures are always decoded as unary.

Observations like these lead Rollings (2004: 64) to regard <ck> as a *non-identical geminate* in English and Eisenberg (2006: 314) to regard <ck> as a geminate in German. Let us thus assume that there is a subregularity of GEMINATE for <ck>.

Another peculiarity is the coding of ambisyllabic nasal velars or affricates in German and English. Let us begin with German. The velar nasal /ŋ/ corresponds to the sequence <ng> in, for instance, <lang> – [laŋ] 'long'. If that nasal is ambisyllabic, for example in [laŋ̩ə], the corresponding sequence is not geminated, cf. <lan.ge> but not *<lang.nge>. But note that in <lan.ge>, the first letter of <ng> is in the nuclear C-position of the first g-syllable and <g>, the second letter, is dominated by the onset of the second syllable.

5 I mark line breaks with <-> while syllables boundaries are indicated by <.>. Line breaks and graphematics syllable boundaries often correspond exactly to each other, but as I will show later in this section, this is not always the case.

The graphematic correspondents of affricates are also not geminated. The affricate /p͡f/ corresponds to the grapheme sequence <pf> in which the first letter is dominated by the nuclear C-position of the first graphematic syllable and the second letter is dominated by the onset of the second g-syllable, cf. e.g. <Hop.fen> 'hop.' In contrast to /p͡f/, there are two spellings for /t͡s/ in German. The affricate /t͡s/ word-initially corresponds to <z> as in <Zeh> [t͡seː] 'toe'. In a word like [ˈkat͡ṣə] 'cat' with an ambisyllabic affricate, /t͡s/ corresponds to <tz> as in <Kat.ze> and not to <zz>.[6] The short list in (16) gives some more examples with indicated lined breaks.

(16) a. *Ben.gel* 'rascal', *bon.gen* '(to) ring (sth.) up', *Dün.ger* 'fertiliser', *Fin.ger* 'finger', *Hän.ger* 'trailer', *Wan.ge* 'cheek', *Zun.ge* 'tounge'
b. *Bat.zen* 'lump', *glot.zen* '(to) stare', *Kat.ze* 'cat', *Ket.zer* 'heretic', *Nut.zen* 'advantage', *Pet.ze* 'telltale', *Wit.ze* 'jokes'

As we can see from the list above, the first letters of <ng> and <tz> are dominated by the nuclear C-positions of the first syllables and the second letters are dominated by the onset of the second syllable. We can thus regard the coding of ambisyllabic velar nasals and affricates in German as conforming to a more general constraint that demands that the nuclear C-position and the onset of the following syllable is occupied by the graphematic correspondent of the ambisyllabic element. Eisenberg (2006: 314) thus considers the coding of ambisyllabic velar nasals and affricates in German to be regular according to subregularities of the ambisyllabicity constraint.

We can find similar instances of ambisyllabicity coding in English. Like in German, velar Nasals usually are coded <ng> in English; this is also true when a velar nasal corresponds to an ambisyllabic consonant: [sɪŋ], <sing> – [sɪŋ̣ər], <singer>. I assume that in words like <singer> the <n> is dominated by the nuclear C-position of the first g-syllable, although the line break for this word is <sing-er>. This is because the word <singer> comprises the suffix *+er* and as mentioned above, suffixes are hyphenated in English.[7]

In English, two affricates are usually considered, /t͡ʃ/ and /d͡ʒ/. The affricate /t͡ʃ/ is usually spelt <ch> word-initially and -finally as in *chicken, each*. If /t͡ʃ/ is ambisyllabic, however, it is spelt <tch> as in <kitchen> or <satchel>. Rollings (2004:

6 <zz> as correspondent to an ambisyllabic consonant only appears in some Italian borrowings such as <Pizza> 'pizza'.

7 I will readdress the question of how graphematic syllables relate to syllables that emerge in word division in chapter 5.

127) calls this the geminated form of <ch>[8]; however, line breaks do not support the interpretation of <t> being dominated by the nuclear C-position of the first syllable and <ch> being dominated by the onset of the second syllable. The monomorphemic words mentioned above are hyphenated <kitch-en> and <satch-el>. Yet, it has to be noted that <tch> closes the first g-syllables in the words mentioned above (cf. the case of <ck>, see above).

The primary spelling of the affricate /d͡ʒ/ is <g> as in *engine, gin, rage, energy* (Rollings 2004: 128). An ambisyllabic /d͡ʒ/ is usually coded <dg> as in <bud.get> or <gad.get>. The first syllable of <dg> is dominated by the nuclear C-position of the first syllable and thus closes the first syllable. This is also the reason why <dg> appears in words like <bridge> or <badge>. The <d> occupies the nuclear C-position and thus blocks the decoding of the v-letter of the first g-syllable as binary.

We have acknowledged the coding of ambisyllabic velar nasals and affricates in German as subregularities of the constraint Geminate. Given the obvious similarity in coding ambisyllabic velar nasals and affricates in English, it is fair to say that their coding is a subregularity in English as well.

After having discussed how geminates are defined and which subregularities exist, let us have a look at the data. In §3.2.1, I presented examples of English words whose first syllables are coded due to the constraints Unary and Binary, cf. table 3.11. I repeat some of these examples in table 4.2. In the left column, there are words with ungeminated c-letters between two v-letters in a canonical bisyllabic g-foot. This means that the first g-syllables of the g-feet on the left side are graphematically open; the v-letters of the first g-syllables thus correspond to binary p-vowels due to the constraint UnaryBinary. In the right column are similar words, and sometimes even graphematic minimal pairs, which display c-letter gemination or <ck>. Their first syllables are graphematically closed. Due to the constraint UnaryBinary, the v-letters of the first g-syllables of the words on the left-hand side of the table correspond to binary phonological vowels, while the v-letters of the first g-syllables of the words on the right-hand side of the table correspond to unary phonological vowels.

All these words have in common that the mute <e> creates a canonical graphematic foot, i.e. a strong g-syllable followed by a reduced one. Some of these structures are used for representing a binary vowel such as *mate* and *site* (cf. §3.4). Others, such as *tittle, single, table* and *noble* are motivated by the constraint that every graphematic syllable has a v-letter in its peak. The first g-syllable of *tittle*,

8 Rollings (2004: 127) also highlights the word-final spelling of /t͡ʃ/ as <tch> in words like *itch, witch*. He considers this spelling to be a requirement of a three letter rule that states that final stressed unary vowels in closed syllables must be spelt with exactly three letters. For an analysis of such rules in a supra-segmental view, cf. §4.3.

<tit->, and *single*, <sin->, is closed; it thus represents a unary vowel. In *table, noble, waste* and *chaste*, the first g-syllable is open and, hence, it signals a binary vowel. The c-clusters <bl> and <st> form the onset of the second syllable due to onset maximisation and to the fact that they are legitimate onsets in English, both phonologically (cf. Giegerich 1992: 153) and graphematically, cf. <bleed>, <humble>, <stem>, <spin-ster>, <mon-ster>. Some graphematic onsets, like <tl> or <dl> are not attested word-initially or as onsets of strong syllables. Nevertheless, these onsets are well-formed regarding phono- and graphotactics, cf. <cas-tle>, <candle> (Evertz & Primus 2013: 8f.).

Tab. 4.2: The graphematic representation of the vowel contrast in canonical graphematic feet in English

v-letter in open strong g-syllable ↔ binary vowel	**v-letter in closed strong g-syllable ↔ unary vowel**
lake, shake, lane, mane, sane, late, mate; safer, saner, later; table	*lack, sack, van, man, fan, lad, mat; gaffer, latter, trapper, matter; baffle*
gene, scene, these, mete; meter, Peter	*bed, fed, gem, pen, hen, bet, met; blesser, better; mettle, pebble*
ride, ripe, dine, shine, bite, site, white; hider, riper, diner, biter, finer; rifle, title	*rid, hid, rip, din, sin, thin, bit, sit, wit; hidden, ripper, dinner, bitter; riffle, tittle*
node, smoke, cone, tone, dope, hope, rope; doper, choker, hoper; noble	*nod, smog, hock, con, ton, drop, hop; nodder, shocker, hopper; hobble*
nude, rude, use, cute, fume, tune; tuner, cuter	*mud, us, cut, nut, hum, fun; tunnel, cutter; muffle*

Let us also have a look at the German data. In contrast to minimal syllables in English, minimal g-syllables, i.e. reduced g-syllables ending in <e>, correspond to phonological nuclei in the German writing system (cf. section 3.2.2 for an OT-model). Apart from this fact, table 4.3 strikingly resembles table 4.2.

C-letter geminates thus code ambisyllabicity; and because unary vowels in the first syllable are a prerequisite for ambisyllabicity, they also code unary vowels. Moreover, since ambisyllabicity correlates with stress, c-letter geminates are also a reliable indicator for foot structure: the v-letter immediately preceding a geminate is dominated by the V-position of a strong syllable; cf. also Rollings (2004: 66), who notes one of the functions of geminates "is to mark the [preceding] vowel as almost certainly stressed."

Tab. 4.3: Graphematic representation of ambisyllabicity and its correlates in canonical graphematic feet in German (Evertz & Primus 2013: 10)

ambisyllabicity (→ unary vowel) → graphematic c-geminate	**no graphematic c-geminate → no ambisyllabicity (→ binary vowel)**
Krabbe 'crab', *Paddel* 'paddle', *Affen* 'monkeys', *Bagger* 'excavator', *Walle* 'ramparts', *Panne* 'breakdown', *Rassen* 'races', *lassen* 'to let', *Watte* 'wool cotton', *Ratten* 'rats'	*Wabe* 'honeycomb', *Adel* 'nobility', *Hafen* 'port', *Lager* 'storehouse', *Wale* 'whales', *Plane* 'tarpaulin', *Rasen* 'grass', *lasen* '(we) read PAST', *wate* '(I) wade', *raten* 'to guess'
Ebben 'low tides', *fleddern* 'to rummage', *Neffe* 'nephew', *eggen* 'harrows', *Stelle* 'place', *essen* 'to eat', *Betten* 'beds', *fette* 'fat'	*leben* 'to live', *Federn* 'feathers', *Hefe* 'yeast', *fegen* 'to sweep', *Stele* 'stela', *lesen* 'to read', *beten* 'to pray', *Fete* 'party'
bibber '(I) shiver', *Widder* 'ram', *Brille* 'glasses', *Kimme* 'notch', *irren* 'to err', *Wirren* 'confusions', *Risse* 'cracks'	*Biber* 'beaver', *wider* 'against', *Chile* 'Chile', *Mime* 'actor', *Iren* 'the Irish', *Viren* 'viruses', *Krise* 'crisis'
Robbe 'seal', *offen* 'open', *Roggen* 'rye', *Pollen* 'pollen', *Trommel* 'drum', *Sonne* 'sun', *Rosse* 'steeds', *Schotte* 'Scot'	*Robe* 'robe', *Ofen* 'stove', *Vogel* 'bird', *Polen* 'the Polish', *Omen* 'omen', *Krone* 'crown', *Rose* 'rose', *Schote* 'pod'
schrubben 'to scrub', *buddeln* 'to dig', *Puffer* 'buffer', *Hummer* 'lobster', *müssen* 'must', *Fussel* 'fluff', *Busse* 'busses'	*Stuben* 'rooms', *Nudeln* 'noodles', *Ufer* 'shore', *Blume* 'flower', *Musen* 'muses', *Fusel* 'bad liquor', *Busen* 'bust'

The correspondences shown in table 4.2 and table 4.3 are obscured in some instances due to independent, higher ranking constraints, which will be discussed in the remainder of this subsection.

One relevant constraint for English is *<vv>, which forbids the gemination of the letter <v>. This constraint blocks the gemination of intervocalic c-letters in words like *clever, drivel, giver, lover, swivel*. Such words are thus opaque with respect to vowel quantity decoding, cf. e.g., *diver* vs. *liver*. Words, such as *navvy* and *skivvy* are marginal (cf. Cook 2004: 60), but they show the tendency to violate the highly ranked constraint (*<vv>) in order to conform to the gemination constraint presented here (cf. also Ryan 2010: 31). Intervocalic <v> is relatively rare in canonical German words with a unary first p-vowel (among the few I could find are the English borrowing *clever* and *cover*). The constraint *<vv> thus does not play a major role in German ambisyllabicity coding.

A further constraint that has been regularly noted in the literature is the ban of geminated complex graphemes (cf. e.g. Fuhrhop 2005, Eisenberg 2006). In §2.3 we defined graphemes as smallest supra-segmental units within a graphematic hierarchy. Thus, graphemes can be identified with the structural positions in a graphematic syllable. Those graphemes which feature umlaut marks like <ä, ü, ö> in German or that consist of more than one letter, like, e.g., <sh> in English or, e.g., <ch> in English and German, are called complex graphemes, cf. §2.3.

Neef & Primus (2001) and Primus (2003, 2010) do not assume that there is a constraint directly banning the gemination of complex graphemes; rather, they derive the fact that complex graphemes are not geminated from the constraint *COMPL-C_{gN}, which is a structural restriction for graphematic syllables; cf. (16) repeated here as (17) for convenience.

(17) *COMPL-C_{gN}: The second nuclear position of a g-syllable is barred for complex graphemes (Primus 2003: 40; 2010: 12).

Let us recall the reasons why we adopted this constraint in chapter 3. In §3.4, we noted that letters with umlaut marks do not appear in the second position of a graphematic diphthong; for example, the plural of <Baum> 'tree' is <Bäume> and not *<Baüme> although the latter would be graphematically closer to the corresponding phonological diphthong (cf. Wiese 2000, Primus 2003). Furthermore, v-letters of graphematic syllables containing <ß> correspond to binary phonological vowels. In a graphematic syllable model we can explain this by two constraints: i) by *COMPL-C_{gN} that bars complex graphemes from the nucleus and ii) by BRANCHING-GN requiring that nuclei of strong graphematic syllables are branching, i.e. nuclei of strong syllables must dominate two structural positions. A graphematic syllable like <Maß> can satisfy both constraints by having a branching nucleus whose structural positions are both associated with the v-letter and by a coda that dominates the complex graphemes <ß>, cf. §3.4 for an analysis.

Neef & Primus (2001) and Primus (2003, 2010) argue that this constraint is also responsible for the fact that complex graphemes are not geminated. Primus (2003) illustrates this with the example <lachen> – [ˈlax̣n̩] '(to) laugh'. The constraint GEMINATE requires that the correspondent of the ambisyllabic consonant /x/, <ch>, is geminated. The constraint *COMPL-C_{gN}, however, demands that the nuclear C-position may not dominate complex graphemes such as <ch>. A third relevant constraint, BRANCHING-GN, requires that the nucleus of a strong graphematic syllable branches (see above). This means there are two diametrical forces: two constraints, GEMINATE and BRANCHING-GN demand that <ch> is dominated by the nuclear C-position and *COMPL-C_{gN} requires this not to be the case. To be more consistent with the mapping analyses in §3.2.2, I will replace BRANCHING-GN with UNARYBINARY. The effect of the constraints is the same given the input [ˈlax̣n̩]: the input has a unary p-vowel in its strong syllable, a candidate thus has to have a closed corresponding g-syllable in order to satisfy the constraint. Tableau 4.4 illustrates the evaluation of the graphematic correspondence of [ˈlax̣n̩] based on the model of Primus (2003).[9]

Tab. 4.4

[ˈlax̣n̩]	*COMPL-C_{gN}	SYLL	*GRAPHAMBI	UNBIN	GEM
a. <lach.chen>	*!				
b. <lach.en>	*!	*			*
c. <lac̣hen>			*!		*
☞ d. <la.chen>				*	*

In candidate a., <lach.chen>, the complex grapheme <ch> is geminated. This means that one complex grapheme is dominated by the onset of the second g-syllable of the candidate and that the other complex grapheme is dominated by the nuclear C-position of the first g-syllable. It is thus the only candidate satisfying the constraint GEMINATE (labelled GEM in the tableaux henceforth). This leads to a violation of *COMPL-C_{gN}. In candidate b., the grapheme is not geminated; the complex grapheme <ch> is dominated by the C-position of the first g-syllable. Like in candidate a., this leads to a violation of *COMPL-C_{gN}. Furthermore, because the second syllable does not start with one grapheme, candidate b. also violates SYLLABIFY (labelled in the tableaux as SYLL). We introduced this constraint in §3.3. This constraint is based on the 'one grapheme rule' for German that states that a hyphenated graphematic syllable begins with exactly one grapheme (consisting of c-letters). Candidate c. comprises an ambisyllabic grapheme. The candidate therefore incurs one violation of the constraint in (11) demanding that there are no ambisyllabic graphematic elements (labelled here as *GRAPHAMBI). The winning candidate d. incurs one violation of UNARYBINARY (labelled UNBIN in the tableaux henceforth) since the complex grapheme is dominated by the onset of the following syllable and the v-letter is not associated with both structural positions of the nucleus.

The analysis of Primus (2003) as sketched above is appealing because it can account for the absence of the gemination of complex graphemes by a structural constraint that is also relevant for other phenomena in written language; how-

9 Tableau 4.4 generally corresponds to tableau 5 in Primus (2003: 45). I follow Primus (2003) in assuming that there are phonetic information in the input.

ever, although this analysis is sound for German, it cannot account for English data. Let us consider an example of an English bisyllabic canonical trochee with an ambisyllabic consonant corresponding to a complex grapheme, for instance, [ˈbrʌðər].

If we consider only the constraints from the analysis above for the analysis of English, there is no way that the grammatical candidate <broth.er> (cf. Gove 2002) would be selected as optimal for an input [ˈbrʌðər]. This is because the grammatical candidate <broth.er> is harmonically bounded to the ungrammatical candidate <broth.ther>. Consider tableau 4.5, which compares the two candidates without a ranking of the constraints in discussion.

Tab. 4.5

[ˈbrʌðər]	*COMPL-C_{gN}	SYLL	*GRAPHAMBI	UNBIN	GEM
a. <broth.ther>	*				
b. <broth.er>	*	*			*

Both candidates violate *COMPL-C_{gN}. Furthermore, <broth.er> violates SYLLABIFY and GEMINATE. This means that regardless of the constraint ranking, <broth.er> cannot perform better than <broth.ther>. As we have seen in §3.3, word division in English is not guided by SYLLABIFY but by UNARYBINARY. But even if we disregard SYLLABIFY (what is not allowed in a strict sense since each constraint is universal in OT, cf. §1.4), <broth.er> is still harmonically bounded to the ungrammatical candidate <broth.ther>.

If we introduce the faithfulness constraint DEP into this ranking, the two candidates are no longer bounded, since the candidate <broth.ther> violates DEP more often than <broth.er>. However, a consistent ranking cannot be found with DEP as decisive constraint, cf. the mini-tableaux 4.6 and 4.7.

Tab. 4.6

[ˈbrʌðər]	DEP	*COMPL-C_{gN}	GEM	SYLL
a. <broth.ther>	*	*		
☞ b. <broth.er>		*	*	*

Tab. 4.7

[ˈlætər]	DEP	*COMPL-C_{gN}	GEM	SYLL
a. <lat.ter>	*!			
(☞) b. <lat.er>			*	*

A high-ranking DEP would not only block the gemination of complex graphemes as in tableau 4.6, it would block gemination altogether as demonstrated in tableau 4.7.

Thus, we need to introduce another constraint that can block the gemination of complex graphemes in English. The most obvious choice is an antithesis to the constraint GEMINATE, which applies to complex graphemes, cf. (18).

(18) *GEMINATE-COMPLEX: Complex graphemes are not geminated.

As mentioned above, this constraint is commonly found in the literature, cf. e.g. Wiese (2004: 321) and Eisenberg (2006: 314) for German; Rollings (2004: 77) for English.

Let us re-examine the evaluation of the coding of [ˈbrʌðər] above, this time with the new constraint and more plausible candidates, cf. tableau 4.8.

Tab. 4.8

[ˈbrʌðər]	*GEMCOMPL	*GRAPHAMBI	UNBIN	*COMPL-C_{gN}	GEM	SYLL
a. <broth.ther>	*!			*		
☞ b. <broth.er>				*	*	*
c. <brother>		*!			*	
d. <bro.ther>			*!		*	

If we introduce this constraint for the analysis of English cases, this constraint is also relevant for German, of course. Introducing *GEMINATE-COMPLEX in the analysis of German does not change anything in the results of the evaluation but it has an interesting effect: it renders the constraint *COMPL-C_{gN} unnecessary for the evaluation, cf. tableau 4.9 in which *COMPL-C_{gN} is replaced by *GEMINATE-COMPLEX.

Tab. 4.9

[ˈlaxn̩]	*GemCompl	Syll	*GraphAmbi	UnBin	Gem
a. <lach.chen>	*!				
b. <lach.en>		*!			*
c. <lachen>			*!		*
☞ d. <la.chen>				*	*

Let us return briefly to the discussion in §3.2.1. I repeated the reasons we introduced this constraints in the beginning of the current discussion. In §3.2.1 we noted that *COMPL-C_{gN} leads to contradictory results in evaluating the syllable structure of syllables like <Maß> 'measure' and <Fisch> 'fish': <Maß> complies to the structural constraints *COMPL-C_{gN} and BRANCHING-GN by associating the v-letter to two structural positions. The v-letter of < Maß> therefore maps onto a binary vowel. <Fisch>, on the other hand, violates BRANCHING-GN since its v-letter is associated to one structural position only. We argued that the make-up of the complex grapheme (consisting of more than one segment vs. being a ligature) has influence on whether the nuclear C-position is deleted or not.

In light of the analysis above, we can offer another analysis: if we assume that complex graphemes consisting of more than one letter are licensed in the nuclear C-position and if we introduce the constraint *GEMINATE-COMPLEX, we can account for the evaluations of syllables like <Maß> and <Fisch> and for the ban of the gemination of complex graphemes. In an analysis like that, the constraint *COMPL-C_{gN} must be reformulated into a group of constraints similar to the constraint barring <h> from the nuclear C-position, *NUCLEAR-<H>, cf. §3.2.2.

4.1.3 Regularity of Ambisyllabicity Coding

In the literature, ambisyllabicity coding is described as being very regular in German (e.g Fuhrhop 2005, Eisenberg 2006, Evertz & Primus 2013) and in English (Rollings 2004, Evertz & Primus 2013). In order to find out how regular ambisyllabicity coding is, I conducted a search in the CELEX database of English phonological lemmas (Baayen et al. 1995). I searched for bisyllabic phonological words which are stress-initial, have a unary p-vowel in their first p-syllable, and have only one consonant between the p-vowel of the first syllable and the p-vowel of the second syllable. In this way, I found every bisyllabic lemma with an ambisyllabic consonant. In order to restrict the search to canonical graphematic feet, the graphematic form of the search result had to be graphematically bisyllabic and the second g-syllable had to contain <e> as single v-letter. I excluded compounds from the search results. The summary of the search results is displayed in table 4.10.

Tab. 4.10: Coding of ambisyllabic consonants within bisyllabic canonical words with ambisyllabic p-consonant in English

Total	%	Correspondent to ambisyllabic consonant	examples
852	100	canonical bisyllabic words with ambisyllabic consonant	
489	57.4	c-letter gemination	*better, snuffle, turret*
97	11.4	<ck>	*bracket, heckle, nickel, rocket, tucker*
19	2.2	<tch>	*butcher, kitchen, watcher*
57	6.7	nuclear C-pos. and onset filled	*banger, budget, crescent, finger, gadget, glisten, often, shepherd*
50	5.9	complex grapheme	*brother, hither, riches, ashen, usher*
40	4.7	nuclear C-pos. filled by v-letter	*double, roughen, sweater, treadle, wooden*
50	5.9	<v>	*ever, gravel, shiver, novel*
50	5.9	single c-letter	*camel, desert, honest, linen, modest*

Table 4.10 is subdivided into four parts. The top stratum displays search results pertaining to words that are coded according to GEMINATE or that feature <ck> or <tch>, which can be seen as geminates as well (e.g. Rollings 2004, cf. the discussion in §4.1, above). The next stratum displays results that have a filled nuclear C-position and a filled onset of the next syllable. The first two strata can be seen as regular concerning ambisyllabicity coding, since they comply either to the primary constraint or to subregularities as described in the subsection above. The results of the first two strata make up 662 words = 77.7%.

The next stratum displays the frequency of words which contain ambisyllabic consonants whose correspondents were hindered from blocking: either because of the ban of geminated complex graphemes, or because of the ban of geminated <v>, or because the nuclear C-position is already filled by a v-letter. The sum of the results of this stratum is 140 = 16.4%.

This leaves an exceptional rest of 50 words = 5.9% with an ambisyllabic consonant whose correspondent is a single c-letter.

Let us now turn to German data. In order to test the claims about the regularity of ambisyllabicity (de-)coding in canonical foot structures in German, I conducted a similar CELEX search. As described above, I searched for bisyllabic phonological words in the database of German phonological lemmas which are stress-initial, have a unary p-vowel in their first p-syllable, and have only one consonant between the p-vowel of the first syllable and the p-vowel of the second syllable. In order to restrain the search to canonical graphematic feet, the graphematic form of the search result had to be graphematically bisyllabic and the second g-syllable had to contain <e> as single v-letter. I excluded compounds from the search results. The summary of the search results is displayed in table 4.11.[10]

Tab. 4.11: Coding of ambisyllabic consonants within bisyllabic canonical words with ambisyllabic p-consonant in German

Total	%	Correspondent to ambisyllabic consonant	examples
1382	100	canonical bisyllabic words with ambisyllabic consonant	
785	56.8	c-letter gemination	*Brille* 'glasses', *Noppe* 'nub', *Wette* 'bet'
200	14.5	<ck>	*schmecken* 'to taste'
248	17.9	nuclear C-pos. and onset filled	*Bengel* 'rascal', *Mütze* 'cap', *Tropfen* 'drop', Städter 'city dweller'
148	10.7	complex grapheme	*Bresche* 'breach', *kuscheln* 'to cuddle', *Kachel* 'tile', *Sichel* 'sickle', *Zither* 'zither'
1	0.1	single c-letter	*proper* 'trim'

Table 4.11 is organised like table 4.10 for English above. The first two strata display results that can be attributed to the ambisyllabicity coding constraint or to subregularities of that constraint. The sum of these results is 1233 = 89.2%.

The next stratum displays the search results of words that do not feature c-letter gemination due to the constraint banning the gemination of complex graphemes. The sum of these results is 148 = 10.7%. This leaves a rest of one word, *proper* 'trim'. This is the only instance of an exceptional ambisyllabicity coding in the whole sample.

10 <ck> is listed separately because its status as a complex grapheme can only be claimed for the norm system after 1996.

Summarising, it is fair to say that the coding of ambisyllabicity in canonical graphematic structures in English is fairly regular with a rate of 5.9% of words whose coding is not explicable by the analysis provided here. The coding of ambisyllabicity in canonical graphematic structures in German has virtually no exceptions that cannot be explained.

4.1.4 Summary

The analysis in this section shows that canonical graphematic foot structures can reliably be identified by cues such as reduced graphematic syllables and c-letter geminates. Graphematic foot structure is essential for vowel quantity (de)coding and, connected with that, ambisyllabicity (de)coding. The optimality theoretic analysis of ambisyllabicity coding in German and English provided in this section illustrates the interaction of constraints promoting and blocking c-letter gemination. Finally, a quantitative analysis of the CELEX database confirms the regularity of ambisyllabicity coding in canonical bisyllabic g-feet in German and English.

The analysis provided in this section also shows that an indication of binary vowels by, for instance, g-diphthongs, is not necessary in canonical graphematic feet in English and German. By logical contraposition it is possible to deduce that the absence of c-gemination also means the absence of ambisyllabicity, cf. (13b). In words with a single consonant between two vowels, absence of ambisyllabicity entails the binarity of the first vowel.

This means that 'length marker', such as <h> in *Kühe* 'cows' or v-letter diphthongs as in *Boote* 'boats' are redundant in canonical word forms. In fact, those marking devices are less regular and less productive in canonical word forms (Primus 2010). It is thus sensible to assume that these markers have a different function. One function can be the optimization of syllable weight (for example in *Kuh*, *See* 'sea, lake', Ramers 1998: 30, cf. §4.2); another function can be the tendency to avoid homographs cf. *Beten* 'praying' vs. *Beeten* 'patches', *wider* 'against' vs. *wieder* 'again' and *Iren* 'the Irish' vs. *Ihren* '(politely) yours' (Evertz & Primus 2013: 10). We will explore the use of such markers in the next section on non-canonical feet.

4.2 The Non-Canonical Foot

We can define non-canonical graphematic feet complementarily to canonical graphematic feet, cf. (1): A g-foot is non-canonical if it is bisyllabic but does not end in a reduced g-syllable. Non-canonical words either consist of exactly one non-canonical foot or they consist of more than one foot and end in a monosyllabic g-foot.

In contrast to canonical g-feet, heads of non-canonical feet are not marked consistently. Thus, there are no reliable visual cues for phonological foot structures, cf. the following English examples:

(19) a. Initial stress: *lily, camera, salad, atom, penguin*
b. Medial stress: *veranda, aroma, astonish*
c. Final stress: *July, apply, robust, consist*

4.2.1 Vowel Quantity and Ambisyllabicity

According to Evertz & Primus (2013) c-gemination as means of ambisyllabicity (de-)coding is also not employed systematically in non-canonical word forms. Let us begin with a survey of the English data, cf. table 4.12.

Tab. 4.12: Graphematic representation of ambisyllabicity and its correlates in non-canonical word structures in English (Evertz & Primus 2013)

ambisyllabicity (→ unary vowel) → graph. c-geminate	**no graph. c-geminate → no ambisyllabicity (→ binary vowel)**	**binary vowel → graph. diphthong**
a. *ballot, callus, witty, coffin, bottom, summit, muffin*	a. *data, fatal, final, minus, fetish, pubic*	*engineer, referee, agree, balloon, platoon, tattoo, bazaar*
b. counterexamples: *camera, canon, medal, blemish, fetid, limit, pity, pumice, public*	b. as in b. in the first column	

The counterexamples in table 4.12(b) show that the (de-)coding of ambisyllabicity by the gemination of c-letters is irregular in non-canonical word forms. This means that the contrast between binary and unary vowels is also represented irregularly.

In order to back up the claim that ambisyllabicity (de)coding is unsystematic in non-canonical feet, I conducted a CELEX (Baayen et al. 1995) search. I searched in the database of English phonological lemmas for bisyllabic phonological words which are stress-initial, have a unary p-vowel in their p-syllable, and have only one consonant between the p-vowel of the first syllable and the p-vowel of the second syllable. The second v-letter of the graphematic form of this word could be anything but <e> – including binary g-diphthongs. With this search criteria it should be possible to find all non-canonical bisyllabic lemmas which correspond to a p-word with an ambisyllabic consonant. I excluded compounds from the search results. The summary of the search result is displayed in table 4.13.

Tab. 4.13: Graphematic correspondences of ambisyllabic consonants in non-canonical bisyllabic words in English

939	**100**	**non-canonical bisyllabic words with ambisyllabic consonant**	
541	57.6	c-letter gemination	*affix, cello, ferry, summit, willow*
46	4.9	<ck>	*cuckoo, jockey*
16	1.7	<tch>	*itchy*
33	3.5	nuclear C-pos. and onset filled	*clingy, edgy, fascist, pidgin*
48	5.1	complex grapheme	*ethic, echo, pushy*
24	2.5	nuclear C-pos. filled by v-letter	*bloody, heavy, ready, rookie*
20	2.1	<v>	*avid, covey, livid*
211	22.5	single c-letter	*cabin, epic, relish, widow*

The table above is organised analogously to the tables in the preceding sections. In the top stratum, the frequency of words which conform to the ambisyllabicity coding constraint is displayed (for a discussion whether <ck> and <tch> are geminates see above). In the next stratum, the frequency of words which conform to subregularities of the ambisyllabicity constraint is displayed. Taken together, 67.7% of the results conform to the ambisyllabicity constraint or a subregularity thereof.

The next stratum displays the results of words that do not feature a c-letter geminate due to the fact that the nuclear C-position is already filled by a v-letter or due to independent constraints such as *<vv> or a constraint banning the gemination of complex graphemes. These cases are 9.7% of the results.

Finally, in the last stratum are words that display a single c-letter as graphematic correspondent to the ambisyllabic consonant. In contrast to the situation in canonical bisyllabic words in English, 22.5% of words with ambisyllabic consonant are coded with a single c-letter. There are no other constraints which can explain this irregularity. The coding and decoding of ambisyllabicity in non-canonical words in English is thus not reliably predictable. Differently from the situation found in canonical graphematic structures, table 4.12 suggests that the (de-)coding of binary vowels by graphematic diphthongs is regular and productive in non-canonical words forms.

Let us now turn to German. Considering table 4.14, we see a similar picture compared to the English data in table 4.12.

Tab. 4.14: Graphematic representation of ambisyllabicity and its correlates in non-canonical word structures in German (Evertz & Primus 2013)

ambisyllabicity (→ unary vowel) → graph. c-geminate	**no graph. c-geminate → no ambisyllabicity (→ binary vowel)**	**binary vowel ↔ graph. diphthong**
a. *Teneriffa* 'Tenerife', *Rollo* 'blind', *Komma* 'comma', *Anna*, *Regatta* 'regatta', *Kalkutta* 'Calcutta', *Motto* 'motto', *Otto*	a. *Klima* 'climate', *Koma* 'coma', *Lima* 'Lima', *Lotus* 'lotus', *Puma* 'cougar'	*Allee* 'alley', *Kanapee* 'sofa', *Schikoree* 'chicory', *Chemie* 'chemistry'; *Magie* 'magic', *Paradies* 'paradise'; *Barbier* 'barber'
b. counterexamples: *Limit* 'limit', *Kamera* 'camera', *Papa* 'daddy'	b. as in b. in the first column	

The counterexamples in table 4.14 are evidence that ambisyllabicity (de)coding with the help of c-letter geminates is not as systematic in non-canonical foot structures as in canonical foot structures. Let us have a closer look at the counterexamples the table provides.

In contrast to the counterexamples in the English data, the counterexamples in German are rather scarce. In order to test how irregular ambisyllabicity coding in non-canonical graphematic feet in German is, I conducted another CELEX-search. I searched in the German database of phonological lemmas for bisyllabic phonological words which are stress-initial, have a unary p-vowel in their p-syllable, and have only one consonant between the p-vowel of the first syllable and the p-vowel of the second syllable. The second g-syllables of the corresponding graphematic words have to contain <e> as sole v-letter. The summary of the search result is displayed in table 4.15.

Tab. 4.15: Graphematic correspondences of ambisyllabic consonants in non-canonical bisyllabic words in German

308	**100**	**non-canon. bisyllabic words with ambisyllabic consonant**	
238	77.3	c-letter gemination	*affig* 'affected', *Bussard* 'buzzard', *Komma* 'comma', *Motto* 'motto, *Phallus* 'phallus', *Wallach* 'gelding'
32	10.4	nuclear C-pos. and onset filled	*Ätzung* 'cauterization', *kitschig* 'kitschy' *Schöpfung* 'creation', *Sprengung* 'blasting', *städtisch* 'municipal', *witzig* 'funny'
19	6.2	complex grapheme	*Bischof* 'bishop', *Fasching* 'carnival', *Köchin* '(female) cook', *tschechisch* 'Czech'
19	6.2	single c-letter	*Ami* 'yank', *britisch* 'british', *Limit* 'limit', *Logos* 'logos' *mini* 'mini', *spritig* 'spirity', *Zloty* 'zloty'

The CELEX search yielded 308 instances of non-canonical phonologically bisyllabic words with an ambisyllabic consonant. Of these 308 words, 77.3% (238 words) have a c-letter geminate. In a further 10.4% (32 words), the nuclear C-position and the onset of the following syllable is occupied by the letters corresponding to the ambisyllabic consonant. The first two strata of the table thus display results corresponding either to the ambisyllabicity coding constraint or to its subregularity. 19 words = 6.2% of the results contain a complex grapheme. These words do not display a geminate because of a constraint hindering complex graphemes from geminating (cf. §4.1.2, above).

This leaves 6.2% (19 words) as exceptions with single c-letters as correspondents to ambisyllabic consonants. It has to be considered, however, that the sample I investigated comprises only bisyllabic non-canonical trochees in bisyllabic words. There are also bisyllabic non-canonical trochees in trisyllabic words, e.g. *Anorak* 'anorak', *Ananas* 'pineapple', *Kamera* 'camera', *Kapitel* 'chapter'. All of these words comprise an initial non-canonical trochee with a phonological ambisyllabic consonant which is not coded by a c-letter geminate. Furthermore, I have only considered the coding perspective. While it seems that in canonical feet, the relationship between c-letter geminates and ambisyllabic consonants is bidirectional, this does not seem to be the case in non-canonical structures: in non-canonical structures, there are c-letter geminates within bisyllabic non-canonical g-words that do not map onto ambisyllabic consonants. Consider, e.g., *Akkord* 'chord', *Allee* 'alley', *Affekt* 'affect'. Note, however, that these occurrences of c-letter geminates not corresponding to ambisyllabic consonants are no violations of the proposed constraint GEMINATE, as this constraint has the form of a conditional ('if there is an ambisyllabic consonant, then it is coded by a c-letter geminate').

Although the many examples found in the CELEX search show that ambisyllabicity coding is far from being chaotic in non-canonical graphematic structures in German, it is fair to say that it is less systematic in non-canonical structures than in canonical ones.

We can summarise at this point that there is a difference between canonical and non-canonical graphematic structures in English and German. First, ambisyllabicity (de)coding differs in canonical and non-canonical graphematic feet in English and German. While in canonical g-feet ambisyllabic consonants are regularly coded by c-letter geminates, the coding of ambisyllabicity in non-canonical feet is less systematic. Second, binary phonological vowels are regularly coded by graphematic diphthongs in both writing systems as we will further explore in the next subsection.

4.2.2 Graphematic Diphthongs

There are basically three functions of graphematic diphthongs (for an inventory of g-diphthongs, cf. §3.2.1.1). First, graphematic diphthongs generally map onto binary phonological vowels, while graphematic monophthongs map onto unary or binary phonological vowels depending on graphematic syllable and foot structure, cf. §4.1 above. In, e.g., <m**e**te>, <m**ee**t> and <m**ea**t>, the g-monophthong <e> and the g-diphthongs <ee> and <ea> map onto to the same phonological vowel, /iː/ (in fact, all three g-words map onto the same phonological form, /miːt/. But the g-monophthong <e> can also map onto /ɛ/ in a strong and closed g-syllable like in the past participle of <meet>, <met>, cf. for the phonological function of graphematic diphthongs §3.2.1.

Second, as seen above, graphematic diphthongs serve to differentiate between homophones, e.g. <mete> vs. <meet> vs. <meat>.

Third, g-diphthongs mark graphematic foot structure. Consider <secret> vs. <discreet>. <secret> is a bisyllabic word with a final reduced g-syllable. The reduced g-syllable marks the preceding g-syllable as strong. The preceding g-syllable thus maps onto a strong p-syllable, cf. [ˈsiːkrɪt]. <discreet>, on the other hand, cannot be analysed as canonical word because the word does not end in a reduced g-syllable, but in a full syllable with a g-diphthong. The second g-syllable is strong and maps onto a strong p-syllable, cf. [dɪˈskriːt].

Why do g-diphthongs mark graphematic foot structure? The only difference on segmental level between a g-monophthong and a g-diphthong is the additional v-letter in the g-diphthong. Drawing on parallels to phonological weight, a syllable which contains a g-diphthong like <creet> in <discreet> is graphematically heavier than a syllable with only a g-monophthong like <cret> in <secret>. We can thus provisionally define that graphematic weight correlates with the number of segments, i.e. letters, dominated by the rhyme. The increased weight of a g-syllable with a graphematic diphthong marks this syllable as head of a foot.

In order to demonstrate how the graphematic weight of g-diphthongs influences foot structure, let us consider the trisyllabic graphematic structures in (20). The figure in (20a) represents the non-canonical graphematic structure of *Kanapee* 'sofa' and the figure in (20b) represents the canonical graphematic structure of *Karate* 'karate'.

(20)

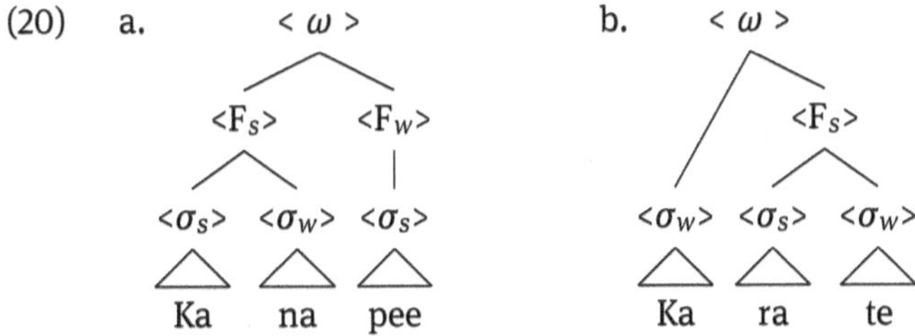

The syllables <ka>, <na>, <ra>, and <te> each have one segment dominated by the onset and one segment dominated by the rhyme; <pee> has one additional segment in the rhyme. <ka>, <na>, <ra> and <te> have the same graphematic weight according to the provisionally definition of graphematic weight (see above); <pee> is heavier than these syllables because it has one more segment in its rhyme. In contrast to the light syllables <ka>, <na>, <ra>, and <te>, <pee> is heavy enough to constitute a foot of its own. The structure in (20a) thus is bipedal, or a *two foot structure*, while the structure in (20b) is monopedal, or a *one foot structure*. Tables 4.12 and 4.14 give more examples of graphematic diphthongs constituting monosyllabic graphematic feet in English and German.

The provisional definition of graphematic weight states that graphematic weight correlates with the number of letters dominated by the rhyme of a graphematic syllable. As we have seen in §1.2.2, phonological weight also correlates with phonological segments in the rhyme. To be more precise, it is commonly assumed that phonological weight in English is defined by morae, that is, every structural position occupied in the rhyme contributes one mora to phonological weight. Bimoraic syllables count as heavy in English. The exact definition of phonological weight in German is disputed. According to Vennemann (1990), closed syllables and syllables with phonological diphthong are heavy in German.

How can we test the provisional definition of graphematic weight? After all, we have to consider that phonological and graphematic segments map onto each other. A g-syllable with many segments in its rhyme can thus just be the result of a mapping relation of heavy *phonological* syllable onto a graphematic syllable.

In order to test whether there is a purely graphematic syllable weight, we need to consider cases in which the number of phonological and graphematic segments in the rhyme do not match. This is the case in words with 'lengthening'-<h> in German, g-diphthongs, doubled c-letters at the end of a word, and complex graphemes, which consist of several segments graphematically but correspond only to one phonological segment (e.g. <sh> - /ʃ/ in *mash*).

In the following sections, I will present two pseudoword production studies in German (Röttger et al. 2012 and Evertz & Primus 2013) which looked into graphematic weight and foot structure. After that, I will present a lexical database study which tries to shed light on minimality restrictions of monosyllabic graphematic feet.

4.3 Graphematic Weight

As we have seen in the previous section, graphematic weight indicates heads in non-canonical feet. This section is devoted to graphematic weight and its influence on graphematic foot structure.

In the first part of the section, I will present two experimental studies. These studies show that the increase of purely graphematic weight by adding silent letters influences graphematic foot structure and by mapping relations also influences phonological foot structures. These experiments thus demonstrate that graphematic weight and graphematic foot structures are relevant and real.

In the second part of the section, we will have a look at monosyllabic graphematic words in English and German and try to test whether there is a minimality constraint for monosyllabic graphematic feet. Based on the discussion so far and the insights the experimental studies and the database studies provide, I will try to formulate a graphematic counterpart to FOOT-BINARITY, cf. §1.2.

4.3.1 Experimental Evidence from German

In this section I will present experimental evidence for the existence and relevance of the graphematic foot and of graphematic weight. One experiment was published in Röttger et al. (2012), the results of the other study were published prior to this work in Evertz & Primus (2013).

The two studies I will present in this section are similar in that they investigate the influence of graphematic weight on graphematic foot structure in German with the help of pseudoword reading tasks. The graphematic weight of the pseudowords is manipulated while the phonological weight is kept stable. Experiments like these cannot be carried out with canonical word structures ending in a reduced syllable. A canonical g-word structure always maps onto a canonical p-word structure. Adding weight to a reduced g-syllable will change it into a full, more salient g-syllable (cf. *alle* [ˈʔal̩ə] 'all' vs. *Allee* [ʔaˈleː] 'alley'). Therefore, the experiments presented here use trisyllabic test items containing only full vowels in which each syllable is liable to carry stress (e.g. <Fuponsas> see below).

Both experiments are based on the following assumptions: i) in a trisyllabic word (where each syllable is equally liable to carry stress), an increase in graphematic weight of the last syllable (ult) has the same effect on the graphematic foot structure like an increase of phonological weight of the ult on the phonological foot structure of a trisyllabic word (cf. §1.2.2 and see below). ii) Graphematic foot structure bidirectionally corresponds to phonological foot structure. This means that a change in graphematic foot structure results in a change in phonological foot structure (and vice versa).

Both experiments manipulate graphematic weight with the help of letters which do not correspond to phonological segments: Röttger et al. (2012) manipulate graphematic weight with the help of complex graphemes or by a sequence of graphemes which correspond to exactly one phonological segment (e.g. <Fuponsas> vs. <Fuponsasch>), Evertz & Primus (2013) manipulate graphematic weight by silent <h> (e.g. <Ranuko> vs. <Ranukoh>) or by a geminated c-letter (e.g. <Turonsas> vs. <Turonsass>).

Before we begin to discuss the actual experiments, let us have a look at phonological feet in trisyllabic words in German.

4.3.1.1 Phonological feet in trisyllabic words in German

I will repeat the most important facts for foot assignment in trisyllabic word in German here for convenience; cf. §1.2.2 for a broader discussion.

Stress assignment in German is dependent on two factors, the preference for trochees and syllable weight. The weight of a full syllable depends on its rhyme structure. This entails that open syllables with a monophthong vowel, such as /pa/, count as light while open syllables that contain diphthongs and closed syllables, such as /pat/, count as heavy (cf. Vennemann 1991, Restle & Vennemann 2001, Knaus & Domahs 2009, Domahs et al., 2014).

(21) a. The rhyme of a light syllable contains only one segment.
b. The rhyme of a heavy syllable contains more than one segment.

There are three phonological foot structures for trisyllabic words containing only full vowels (Alber 1997, Domahs et al. 2008, Knaus & Domahs 2009, Röttger et al. 2012, Domahs et al., 2014). I repeat the structures of §1.2.2 in (18) as (22). The structures in (22) are 1-foot-structures, they contain only one foot. The first syllable is not parsed as a foot and the final syllables form a trochee.

(22)

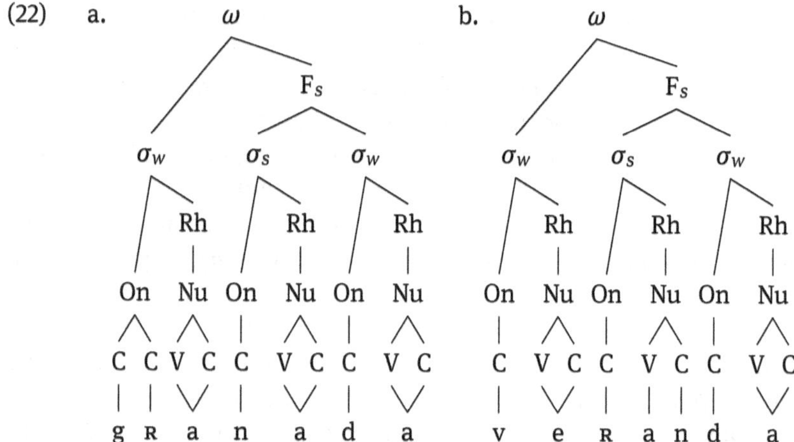

The structures in (23) (=(19)) are examples of 2-foot structures. In 2-foot structures, all syllables are parsed into feet and the last syllable constitutes a monosyllabic foot.

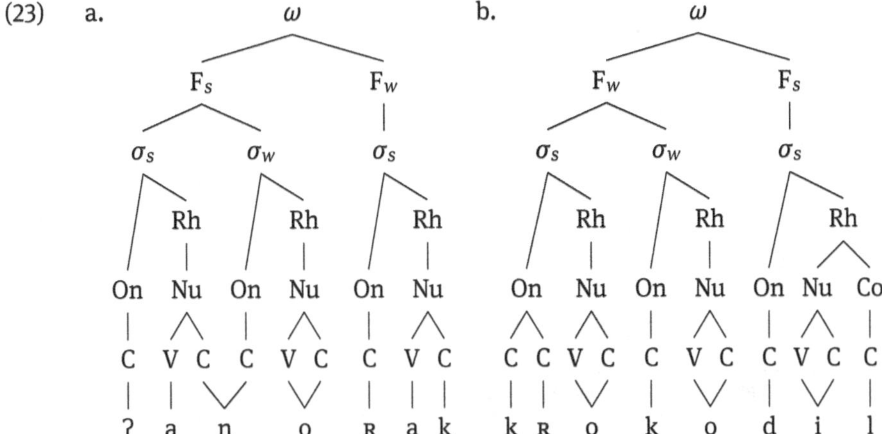

The structures in (23) differ in the prominence relations of their feet. In (23a), the first foot is stronger (i.e., more prominent) than the other foot, as indicated by the subscript "s". Therefore, the strong syllable in this foot bears the main stress. In (23b), the last foot is stronger, so that its only syllable bears the main stress. Whether a 1-foot or a 2-foot structure is selected depends mainly on the distribution of phonological weight, cf. (24):

(24) a. If the ultimate syllable is light or the penultimate syllable is heavy, a final trochee is built up. A 1-foot structure emerges (see (22)). Word stress is on the penultimate syllable.

b. If the ultimate syllable is heavy, the ultimate syllable builds up a monosyllabic foot and an initial trochee emerges (see (23)). Word stress may be on the antepenultimate or the ultimate syllable, though stress on the ultimate syllable is dispreferred (Noel 2002).

These generalisations are not strict rules but describe preferences. Exceptions to these generalisations are for instance words like *Indigo* 'indigo' with a light ultimate and penultimate syllable but stress on the antepenultimate syllable, contrary to the prediction in (24a). In this case the departure from the generalisation may be explicable by the segmental influence of /i/ (cf. Jessen 1999, Janßen 2003).

4.3.1.2 Complex graphemes (Röttger et al. 2012)

4.3.1.2.1 Hypothesis & Method

Röttger et al. (2012) examine several factors on stress assignment in German. One of the factors they investigate is graphematic weight. Their reasoning is that graphemes such as <s> and <sch> both correspond to one phoneme, [s] and [ʃ], respectively. <s>, however, consists of one letter, while <sch> consists of three letters. Syllables such as [sas] and [saʃ] do not differ in phonological weight, the corresponding graphematic syllables <sas> and <sasch>, however, should differ in graphematic weight because the rhyme of <sasch> dominates two more c-letters than the rhyme of <sas>.

The test items are therefore identical in phonological weight but differ in the number of letters dominated by the graphematic rhyme of the ultimate syllable, cf. table 4.16.

Tab. 4.16: Item groups in Röttger et al. (2012)

Condition	Letters per graph. syllable	Example	Subgroup
a.	cv.cvc.cvc	Fo.pun.sas	[s]
		Do.san.rax	[ks]
b.	cv.cvc.cvccc	Fo.pun.sasch	[ʃ]
		Do.san.racks	[ks]

The experimental hypothesis of Röttger et al. (2012: 67) is as follows: "If orthographic weight does have an effect on stress assignment, we expect a significantly different distribution of stress patterns related to conditions [a.] and [b.]. Specifically, if orthographic complexity constitutes something similar to visual quantity, we expect that the frequency of final stress should significantly increase and the frequency of penultimate stress should significantly decrease from [a.] to [b.]."

In order to test this hypothesis, Röttger et al. (2012) conducted a pseudoword reading experiment. Forty monolingual native speakers of German (30 women, 10 men; mean age 23) participated in the experiment. All participants were students at the University of Cologne.

There were twenty test item pairs of the graphematic weight item group. The test items were presented in a carrier sentence, *Ich habe gehört, dass Peter ... gesagt hat.* 'I have heard that Peter said ...'. The participants were asked to read the sentence with the test item aloud. The experiment had a counterbalanced design, so that no participant saw both parts of a test item pair. The first author and an independent rater listened to the recorded responses of the participants and transcribed them for main stress positions.

4.3.1.2.2 Results

Röttger et al (2012: 75) report a significant effect of orthographic complexity of the final rhyme structure on the distribution of antepenultimate, penultimate and final stress. Between a simple (such as <s>) and a complex orthographic rhyme (such as <sch>), the proportion of items with antepenultimate stress increased from 24.7% to 43.4%, the proportion of items with penultimate stress decreased from 52.7% to 26.1%, and the proportion of items with final stress increased from 22.6% to 30.6%, cf. figure 4.1.

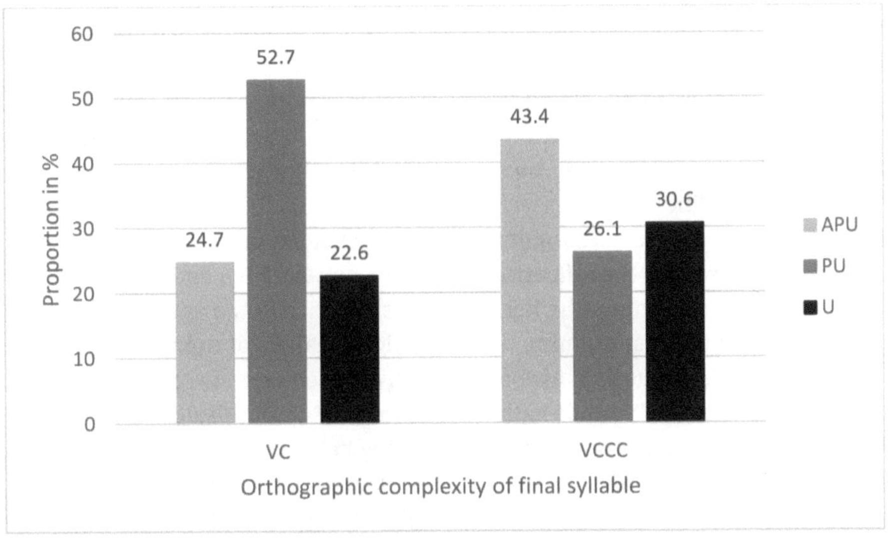

Fig. 4.1: Distribution of stress assignment for two types of trisyllabic pseudowords manipulated for graphematic complexity (Röttger et al. 2012: 76; my reconstruction)

4.3.1.3 <h> and c-letter gemination (Evertz & Primus 2013)

4.3.1.3.1 Hypothesis & Method

The experimental hypotheses of Evertz & Primus (2013) are summarised in (25):

(25) *Experimental hypotheses* (Evertz & Primus 2013)
An increase of graphematic weight in the ultimate syllable leads to an enhanced proportion of phonological structures with a final monosyllabic foot

i. in trisyllabic words with a final mute <h> compared to an ultimate syllable without final <h>;

ii. in trisyllabic words with a final graphematic geminate (e.g., <pp>) compared to an ultimate syllable without a final graphematic geminate.

In order to test this hypothesis, Evertz & Primus (2013) conducted a pseudoword production experiment with 18 monolingual native speakers of German (14 women, 4 men). The participants were students at the University of Cologne. Their mean age was 23.34 (ranging from 20 to 29). The participants received small gifts for their participation.

In accordance with the hypotheses in (25), two groups of items as shown in table 4.17 were created.[11] In order to ensure that every syllable is equally able to bear stress, no item contained <e> since reduced syllables are not stressable in German and <e> is often related to schwa. Furthermore, no item contained <i>. Words with an open penultimate syllable ending in /i/ are often stressed on the antepenultimate syllable, e.g. *Ánimus* 'soul', *Álibi* 'alibi', *Défizit* 'deficit', *Éskimo* 'Eskimo', *Índigo* 'indigo' (cf. Jessen 1999, Janßen 2003). To avoid segmental influence of the vowel on stress assignment, <i> was avoided in the stimuli.

In order to reduce the influence of analogy, non-nativity, and morphological complexity to a minimum, the items were tested prior to the actual experiment in two ways. In the first norming test, 59 native speakers of German were asked to rate the item's status as native or non-native based on a five-point-scale. The scale ranged from 5 = "sounds native/ German" to 1 = "sounds utterly not native/ German." All potential items with a mean rating below two were eliminated. The surviving items were tested in another pretest by 47 native speakers of German. The informants were asked to name existing words (German or another language) that they associated with these items. Items that were associated by two or more informants with the same existing word were excluded. Also, items that were associated with a morphologically complex word by at least one informant were excluded.

48 test items were used in total. They were organised in 24 pairs (e.g. *Ranuko, Ranukoh*). The pseudowords did not violate any German phono- or graphotactical constraint and their syllable boundaries were unambiguous.

The items of group 2 differ from the items of group 1 in two ways. First, their ultimate syllables are formed according to the hypotheses in (25): The items of group 1 have a phonologically open ultimate syllable that is graphematically open in the a-condition and graphematically closed in the b-condition. The items of group

11 The lower-case characters 'v' and 'c' in table 4.17 and in the labeling of the x-axes of the charts do not refer to skeletal positions of syllables but to segments, i.e. letters. 'c' denotes a c-letter, 'v' a v-letter.

Tab. 4.17: Item groups in Evertz & Primus (2013)

	Item group 1: final <h>		*Item group 2: graph. gemination*	
	letters in ult. syll.	examples	letters in ult. syll.	examples
a.	cv	Ranuko, Bodalu, Funusa, Posuto	cvc	Baruntap, Turonsas, Karantul, Kuranlup
b.	cvc	Ranukoh, Bodaluh, Funusah, Posutoh	cvcc	Baruntapp, Turonsass Karantull, Kuranlupp

2 have closed ultimate syllables. Phonologically they are closed by one consonant in both conditions, graphematically they are closed by one letter in the a-condition and by two letters in the b-condition. The second difference is the structure of the penultimate syllable. The items of group 1 have light penultimate syllables, while the items of group 2 have heavy penultimate syllables. Because the ultimate syllables are already heavy in the paradigm of group 2, the penultimate syllables also had to be heavy. If the penultimate syllables had been light, a 2-foot structure would have emerged with high likeliness. By creating items with heavy penultimate syllables and heavy ultimate syllables, a situation is generated where the options for a 1-foot structure and for a 2-foot structure are conflicting.

To avoid the emergence of stress routines, 29 filler items were interspersed into the sequence of experimental items. Those fillers were designed in a way that their main stress was predictable with a high likeliness (this was mainly archived by manipulating the syllable structure and by graphematic cues, such as <e> as syllable nucleus).

The experiment was implemented with a counterbalanced design. The participants were divided randomly into three groups where each group received a different set of stimuli. Every set consisted of filler items that served as distractors and of experimental items. The items and fillers were divided into blocks. Every set consisted of 4 blocks. Two of these blocks consisted of 11 experimental items and 6 fillers, and two blocks consisted of 12 experimental items and 6 fillers. All sets were pseudorandomised for syllable number, item group, condition, expected stress pattern and experimental status (filler vs. experimental item). In order to avoid priming effects, no set of stimuli contained both the a- and b-form of an item. This made sure that no participant had to produce a minimal graphematic pair like *Ranuko* and *Ranukoh*.

The participants were instructed to read aloud three training items and the actual items from a computer screen. The actual items consisted of 46 test items and 24 fillers. In order to familiarise the participants with the items, every item was shown in isolation for three seconds. After this introduction, the item was presented embedded in a carrier sentence (*Er hat den ... gemurft* 'He murfed the ...'). The participants were asked to read the whole sentence (but not the word in isolation) aloud. The verb of the carrier sentence is also a pseudoword. By using a pseudo carrier sentence containing German function words and inflectional affixes, we could avoid a metalanguage context and we familiarised the participants with producing pseudowords. This minimised the probability that the test item was interpreted as belonging to a language different from German.[12]

After every second block, participants had to solve two mental arithmetic tasks. After solving the tasks, there was an obligatory break of 30 seconds. The procedure (including the instruction) took approximately 20 minutes. The responses of the participants were recorded digitally with 44.1 kHz using a PC and a microphone. Martin Evertz and an independent person trained in phonetic analysis transcribed the data for main stress position. Items whose positions of main stress were judged differently by the two transcribers were excluded from the analysis. Furthermore, we excluded all items which were produced erroneously with respect to their segmental structure (e.g., *Ran.un.ko* instead of *Ra.nu.ko*). In this way 3.65% of the items were excluded. All remaining relevant pairs of items (e.g., *Baruntap* - *Baruntapp*) did not exhibit phonological differences other than stress.

The following method was used to calculate a ratio of stress positions of the target items: the number of responses for each stress position per item was divided by the number of all analysable responses for that item. This resulted in a proportion of responses for each stress position and pseudoword. These stress-ratios were subjected to t-tests for specific contrasts. Since we tested directed hypotheses, all t-tests were performed one-tailed (cf. Röttger et al. 2012 for a similar statistical analysis).

4.3.1.3.2 Results

The chart in Figure 4.2 illustrates the frequency distribution of main stress in pseudowords with and without final <h>. The columns on the left represent the distribution of main stress in items with a graphematically light ultimate syllable (e.g., *Ranuko*). The columns on the right show the distribution of main stress in items with higher graphematic weight (e.g., *Ranukoh*).

12 An example of a metalanguage context is the carrier sentence of Janßen (2003): *Ich habe gehört, dass Peter ... gesagt hat* ('I have heard that Peter said ...'). A sample of six participants in a design with a metalanguage carrier sentence showed strong differences in the distribution of main stress compared to the design presented in this paper. The carrier sentences of both designs

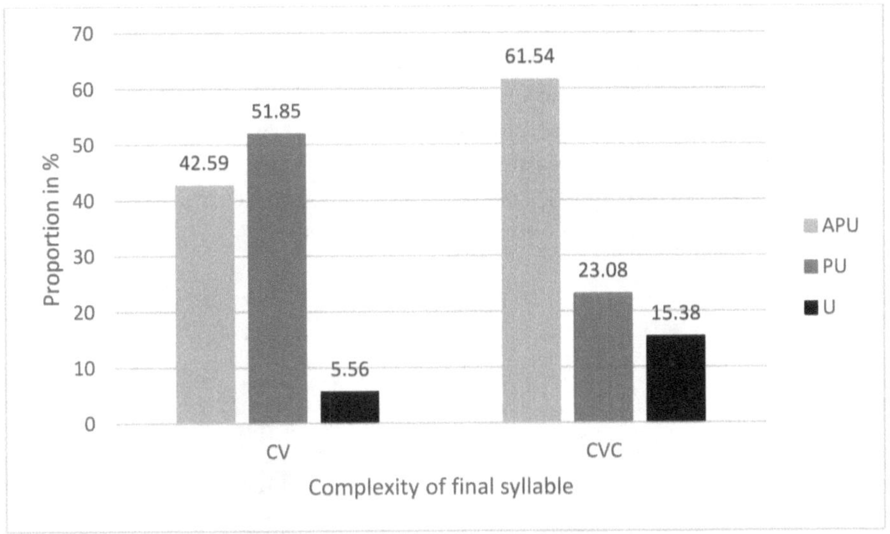

Fig. 4.2: Frequency distribution of stress patterns against graphematic complexity of the ultimate syllable (Item group 1: final <h>).

If the ultimate syllable was graphematically light, the penultimate syllable received main stress in the slight majority of cases (51.85%). In 42.59% of cases the antepenultimate syllable was stressed, in 5.56% of cases the ultimate syllable received stress. If the ultimate syllable was graphematically heavy, the distribution of the main stress was different. The penultimate syllable was stressed in only 23.08% of cases. The antepenultimate and ultimate syllable were stressed more often. The main stress was on the antepenultimate syllable in 61.54% and on the ultimate syllable in 15.38% of cases.

Let us now examine the paired comparisons: The differences in the distribution of stress on graphematically heavy vs. light penultimate and ultimate syllables are significant. The frequency of stressed graphematically light penultimate syllables differs from the frequency of stressed graphematically heavy penultimate syllables with $p = 0.015$ ($t = 2.38$, $df = 16$). In the case of the ultimate syllables,

---

are very similar in regard to their prosodic make up (*Ich habe gehört, dass Peter ... gesagt* hat vs. *Er hat den ... gemurft*). The only considerable difference in their make-up is the semantic context; therefore metalanguage could be an independent parameter.

the p value is $p = 0.041$ ($t = -1.857$, $df = 16$). The difference in the distribution of stress on graphematically light vs. heavy antepenultimate syllables is nearly significant with $p = 0.077$ ($t = -1.498$, $df = 16$).

Main stress on the antepenultimate or ultimate syllable indicates a 2-foot structure, whereas main stress on the penultimate syllable indicates a 1-foot-structure (cf. section 4.1 above). Therefore, we can count the relative frequency of stressed antepenultimate and ultimate syllables together.

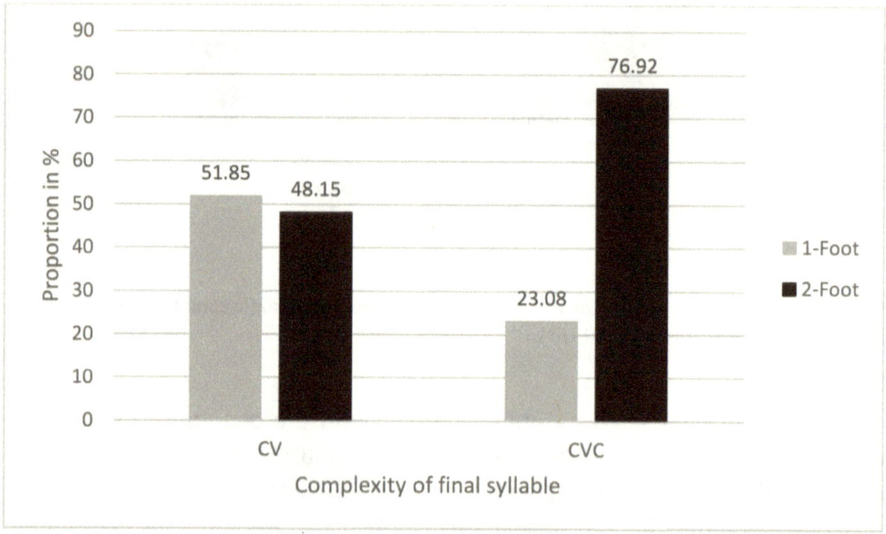

Fig. 4.3: Frequency distribution of foot structures against graphematic complexity of the ultimate syllable (Item group 1).

With a graphematically light ultimate syllable, 1-foot structures and 2-foot structures were selected nearly at the same rate (51.85% 1-foot structures, 48.15% 2-foot structures). By increasing the graphematic weight of the ultimate syllable, the selection of a 2-foot structure was increased to 76.92%. The difference between the frequency distributions of the graphematically light and heavy ultimate syllables is significant at a $p=.015$ level.

The picture for graphematic gemination (second item group) looks slightly different. The effect we see here is not as strong as in the first item group, but is nevertheless observable, cf. figure 4.4.

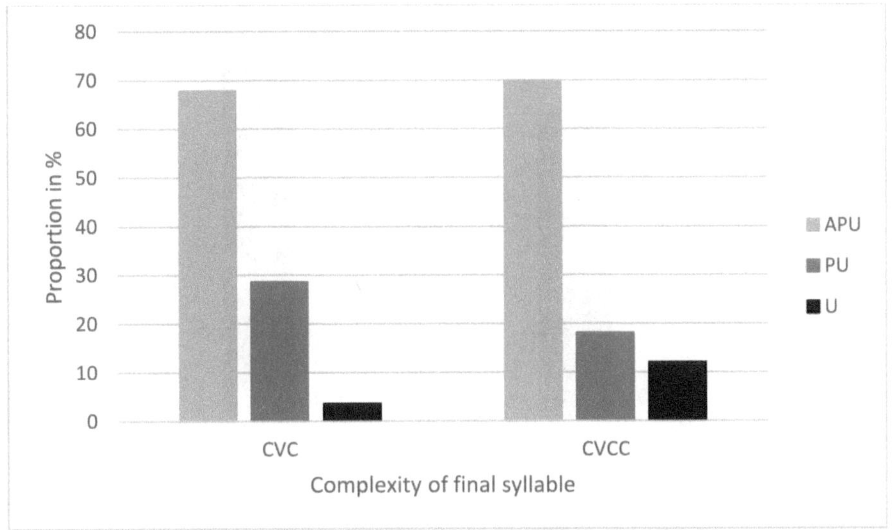

Fig. 4.4: Frequency distribution of stress patterns against graphematic complexity of the ultimate syllable (Item group 2).

The frequency of stressed antepenultimate syllables stays nearly stable, irrespective of the graphematic weight of the ultimate syllable (67.86% to 69.88%). But like in the first item group, the frequency of stressed penultimate syllables decreases (28.57% to 18.07%), while the frequency of stressed ultimate syllables raises (3.57% to 12.05%) when the graphematic complexity of the ultimate syllable is increased.

If we count stressed antepenultimate and ultimate syllables together as 2-foot structures, we see that the 2-foot structure is also preferred in the <cvc>-condition (Baruntap) and only gains more dominance in the <cvcc>-condition (Baruntapp). Though there is a tendency at the descriptive level, the differences in the distributions are statistically observable, but not significant.

4.3.1.4 Discussion

The hypothesis that graphematic weight influences the phonological foot structure of trisyllabic pseudowords has been confirmed by the experiments of Röttger et al (2012) and Evertz & Primus (2013).

The effects of mute <h> and the complex graphemes were clearer than those of graphematic gemination. This difference is explicable by the different weight contrasts in the item groups. Adding a mute <h> to a word like <Ranuko> turns

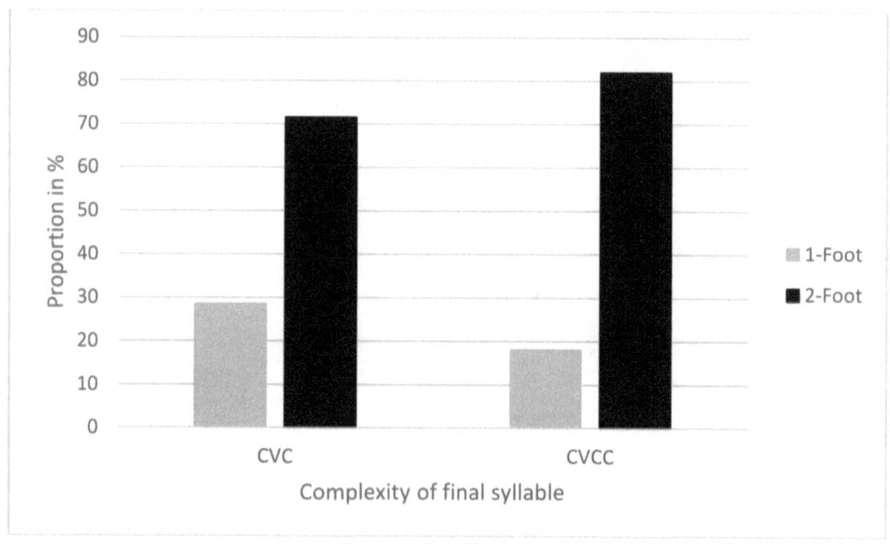

Fig. 4.5: Frequency distribution of foot structures against graphematic complexity of the ultimate syllable (Item group 2).

a graphematically light ultimate syllable into a heavy ultimate syllable. In the experiment of Röttger et al. (2012) two c-letters were added to an already closed g-syllable (cf., e.g., <Fuponsas> – <Fuponsasch>). Graphematic gemination, however, adds only one c-letter to an ultimate syllable that is graphematically already heavy (cf., e.g., <Baruntap> – <Baruntapp>). These findings are in line with Janßen's observations (2003: 71) pertaining to phonological weight differences. Janßen (2003) manipulated phonological weight in her pseudoword production study and found that the effect of phonological weight on stress assignment is not as strong between item groups consisting of trisyllabic words with an already closed ultimate syllable and item groups with a complex ultimate syllable as the effect of graphematic weight on stress assignment between item groups with open ultimate syllables and closed ultimate syllables, or item groups with ultimate syllables with a simple coda and item groups with a super-heavy ultimate syllable.

In all item groups of the two experiments presented here, the number of letters in the ultimate syllable was increased in the b.-condition, while the phonological weight was kept stable. What is remarkable is that it was not the ultimate syllable with the increased graphematic weight that was stressed most frequently, but the antepenultimate syllable. On first sight, this might look puzzling since one could think that the syllable with the highest graphematic weight should attract stress, but, if we take foot structure into consideration, we can explain these results.

The explanation is as follows: Mute letters, including <h>, geminated letters, and letters in complex graphemes, increase the visual weight of the ultimate syllable. A heavy ultimate syllable is likely to form a graphematic foot of its own. An increase in the graphematic weight of the ultimate syllable does not directly lead to main stress on this syllable. The graphematic weight of the ultimate syllable directly influences graphematic foot structure, as mentioned; the default assumption of a close correspondence between graphematic and phonological foot structure leads to an analysis in which a phonological 2-foot structure is built that matches the graphematic 2-foot structure of words with a visually heavy ultimate syllable. Once a phonological 2-foot structure is assumed, stress may fall on the first foot, i.e., the antepenultimate syllable in the cases under discussion, or on the second foot (the ultimate syllable) in German. Due to the fact that ultimate syllable stress is slightly dispreferred (cf. Noel 2002), stress on the antepenultimate syllable is also possible, as shown in (23) above. This may account for the stress variation found in pseudowords with graphematically heavy ultimate syllables (e.g., *Ranukoh* with antepenultimate or ultimate syllable stress). This stress variation is also attested with proper words that have a graphematically heavy ultimate syllable. There are words with antepenultimate syllable stress, such as *Kanapee* 'sofa', *Inschallah* 'god willing', words with ultimate syllable stress, such as *Frikassee* 'fricassee' and also words with a shifting antepenultimate or ultimate syllable stress, such as *Schikoree* 'chicory' or *Nargileh* 'narghile'.

In the experiments, only graphematic weight was manipulated. There was no increase in the phonological weight of the corresponding p-syllable. Thus, both *Ranuko* and *Ranukoh*, for example, encode an open final p-syllable with a tense monophthong that counts as light for stress purposes in German (cf. Vennemann 1991; Restle & Vennemann 2001; Knaus & Domahs 2009). Both *Baruntap* and *Baruntapp* and *Fuponsas* and *Fuponsasch*, for instance, encode a heavy final p-syllable. These experiments therefore strongly suggest that graphematic weight and graphematic foot structure are relevant graphematic units that may influence the analysis of the corresponding phonological foot structure.

4.3.2 Evidence based on lexical databases

This section investigates whether there is evidence based on lexical databases for a graphematic counterpart of the following phonological constraints.

(26) LEXWD=PRDWD: Every lexical word corresponds to a prosodic word (Prince & Smolensky 1993: 101).

(27) FOOT-BINARITY: Feet are binary at a syllabic or moraic level of analysis (McCarthy & Prince 1995a: 320-24).

Due to the (rather high-ranking) constraint LEXWD=PRDWD, every lexical word corresponds to a phonological word. And due to the phonological hierarchy, every prosodic (phonological) word comprises at least one phonological foot, and every phonological foot comprises exactly one strong syllable. A lexical word must therefore be footed and thus display stress.

The other constraint, FOOT-BINARITY, is simultaneously a minimality and maximality constraint for phonological feet. A phonological foot comprises either two syllables of any weight or one heavy syllable.

Before we begin with a survey of a lexical database, it is important to consider that not all words behave in the same way, both in written and in spoken language. The constraint LXWD=PRWD, for instance, applies only to lexical words and not to function words. Traditionally, function words are defined as words that have little lexical meaning but serve grammatical functions. An example of a typical function word in this sense is a preposition like *to*, and an example of a typical lexical or content word is a noun like *house*. However, there is no sharp distinction between these categories (cf. e.g. Fronek 1982).

According to LXWD=PRWD, there are phonological differences between lexical words and some function words (e.g., Selkirk 1984, 1996 for English, Nespor and Vogel 1986 for various languages, Zec 1993 for Serbo-Croatian, Booij 1996 for Dutch, Hall 1999 for German, Vigário 1999 for Portuguese). Function words tend to be prosodically weak and subminimal, i.e. they do not meet word minimality constraints. Thus, function words are vulnerable to phonological reductions and often undergo cliticization to a prosodically stronger host, namely lexical words (e.g., *I saw* [m̩] 'I saw him'; Kabak & Schiering 2006). It should be noted, however, that not all function words behave this way, for instance, not every monosyllabic function word can appear in a weak form in English (e.g., *too, off*, etc.; Selkirk 1996: 447). Likewise, there are German function words that are monosyllabic but have no reduced variants (e.g., *weil* 'because', *aus* 'out', *bei* 'at', *statt* 'instead of'; Hall 1999: 103).

Since the semantic and syntactical definitions of lexical and function words cannot make a sharp distinction between these two groups of words, I will rely on the phonological differences of the word groups. Those words which can appear in a prosodically weak form, I will call 'weak words' and those words which are not attested in a prosodically weak form, I will call 'strong words'. Thus, words like *Haus*, *house* or *obwohl* 'although', *too* are strong words, whereas words such as *in* (Ger./Engl.), *him*, *for*, *zu* 'to' are weak words. We will see that writing systems are sensitive to this difference, cf. *of* (weak word) vs. *off* (strong word), *to* (weak word) vs. *too* (strong word) (cf. Rollings 2004: 79).

Another group of words that may behave unexpectedly are interjections. Some interjections are exceptional in phonology and graphematics: some interjections that can be found in English and German, e.g., *hm* and *psst*, for instance, do not contain a v-letter in their graphematic representation and do not contain a phonological vowel although they are potentially stressable. Interjections like these can also be counted as belonging to the group of weak words.

A third group that may behave exceptionally are non-native words. Carney (1994), for instance, makes a distinction between native and non-native words and states that native words are subject to other spelling rules than non-native words. Eisenberg (2006) states that "native words are exactly those which do not stand out with reference to their phonological, graphematic and morphological properties" (Eisenberg 2006: 39, my translation). Neef (2010) also makes the distinction between native and non-native words, but his analysis of native words is more finely grained. He assumes that there are several strata within the native vocabulary. Some proper nouns, for instance, are native words but they may violate constraints which words of the core lexicon may not violate, e.g. in the German town names *Bayenthal, Bayreuth* and *Alzey, Loreley*, the v-letter <y> forms g-diphthongs which do not appear in words of the core lexicon. These diphthongs can also be found in German surnames like *Mayer, Meyer, Keyser*, etc.

Summarising, I expect there to be three groups of words that may behave differently from strong native words, 1. weak words (including some interjections), 2. non-native words and 3. proper names (irrespective of whether they are native or non-native).

4.3.2.1 German Data

My starting point for a study of graphematic weight based on lexical databases is a database survey by Ramers (1998). He examined whether there is a minimality restriction for graphematic words in German. His reasoning is as follows: There is a minimality constraint for phonological feet, FOOT-BINARITY (McCarthy & Prince 1995a: 320-24), stating that a foot consists minimally of two syllables or two morae (cf. §1.2), and there is the constraint LXWD=PRWD (Prince & Smolensky 1993: 101) stating that every lexical word is a prosodic (phonological) word. Because every phonological word comprises at least one foot, a minimal word comprises exactly one foot and thereby two syllables or two morae. A monosyllabic word thus has to consist of a heavy syllable. If there are similar restrictions for graphematic words in German, monosyllabic graphematic words should only consist of heavy graphematic syllables.

Ramers found in a corpus of German monosyllabic words (composed of Muthmann 1996 and Duden 1996) that there are no (or only very few) words of the structure *<v>, *<vv>, *<c_0v> (where 'c_0' is zero or more c-letters and 'v' is a v-letter) or of the pattern *<vc> (Ramers 1998: 35).[13] There are, however, words with the structure <cvc>, <cvv>, and <vcc>.

Tab. 4.18: Examples of words with restricted structures (cf. Ramers 1998)

Letters	Examples
<vv>	*Au* (interjection), *Ei* 'egg', *Ai* (interjection)
<cv>	*bi* 'bisexual' (abbr.), *Bö* 'gust', *da* 'there', *du* 'you', *Go* 'go (jap.)', *ja* 'yes', *je* 'each', *(im) Nu* 'in no time', *Po* 'bottom (abbr. of *Popo*)', *Pi* 'pi', *Re* (abbr. of *Rekontra*[14]), *so* 'so', *wo* 'where', *zu* 'to')
<ccv>	*Pli* 'curl', *Gnu* 'gnu', *Klo* 'toilet', *Schi* 'ski', *Schmu* 'rubbish', *Schwa* 'schwa'
<vc>	*ab* 'from', *am* 'at the', *an* 'at', *er* 'he', *es* 'it', *im* 'in the', *in* 'in', *ob* 'whether', *um* 'around'; *Ar* 'are ($100m^2$)', *Öl* 'oil', *Ur* 'aurochs'

Ramers notes that there are only three examples of words with the structure <vv>. Two of these examples, however, are interjections, leaving only one instance of a strong native word. Ramers assumes that this gap in the lexicon is systematic: he concludes that words of this make-up do not fulfil a weight-minimum and are therefore not grammatical.

There are, however, more examples with the structure <cv>. A closer look reveals that the 14 examples listed in table 4.18 consist of 7 weak words (*da, du, ja, je, so, wo, zu*), 3 abbreviations (*bi, Po, Re*) and two loanwords (*Go, Pi, Bö* (Dutch)), leaving only one native strong word, *Nu*; but *Nu* is only used in the expression *im Nu* 'in no time'. While there are (virtually) no strong words of the structure <cv>, weak words (and non-reduced interjections) can seemingly have this structure.

The words with the structure <ccv> listed in table 4.18 are the only ones Ramers (1998: 31) could find in his corpus. Four of these words are loanwords (*Pli, Gnu, Schwa, Schi*), one is an abbreviation (*Klo* from *Klosett*) and one is a colloquial term derived from western Yiddish (*Schmu*). In other words, none of these words can be counted as belonging to the native vocabulary (Ramers 1998: 32).

13 I use lower-case letters to indicate letters and upper-case letters to indicate structural positions.

Strong words with the structure <vc> are also relatively rare in German. Ramers (1998: 34) finds only three[15] native strong words (*Ar* 'are (100m^2)', *Öl* 'oil', *Ur* 'aurochs') which are not abbreviations or attested with a bisyllabic graphematic form (e.g *öd* – *öde* 'dull'); however, there are many weak words with this structure (e.g. *ab* 'off', *am* 'at the', *an* 'at', *er* 'he', *es* 'it', *im* 'in the', *in* 'in', *ob* 'whether', *um* 'around').

I conducted a CELEX-search in order to replicate Ramer's findings. My findings are in line with Ramer's, cf. 4.6.[16]

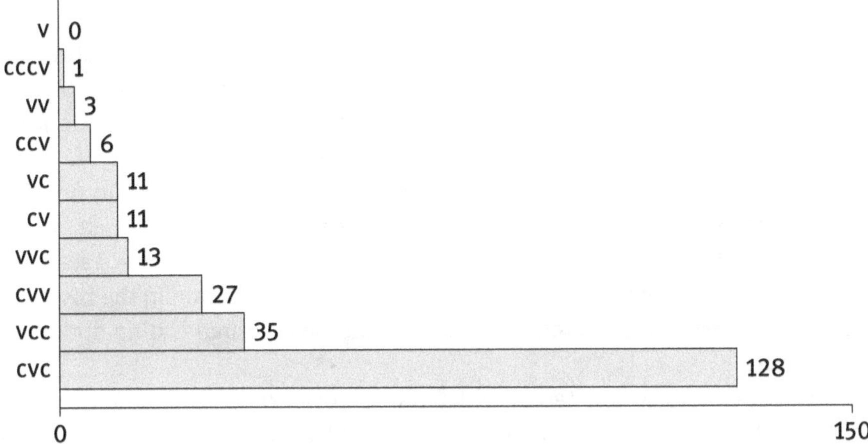

Fig. 4.6: Total numbers of minimal words in the CELEX database of German lemmas

One could object that these gaps in the lexicon are not caused by graphematic constraints but by phonological constraints. In other words, maybe the lack of, e.g., *<c_0v>-words is caused by a lack of phonological words with a corresponding make-up.

Indeed, stressed syllables ending in unary phonological vowels are ill-formed. They occur neither in monosyllabic words nor in polysyllabic words (cf. §1.2). But on the other hand, syllables ending in a binary vowel are well-formed and there are monosyllabic words consisting only of an open syllable with binary vowel, cf. (28).

15 Ramers also finds *As* 'ace' and *iß* 'eat (Imp.)'. This is, however, the spelling prior to the spelling reform in 1996. After 1996 the spelling changed to *Ass* and *iss*, which conforms to the weight theory proposed by Ramers.

16 The frequency chart in figure 4.6 does not list weak words.

(28) a. *Tee* 'tea', *Fee* 'fairy', *Lee* 'lee', *See* 'lake'
b. *Kuh* 'cow', *Rah* 'yard', *Reh* 'deer', *roh* 'raw', *sah* 'saw', *Weh* 'woe', *jäh* 'abrupt', *nah* 'near', *näh* 'sew', *mäh* 'mow', *Loh* 'flames', *Dreh* 'shooting', *droh* 'threaten', *steh* 'stand', *floh* 'escape', *froh* 'happy', *Stroh* 'straw', *Schah* 'shah', *Schuh* 'shoe'
c. *Vieh* 'cattle', *lieh* 'lend', *sieh* 'behold'

The examples in (28) show that there are monosyllabic words consisting of an onset and a rhyme dominating a single segment in phonology. However, these examples do not have a graphematic form that only consists of an onset and a rhyme dominating a single letter. All examples in (28) display at least one additional silent letter (cf. lengthening signs below): The words in (28a) feature a g-diphthong, the words in (28b) feature a silent <h>, commonly called 'lengthening-h' (cf. §3.2.1), and the words in (28c) display <ie> and <h>. The graphematic structure *<c_0v> thus seems to be *graphematically* constrained.

A second structure that seems to be restricted is <vc>. In order to find out whether this structure is phonologically or graphematically restricted, I conducted a search in the CELEX database of German phonological lemmas. I searched for monosyllabic p-words without onset and only one consonant in the rhyme. If there is no constraint blocking <vc>, this should be a normal coding option for such words.

In total, I found 40 lemmas, 27 with binary p-vowel and 13 with unary p-vowel. Only five of these words with binary vowel are coded <vc>, *Ar* 'are', *As* 'A flat', *er* 'he', *Ur* 'aurochs' and *Öl* 'oil'. Of the words with unary vowel, six words are coded <vc> – all of them are weak words: *ab*, *an*, *es*, *in*, *ob*, *um*. All other words have other structures, cf. table 4.19.

With the exception of *Ar*, *As*, *Ur* and *Öl*, only weak words have the structure <vc>, although there are potentially many more strong words that could map onto a monosyllabic graphematic word with this structure. Thus, the data strongly suggest that the structure <vc> is constrained in purely *graphematic* terms.

Ramers (1998) draws two conclusions from his observations (which are reinforced by this study): there are systematic gaps in the lexicon and there has to be something which causes these gaps: Ramers suspects a graphematic minimality constraint that determines the minimal weight of graphematic words.

The second of Ramers' conclusions is based on the observation that there are strong <vcc>- and <cvc>-words but only very few strong <ccv>-words. These kinds of words have the same number of letters, but while two structures, <vcc> and <cvc>, do not seem to be restricted, the <ccv>-structure seems to be a restricted

Tab. 4.19: Coding of monosyllabic phonological words without onset and one consonant dominated by the rhyme in German

	unary p-vowel			binary p-vowel		
	#	%	examples	#	%	examples
<vc>	6	46.2	*ab* 'from', *es* 'it', *um* 'around'	5	18.5	*Ar* 'are', *Öl* 'oil', *er* 'he'
<vvc>				9	33.3	*Aas* 'carrion', *auf* 'on', *Eis* 'ice'
<vcc(c)>	7	53.8	*All* 'space', *eng* 'narrow', *Eck* 'corner'	7	25.9	*Ahn* 'ancestor', *ihr* 'your', *Ohr* 'ear'
<vvcc(c)>				4	15	*auch* 'too', *autsch* 'ouch'
< $\sigma\sigma$ >				2	7.4	*Aide, Ale*

structure. Let us compare the frequency of <vcc>- and <ccv>-words. I found in the CELEX database 6 lemmas with the <ccv>-structure and 27 with the <vcc>-pattern cf. table 4.20.

Tab. 4.20: Examples of German words with the structures <ccv> and <vcc>

Letters	**<ccv>**	**<vcc>**
# of words	6	27
Examples	*Klo* 'toilet', *Pli* 'curl', *pro* 'pro', *Psi* 'psi', *Ski* 'ski', *zwo* 'two'	*Abt* 'abbot', *Ahn* 'ancestor', *Akt* 'act', *Alm* 'mountain pasture', *alt* 'old', *Arm* 'arm', *Ast* 'branch', *Eck* 'corner', *eng* 'tight', *Ohr* 'ear', *Uhr* 'clock'

The only native strong word in the <ccv> paradigm is *zwo*, a more colloquial term for *zwei* 'two'. Although there are relatively few examples of the <vcc>-structure, all examples listed above belong to the core vocabulary.

If this restriction of <vcc>-structure is caused by a weight minimality constraint, it seems that the mere number of letters alone is not sufficient to determine the weight of a graphematic word. The position of the letters with respect to the v-letter is important as well; in other words, it is the graphematic syllable structure that determines the weight of graphematic words.

The structures in table 4.20 above differ in the complexity of their rhyme and onset. While the non-restricted structures <vcc> and <cvc> have two or more segments in their rhyme, the restricted structure <ccv> has a complex onset and only one segment in its rhyme. Let us have a closer look at the onset and the rhyme and how these subsyllabic constituents contribute to graphematic weight.

Most phonologists assume that the onset does not contribute to phonological syllable weight (but cf. Everett & Everett 1984, Davis 1988, Kelly 2004). The picture in graphematics, however, seems to be different. If the graphematic onset had no effect on weight, we would expect that words with the structure <cvc> and <vc> would have the same weight and therefore behave similarly. It appears, however, that <vc>-words are not only relatively rare; there are nearly no native strong words with a <vc> structure. <cvc>-words, however, are huge in number and not restricted. This may lead to the conclusion that <cvc> and <vc> words have different weights: <vc> seems to be a restricted pattern, it is too light for strong words; <cvc>, however, does not seem to be restricted, which indicates that this structure meets the minimality constraint. Therefore, it is the onset-<c> that makes the difference. Thus we may conclude that the onset contributes to graphematic weight.

However, although it seems that the onset contributes to weight, the weight of two letters dominated by the onset and one letter dominated by the rhyme is not sufficient to build a monosyllabic foot, while the weight of the three letters in the rhyme in a word like <arm> 'poor' are sufficient to do the job, cf. table 4.20.

Ramers' (1998) solution to the question of how the graphematic onset contributes to weight is that there is a qualitative difference between weight contributed by the onset and weight contributed by the rhyme: the onset can maximally contribute one weight unit, one *mora*, to syllable weight – regardless of whether there are one, two or even more letters dominated. Furthermore, he states that the total number of morae a monosyllabic foot needs to have in order to be grammatical is three. These assumptions can explain why <ccv>-words are virtually non-existent. They are bimoraic in graphematic terms and thus too light; in other words, they are violating the proposed minimality constraint.

It turns out that the distinction we have made in the introduction of this section is crucial: only graphematic words of at least 3 weight units, morae, are grammatical, exceptions are weak words (e.g. *in*, *ob* 'whether'), loanwords (*Bö* 'gust') or interjections (*ah*, *oh*). Ramers' generalisation is:

(29) *Weight restriction for graphematic words* (Ramers 1998: 37, my translation)
Graphematic words have (generally) three morae.

Ramers illustrates his generalisation with the examples *Tal* 'valley', *Tee* 'tea', *blau* 'blue', *Ort* 'place' (trimoraic) and *da* 'there', *ab* 'from' (bimoraic), cf. (30)

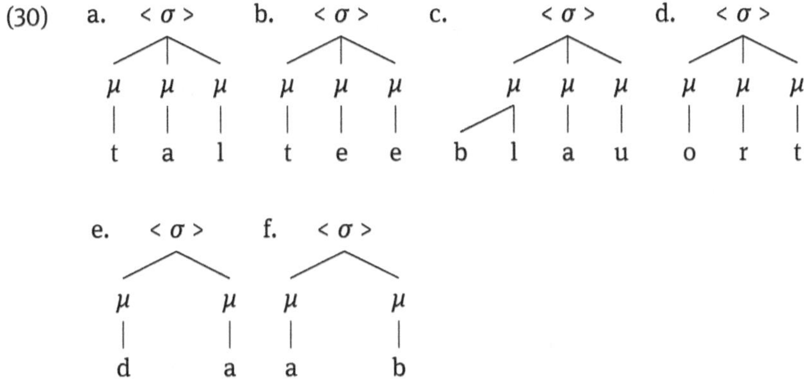

The first example represents the pattern <cvc>, which can be found quite often in the database. All letters equally contribute to the graphematic weight. The example in b. illustrates how a doubled consonant contributes two morae.[17] The example in (30 c) illustrates that even if there is more than one letter in the onset, the onset can only contribute one mora per word and that a diphthong contributes two morae to weight. The word in d. is an example of an onset-less word. The lack of the mora contributed by the onset is compensated in (30b) by two c-letters in the rhyme. The last two words (e and f) are bimoraic. Bimoraic words are usually words of the three exceptional groups, weak words, interjections and loanwords.

Although Ramers' theory is a good starting point, the question of how the onset contributes to syllable weight is not fully answered. Primus (2000) points to the relevance of so called 'lengthening signs' (*Dehungszeichen*) in weight optimization. Let us briefly have a look at lengthening signs. Following lengthening signs can be found in German, cf. (31).

(31) Lengthening signs in German arranged in the order of their frequency (Primus 2000: 19)

<ie> for /iː/	*bieten* 'to offer', *viel* 'much', *Liebe* 'love'
lengthening-h	*ihm* 'him', *Geweih* 'antlers'
Doubling of a vowel letter	*Saal* 'hall', *Boot* 'boat'
<ie> + <h>	*Vieh* 'cattle', *zieh* 'pull'

17 I have changed the tree diagrams in one point. Ramers notates only one letter in the diagram of *tee* because <ee> corresponds to one phonological monophthong (Ramers 1998: 27). However, since it is letters and not graphemes that contribute to graphematic weight, cf. the experimental evidence above, I changed the tree diagram of *tee* accordingly.

These lengthening signs do not have segmental phonological correspondents; because of that, they are often called 'mute' (cf. section 3.2.1). One function of lengthening signs is disambiguation, like in *im* 'in the' vs. *ihm* 'him'. Another function is weight optimization, for instance *Zeh* 'toe', *Fee* 'fairy' (Ramers 1998: 30, Primus 2000: 30, Evertz & Primus 2013: 10). The latter words would be ungrammatical without the lengthening signs, cf. **Ze*, **Fe*. An explanation for the presence of lengthening signs in these words is that the lengthening sign adds one purely graphematic weight unit to the total weight of the syllable. With this additional weight, these monosyllabic words conform to the weight restriction for graphematic words.

Several authors report that the complexity of the onset of a graphematic syllable has an influence on whether lengthening signs appear or not. The more complex an onset is, the less likely is the appearance of lengthening signs in the rhyme of a graphematic syllable (Augst 1980: 313-318, Primus 2000: 30, Eisenberg 2006: 317).

This observation is not only interesting because it contributes to the discussion of whether and how the onset contributes to graphematic weight, it also suggests that there is a *maximality constraint for minimal words*. If there was no maximality constraint, there is no reason why weight units disappear on one side when weight units are added to the other side. So, before we continue with the question of how the onset contributes to weight, we first need to test whether there is a maximality constraint for graphematic feet.

In order to test whether there is a maximality constraint in the writing system of German, we will examine the rhyme, which has undoubtedly influence on graphematic weight (cf. the experimental evidence in §4.3.1, above). Our hypothesis is that if there is a maximality constraint, the complexity of the coda of a graphematic syllable should have an influence on the likeliness of the occurrence of lengthening signs. If a certain weight, i.e. the maximal weight, has been reached, lengthening signs should not occur.

In order to test this hypothesis, I conducted a search for monosyllabic words with binary p-vowels in the German phonological lemma database of CELEX. The words were clustered into groups according to the number of c-letters in the (graphematic) coda. While establishing the groups, lengthening-<h> was ignored for the complexity of the coda, as our hypothesis is that the occurrence of lengthening-<h> is influenced by coda-length. Thus, a word like *Fahrt* 'journey' is placed in the group '2 c-letters in the coda'. I excluded graphematically bisyllabic words (e.g. *Ale, live, Spike*) and words with g-diphthongs because lengthening signs never occur after g-diphthongs. The results of the CELEX search are displayed in table 4.21.[18]

Tab. 4.21: Frequency of lengthening signs in German depending of the number of c-letters in the coda in monosyllabic words with binary vowels

Letters in coda	Words	Lengthening signs							
		<ie>		<h>		<vv>		all	
	total	total	rel.	total	rel.	total	rel.	total	rel.
0	51	7	13.7	18	35.29	7	13.7	32	62.7
1	356	47	13.2	64	18	29	8.1	141	39.6
2	46	4	8.7	1	2.2	0	0	5	10.9
3	11	1	9.1	0	0	0	0	1	9.1
4	4	0	0	0	0	0	0	0	0

With an empty coda (as mentioned above, in this study I did not count lengthening-<h> to the complexity of the coda), lengthening-signs appear in most of the searched words (62.7%). Most frequent was <h> in 32.3% of words, e.g. in *Floh* 'flea', *Kuh* 'cow', followed by <ie> and <vv> (g-diphthongs) with 13.7% each (e.g. *nie* 'never', *Schnee* 'snow'). Words without lengthening signs include weak words (such as *da* 'there', *ja* 'yes'), abbreviations (*Klo* from *Klosett* 'toilet') and loanwords (*Schi* 'ski'), see above.

In a coda of one c-letter, the frequency drops to 39.6%. Still <h> is most frequent with 18 % followed by <ie> (13.2%) and <vv> (8.1%); examples include *Kohl* 'cabbage', *Brief* 'letter' and *Boot* 'boat'.

The percentage of monosyllabic words with binary p-vowel which display lengthening signs drops dramatically from 39.6% to 10.9 % in words with more than two c-letters in the coda. In these words, only <ie> (8.7%, e.g. *Biest* 'beast', *Viech* 'creature') and <h> (only 1 word, 2.2%, *Fahrt* 'journey') appeared as lengthening signs.

In the CELEX database of German lemmas, there were only very few examples of monosyllabic words with binary p-vowel and a graphematic coda with more than two letters; to be precise, there were only 11 lemmas with a coda of three c-letters and only 4 lemmas with a coda of four c-letters. In the former group, there

18 The table does not list <ie> + <h> because there was only one occurrence, *Vieh* 'cattle'. This result, however, is included in the total numbers in the rightmost columns.

was one word (= 9.1%) with a lengthening sign, namely *Dienst* 'work'; in the latter group, there was no word with a lengthening sign. The graph in figure 4.7 gives a visual representation of the results.

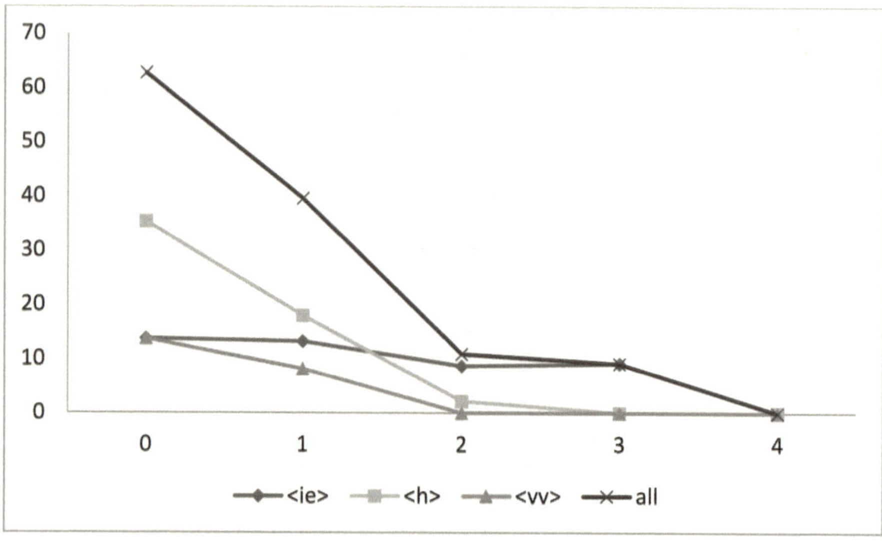

Fig. 4.7: Frequency of lengthening signs in monosyllabic words with binary p-vowel in German depending on c-letters in the coda

The black line in figure 4.7 shows the relative frequency of all words that displayed lengthening signs, the other lines show the frequency of words with the single instances of lengthening signs, i.e. g-diphthongs as indicated by <vv> (triangles), <ie> (diamonds), and <h> (squares).

A χ_2-test confirms that there is a connection between graphematic coda complexity and the frequency of lengthening signs in monosyllabic words with binary phonological p-vowels ($\chi_2 = 34.272$, df = 4, p-value < 0.0001). I refrain from calculating a linear regression model because of the few data points, but it is fair to say that the complexity of the coda has a negative influence on the occurrence of lengthening signs in monosyllabic words with binary p-vowel given the descriptive values and the highly significant result of the χ_2-test.

To sum the results up, if the coda consists of zero or one c-letter (excluding <h>), lengthening signs may appear. From a complexity of two letters on, lengthening signs rarely appear. At first glance, this is surprising because, especially in rhymes with complex codas, the occurrence of lengthening signs is well motivated with respect to vowel quantity coding (because closed syllables are potentially ambiguous with respect to their vowel quantity decoding, e.g. *Weg* 'way' or 'away' with binary or unary p-vowel, cf. §3.2.2).

A (violable) maximality constraint can explain the lack of lengthening signs in words with complex graphematic coda: the graphematic syllable of a monosyllabic word tends to be maximally trimoraic. Note, however, that until now we have only examined the rhyme. We do not know yet how the onset contributes to weight. Thus, it might be best to reformulate the provisional maximality constraint in '*the rhyme* of the graphematic syllable of a monosyllabic word tends to be maximally trimoraic.'

Now that we have evidence that there is some sort of maximality constraint in graphematic g-syllables, let us examine whether the onset has an influence on the occurrence of lengthening signs.

In order to replicate the findings of Augst (1980), who noticed that the complexity of the onset has an influence on the occurrence of lengthening signs, I conducted a CELEX-search similar to the one presented above. I searched for every phonologically monosyllabic word with a binary phonological vowel.[19] The hypothesis is that the occurrence of lengthening letters, such as <h>, depends on the complexity of the g-onset: the more letters the onset consists of, the less frequent are lengthening signs. Confer table 4.22 for results.[20]

Tab. 4.22: Frequency of lengthening signs in German depending of the number of c-letters in the onset in monosyllabic words with binary vowels

Letters in onset	Words total	Words binary	Lengthening signs <ie> total	<ie> rel.	<h> total	<h> rel.	<VV> total	<VV> rel.	all total	all rel.
0	94	26	0	0	10	38	3	12	13	50
1	981	275	35	12.7	57	21	27	10	120	44
2	455	142	19	13.4	11	8	4	3	34	24
3	106	26	3	11.6	4	15	2	8	9	35
4	90	21	2	9.6	0	0	1	5	3	14

19 Like above, I left words with the graphematic diphthongs <au>, <ai>, <eu> and <ei> out because lengthening signs do not appear after g-diphthongs.

20 I left the findings for <ie> + <h> out in this table. In the CELEX database for German phonological lemmas, this combination can only be found once in monosyllabic words with binary vowels: *Vieh* 'cattle'. The result is, however included in the total number in the rightmost columns of the table.

The findings presented in table 4.22 are in line with those of Augst (1980). In total, nearly 50% of words with binary vowel and simple onset (zero or one letter in the onset) show lengthening signs (e.g. *lahm* 'lame', *Rahm* 'cream', *Kuh* 'cow'). With increasing complexity of the onset, the frequency of lengthening signs gradually decreases. Only 14% of words with a highly complex (four letters) onset contain lengthening signs (e.g. without lengthening sign *Schwert* 'sword', *Strom* 'electricity'; with lengthening sign *Schnee* 'snow', *Schmied* 'smith'). The chart in figure 4.8 shows the influence of graphematic complexity of the onset on the frequency of lengthening signs in monosyllabic words with binary p-vowels.

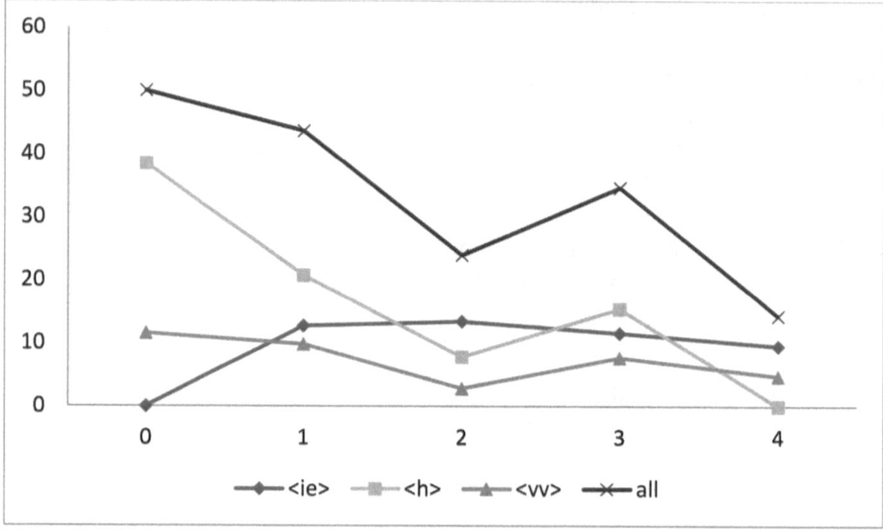

Fig. 4.8: Frequency of lengthening signs in monosyllabic words with binary p-vowels in German depending on c-letters in the onset

The black line in figure 4.8 shows the relative frequency of all instances of lengthening signs, the other lines show the single instances, i.e. <vv> (g-diphthongs, triangles), <ie> (diamonds), and <h> (squares).

A χ_2-test (goodness of fit) reveals that there is a connection between graphematic onset complexity and the frequency of lengthening signs in monosyllabic words with binary phonological vowels ($\chi_2 = 22.25$, df = 4, p-value = 0.00018). For a meaningful linear regression model there are too few data points, but given the clear trend and the highly significant result of the χ_2-test, it is fairly safe to conclude that the hypothesis that the graphematic complexity of the onset negatively influences the occurrence of lengthening signs in monosyllabic words with binary p-vowels is confirmed.

We can explain the results of the second CELEX search as follows: if lengthening signs serve weight optimization and if the complexity of the onset influences the frequency of lengthening signs in graphematic syllables and, finally, if there is a maximality constraint for graphematic weight, two conclusions must be drawn: (1) onsets contribute to graphematic weight and (2) the more letters an onset consists of the more that onset contributes to the graphematic weight of a syllable.

Regarding the first point, our explanation and Ramers' theory agree: the onset contributes to graphematic weight. Regarding the second point, however, there is a disagreement. While Ramers states that the onset can contribute maximally one mora to graphematic weight, the data suggest that there must be a continuum of onset weights.

If our explanation above is right, however, and there is a continuum of onset weights, then why are there systematic gaps (especially <ccv>) in the lexicon as Ramers' and our database analysis revealed? But, if Ramers is right, how can we explain the continuous decrease of the frequency of lengthening signs depending on the increasing complexity of the onset?

The solution I propose lies within syllable structure. Let us recall Ramers' argument: (a) although there is a number of monosyllabic phonologically open words with a single p-vowel, there are (nearly) no instances of strong monosyllabic graphematic words which have only a single v-letter in their rhyme (but may have a complex onset); (b) there are strong graphematic words which have a single v-letter and two or more c-letters dominated by the rhyme and (c) there are strong words of the make-up <cvc>. If the onset can contribute more than one mora, we should expect that words of the structure mentioned in (a) are as unrestricted as words in (b) and (c). The only obvious difference between these words is the onset; the onset is therefore unable to contribute enough weight to license words mentioned in (a).

In actual fact, however, there is another difference between these words: words with the structure <cvc> and <vcc> have a complex rhyme, while words with the structure <c_0v> have a simple rhyme. This observation leads to the conclusion that a syllable with a complex rhyme is a prerequisite for a minimal word and thereby as well for a monosyllabic foot.

(32) *Structural restriction for optimal monosyllabic g-feet*
A monosyllabic graphematic foot dominates a syllable with a rhyme dominating at least two segments.

There are a few (non-native) words like *Bö* 'gust' or *Ra* (ancient Egyptian solar deity), furthermore, there are several weak words (e.g. *zu* 'to', *da* 'there', *du* 'you') in violation of the constraint. Interestingly, so called function words that do not have a weak form (e.g. *weil* 'because', *aus* 'out', *bei* 'at', etc.) conform to the constraint in (32).

Now let us summarise which parts of the syllable contribute to weight:

(33) Every segment dominated by the rhyme or the onset of a graphematic syllable contributes to its weight.

Although the data suggests that segments dominated by the onset contribute to graphematic weight and that there is a continuum of onset weights, it is not clear whether segments dominated by the onset contribute as much to weight as segments dominated by the rhyme. For this reason, morae might not be the adequate units of representation for graphematic onset weight. We will thus just refer to segments (letters) dominated by the onset or the rhyme.

In what way will this change the analysis of Ramers displayed above in (30)? There are no substantial differences in a. *Tal*, b. *Tee*, d. *Ort*, e. *da* and f. *ab*. These words have either a simple onset or no onset at all. Let us consider *Tee* as an example here. Interesting is the comparison of a word with a simple onset with example c. *blau*, consider the illustrations in (34).

(34)

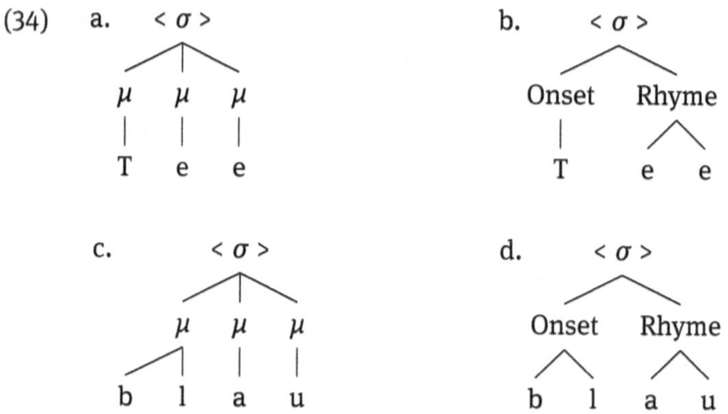

In Ramers' approach, the onset can maximally contribute one mora to the weight of a graphematic syllable. In this analysis, segments dominated by the onset can contribute a continuum of weights. Thus, the advantage of this analysis is that it can account for the fact that the onset has an influence on the presence of lengthening signs in the rhyme.

Because the number of segments dominated by the onset influences the presence of lengthening signs in graphematic syllables, I tentatively conclude that the onset gradually contributes to graphematic weight. However, I will leave the question open whether segments in the onset can contribute as much weight as segments dominated by the rhyme.

Moreover, I conclude that a monosyllabic foot must conform to the *Structural restriction for optimal graphematic feet* (cf. (32)) and must at least have three segments contributing to weight if it corresponds to a monosyllabic g-word. These assumptions explain why <c_0v> and *<vc> are no possible structures for strong words: *<c_0v> and *<vc> are too light to constitute own feet, moreover, *<c_0v> violates the structural restriction for optimal graphematic feet. All other structures satisfy these constraints.

4.3.2.2 English Data

The minimality constraints sketched above also seem to hold for English words: strong native words need to have a certain graphematic weight, in other words, they need to be graphematically heavy. The property that English words need to have a certain weight is not unnoticed in the literature. Cook (2004: 56-57), for instance, formulates the "three-letter rule", which demands that content words must have more than two letters (cf. Venezky 1999: 86 for a similar rule). With this rule, he explains the different spellings of homophonous words like *be* vs. *bee* and *in* vs. *inn*.

I hypothesise that the only difference between English and German regarding graphematic weight is that there are more lexical exceptions in English than in German.

(35) Weight analysis of English monosyllabic g-words

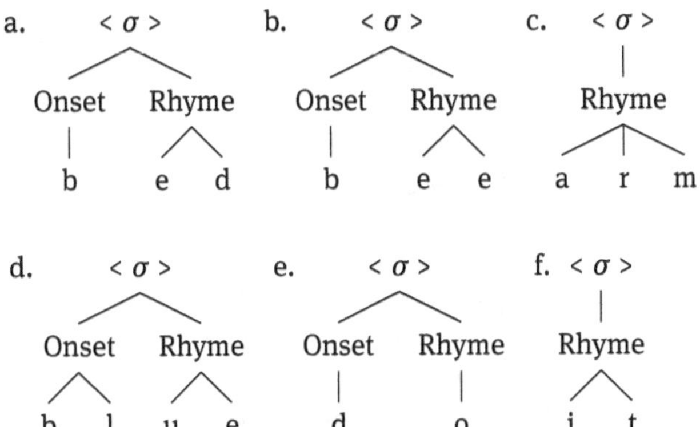

The structures in (35) illustrate how letters contribute to graphematic weight in the weight theory presented above. The first two structures in a. and b. illustrate <cvc>- and <cvv>-words. Both structures are identical in weight. The structure in c. lacks an onset but is as heavy as the structures in a. and b. The structure in d. has a complex onset, it is thus heavier than a. and b. The words in e. and f. are weak words and lighter than strong words.

One difference to the graphematic weight in German is obvious: While two letters seem to be the absolute minimum for German words, the absolute minimum for English words appears to be one letter, although there are only two notable words with only one letter: *I* and *a*.

A search of the CELEX database of English lemmas (Baayen et al. 1995) yielded the results displayed in figure 4.9 (the patterns are sorted by frequency) for monosyllabic graphematic words in English. I excluded acronyms (e.g. *AA, RIP, EEG*), common abbreviations (e.g. *mlle (Mademoiselle), oz, yd*). I checked the list manually and excluded all remaining mistakes. <y> was counted as v-letter in nucleus position and as c-letter in onset position. Table 4.23 lists some examples of the search results.

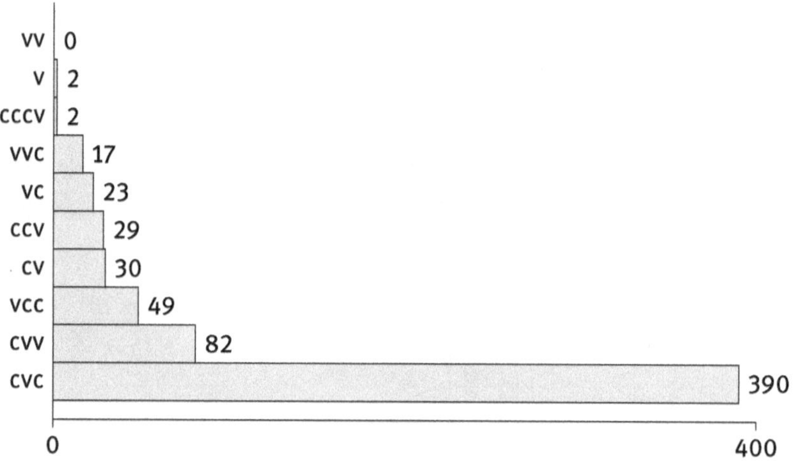

Fig. 4.9: Total numbers of minimal words in the CELEX database of English lemmas (filtered)

It seems that some patterns are restricted. Especially the patterns <vv>, <v>, and <cccv> are virtually non-existent. Words with a complex onset <ccv> or a simple onset <cv> with a single v-letter are also quite few in number. This is also the case with some words without onset, such as <vc> and <vvc>.

Tab. 4.23: Examples for monosyllabic graphematic words in English

Letters	**<v>**	**<cv>**	**<ccv>**	**<cccv>**
# of words	**2**	**30**	**29**	**2**
Examples	*a, I*	*be, by, do, go, hi, ma, pi, ye*	*bra, chi, cry, flu, the, who*	*spry, thru*
Letters	**<vc>**		**<vcc>**	
# of words	**23**		**49**	
Examples	*ad, ah, at, ex, if, in, it, of, or, ox, up, us*		*act, and, ass, egg, ink, inn, its, oft, ohm, old, owl, urn*	
Letters	**<cvc>**			
# of words	**390**			
Examples	*big, cat, cow, dot, fat, fox, gin, hag, her, job, kid, leg, mad, net, now, pen, red,* sad, sex, tan, tin, van, war, wax			

Again, we must ask whether this is a consequence of genuinely graphematic constraints or just a phonological reflex. The restriction of <vv> and <v> seems to be graphematically driven, given that there are words consisting of just binary p-vowels ([ɔː], [aɪ̯], [əʊ̯]) which are, however, not only coded with more than just one v-letter but as canonical feet (<*awe*>, <*aye*>, <*eye*>, <*owe*>).

Let us have a look at monosyllabic phonological words ending in a binary p-vowel. In the CELEX database of English phonological lemmas, there are 314 monosyllabic p-words ending in a binary p-vowel. 64 out of 314 (20.1%) are coded <c_0v> (where <c_0> is zero to any number of c-letters). 13 of these 64 words are weak words (e.g. *a, by, the, to, ye*) and further 24 words are either abbreviations (e.g. *bo, co*), loanwords (e.g. *Ski, Sri, phi, pi*) or interjections (e.g. *ha, ho*). This reduces the number of strong words coded with the graphematic structure <c_0v> to 10 (3.2%).

A further 13 words have a complex onset and end with <y> (*cry, dry, fly, fry, ply, pry, shy, sky, sly, spy, sty, try, wry*). This pattern is already exceptional since its V-position is filled with <y> (recall that according to Fuhrhop & Buchmann (2009) <y> marks graphematic word boundaries, cf. section 2.3). Table 4.24 gives an overview of open monosyllabic phonological words coded with an open graphematic syllable.

The vast majority of graphematic words corresponding to monosyllabic p-words ending in a binary p-vowel avoid the spelling <c_0v> and rather have spellings that add silent letters to their rhymes. Such spellings include <w> in the second nuclear position (e.g. *blow, bow, brew, cow, law*), g-diphthongs (including <ie> and <vy>, e.g. *bee, slay, sloe, woe*) and other graphemes with zero correspondence, such as <gh> (e.g. *bough, high, nigh, though*). These silent letters

Tab. 4.24: Monosyllabic words with open phonological syllables coded with open graphematic syllables

#	%		
314	**100**	**monosyllabic words with open phonological syllable**	
64	**20.4**	**g-words coded <c$_0$v>**	
14	4.6	weak words	*a, be, do, no, the*
29	9.2	abbr., loanword, interjection	*chi, co, gnu, Sri*
17	5.4	ending in <y>	*cry, ply, shy why*
4	1.3	rest	*fro, hi, two, who*

increase the graphematic weight of the words. Some words ending in a binary p-vowel are coded as a canonical g-foot (e.g. *awe, ewe, eye*). These spellings are not subject to a weight restriction because they fulfil the minimality constraint by being bisyllabic.

These findings suggest that <c$_0$v> seems to be a *graphematically* restricted pattern. Let us now turn to the other patterns that seem to be restricted: <vc> and <vvc>. Let us first check which phonological words these graphematic structures correspond to and than how these words are coded. In total, there are 95 monosyllabic words in the CELEX database of English lemmas that have a simple phonological coda and a unary (29 lemmas) or binary phonological vowel (66 lemmas).

Of these 29 lemmas with unary vowel, 14 lemmas are coded with more letters than <vc> (e.g. *add, eff, ill, off; ash, itch; edge*) and 15 are coded <vc> (e.g. *an, as, if, of, on, up*). These 15 words are all either attested with a weak form or they are non-native words (*Al, id*). Of the 68 lemmas with binary p-vowel, only one lemma, *or*, is coded with only two letters. All other words are coded in different ways: <vvc>, i.e. with a g-diphthong (e.g. *air, oil, out*), with a canonical foot, e.g. *ice, ode, ore*, with <w> or <r> in postnuclear position (e.g. *ark, orb*; *owl, own*), some combine aforementioned ways (e.g. *aught, each, earn*). These different ways of spelling all have in common the fact that they have more than two letters in the rhyme of the graphematic syllable, cf. table 4.25.

Thus, it seems that <vc> is a graphematically restricted structure, while <vvc> or other structures with more than two letters in the rhyme do not seem to be restricted to certain word groups. Although <vvc> is not a restricted structure, only 22% of potential corresponding phonological words are coded like this. This may be due to the various spelling possibilities. Some binary vowels, e.g. /aː/ are preferably coded with a nuclear <r>, e.g., /aːm/ - <arm> (cf. Rollings 2004: 93), other frequent spellings include <w>.

Tab. 4.25: Coding of monosyllabic words without onset and one consonant dominated by the rhyme

	unary p-vowel			binary p-vowel		
	#	%	examples	#	%	examples
<vc>	15	51.7	ad, an, of	1	1.5	or
<vcc>	11	37.9	add, ash, ill	14	21.2	all, arm, erg, owl
<vccc>	2	6.9	itch, etch	0	0	
< σσ >	1	3.4	edge	22	33.3	age, ice, urge
<vvc>	0	0		15	22.7	air, oil, out
<vvcc(c)>	0	0		13	21.2	aitch, eight, oath
<cvvc>	0	0		1	1.5	heir

The low total number of monosyllabic graphematic words without onset but with a complex rhyme compared to monosyllabic g-words with onset and a complex rhyme, like e.g. <cvc>, might be explicable by their phonological syllable structure. Phonological syllables tend to have an onset and tend to avoid codas. Furthermore, syllables tend to avoid complex codas and complex onsets. In Optimality Theory, this tendency is expressed by the constraints ONSET, *CODA and *COMPLEX, (e.g. Prince & Smolensky 1993, cf. onset maximisation in §1.2).[21]

Graphematic words that begin with a v-letter usually do not have a phonological onset either (an exception are words beginning with /juː/, e.g., [juːnɪt], <unit>) and words ending in more than one c-letter usually have a complex coda (exceptions are complex graphemes like <sh> that correspond to one phonological segment only). The low frequencies of words with the structure <vccc>, <vvcc>, <vvc> and <vcc> are thus explicable by the marked structure of their phonological correspondents. Words that correspond to graphematic words of the structures <cvv> and <cvc> are less marked.

The reason why words of the pattern <cvc> are more frequent than the equally unmarked <cvv>-pattern may thus be caused by the frequency of corresponding phonological monosyllabic words. There are 1870 monosyllabic lemmas with a simple onset, a binary or a unary p-vowel and a simple coda, but only 215 monosyllabic words with a simple onset, a binary p-vowel (remember that unary p-vowels do not appear in open monosyllabic words in English) but without a coda.

21 The constraints under discussion are defined as follows (Prince & Smolensky 1993: 93, 96):
i. ONSET: A syllable must have an onset.
ii. *CODA: A syllable must not have a coda.
iii. *COMPLEX: No more than one C or V may associate to any syllable position node.

We can summarise the findings for English so far as follows:

- Words consisting of only one letter seem to be highly exceptional. There are only two lemmas in the CELEX database, (*I*, *a*), both of them are weak words.
- Words consisting of two letters (<cv>, <vc>) are rather rare. They are generally weak words, abbreviations, interjections or non-native words.
- Words ending in a single v-letter, <c_0v>, are generally rather rare. A CELEX search revealed that phonological monosyllabic (strong) words ending in a binary vowel have the strong tendency to be coded with more than one graphematic element in the rhyme (e.g. <bow> vs. *<bo>; <nigh> vs. *<ni>). Only weak words, abbreviations and words with a complex onset ending in <y> (e.g. <sky>, <cry>) end in one v-letter.
- The picture for monosyllabic g-words without onset and a complex rhyme, <v(v)cc(c)>, is different. Although there are relatively few words of this structure, they tend to be native strong words. The reason why those words have a relatively low frequency may lie in the fact that the syllable structure of those words is more marked than syllable structures which have an onset and do not have a coda.

These findings fit well into the weight theory I proposed for the German writing system (see above). The lack of words consisting only of one or two letters suggests that there is a minimal weight for English graphematic words. As mentioned above, these findings are in line with earlier observations that strong native words need to have a certain graphematic weight (the "three-letter rule" cf. Venezky 1999: 86, Cook 2004: 56). The main difference to these former analyses is that our analysis is supra-segmental in nature. Researchers like Venezky and Cook only point out that there has to be a certain number of letters in a word. The findings presented here, however, point to the fact that it is not the mere number of letters that constitutes weight; it is the graphematic syllabic structure.

I conclude from the systematic gaps in the lexicon that the structures <v> and <c_0v> are highly restricted. Although there are more strong native words with the latter structure than in German, the relatively low number of this kind of words in total and the even lower number of strong native words with this structure reinforce this assumption. A strong native word needs a complex rhyme dominating at least two letters.

The onset can contribute to weight. This assumption can explain why the <vc>-structure is restricted and why the <cvc>-structure is not: the latter structure has additional weight provided by the onset, which makes a <cvc>-syllable heavy enough to constitute a separate foot and thereby a minimal graphematic words.

4.3.3 Summary

In this section I presented two pieces of evidence for graphematic weight. The experiments of Röttger et al. (2012) and Evertz & Primus (2013) show how graphematic weight influences graphematic foot structure and through graphematic foot structure phonological foot structure. The increase of the graphematic weight of the ultimate syllable in trisyllabic pseudowords with help of mute letters, such as <h>, resulted in enhanced proportions of stress on the antepenultimate or ultimate syllable in the reading experiments. This variation in stress can only be explained by graphematic foot structure. The increased graphematic weight made the ultimate syllable heavy enough to form a foot on its own. Thus, 2-foot structures emerged.

In the database-based survey I investigated the minimality constraint for monosyllabic graphematic words. Systematic gaps in the lexicon which could not be explained by phonological restrictions show that in English and German, structures with a simple nucleus and without coda, <c_0v>, and structures consisting only of a nucleus (i.e. <v>, <vv> or <vc>) are not heavy enough to constitute a monosyllabic word which corresponds to a native strong word. <cvc>-words, however, seem not to be restricted to any group of words. This observation led to the conclusion that the onset can contribute to graphematic weight. Further investigations revealed that a complex onset made the appearance of lengthening signs, which serve graphematic weight optimisation, less likely, which indicates that the onset gradually contributes to graphematic weight.

I therefore tentatively concluded that a monosyllabic g-word must conform to two constraints. 1) It must conform to the (violable) *structural restriction for optimal monosyllabic g-feet* (cf. (32), which states that a monosyllabic graphematic foot dominates at least one syllable with a rhyme dominating at least two segments. 2) A monosyllabic g-word corresponding to a strong native word has at least three segments contributing to weight (cf. *<c_0v>, *<vc>).

It must be noted, however, that the findings of the database-based studies are related to monosyllabic graphematic *words*. Strictly speaking, this means that our conclusions only apply to monosyllabic feet in monosyllabic words. The graphematic word is the next higher level to the graphematic foot in the graphematic hierarchy. This means that due to the strict layer hypothesis (cf. Selkirk 1984, Nespor & Vogel 1986, see §1.2 and §1.3) the smallest graphematic word consists of exactly one foot. If there are no additional constraints concerning graphematic words, the smallest graphematic word is identical to the smallest graphematic foot.

The experimental findings of Evertz & Primus (2013) are in line with the findings of the database study. Consider the experimental items of the <h>-group, e.g. <Ranuko> - <Ranukoh>. The ultimate syllable of the test items have the structure <cv> in the a.-condition and <cvc> in the b.-condition. The <cv>-structure is too light to constitute a foot of its own (it violates the three-segment-constraint and the structural condition for optimal monosyllabic g-feet), the participants of the experiment thus preferred a one-foot-structure. The <cvc>-structure of <Ranu**koh**>, however, is heavy enough (it satisfies both aforementioned constraints) to constitute a separate foot; the participants of the experiment therefore tended to assign a 2-foot structure (77%, cf. chart 4.3).

Returning the question in the introduction of this section, I conclude that there is a graphematic counterpart to FOOT-BINARITY. Based on the findings in this section, I formulate the following (violable) constraint:

(36) *Minimality constraint for graphematic feet*
- i. Graphematic feet are mono- or bisyllabic.
- ii If a graphematic foot is monosyllabic
  - a. it dominates a syllable with a rhyme dominating at least two segments, and
  - b. there are at least three segments contributing to weight.

4.4 An OT-Model of g-Feet

4.4.1 Assigning g-Foot Structures

Let us recall what we know about feet: Phonological and graphematic feet are sequences of at least one and maximally two syllables. In every g- and p-foot there is exactly one syllable that is the head of the foot. In the first chapter, I introduced the foot binarity constraint for phonological feet. It states that every p-foot must be binary under the syllabic or moraic level of analysis (cf. section 1.2). This means that a phonological foot either consists of two syllables or of one heavy syllable.

In the previous section, I investigated graphematic weight (cf. §4.3.2). Let us recall the findings concerning the minimality constraints for monosyllabic graphematic words in English and German. There were three main findings: (i) The English and German writing systems have similar weight systems. The only difference I could find is the higher number of lexical exceptions to the weight minimality constraint for graphematic words in English. (ii) There is a minimal weight for monosyllabic words in graphematics: there must be at least three segments that contribute to weight. (iii) The subsyllabic constituents onset and rhyme contribute to weight: each segment dominated by onset or rhyme contributes to weight.

These findings are in line with the results of the experiments presented in the same section. In the experiments of Evertz & Primus (2013), it turned out that a syllable like <Ranu**ko**> was too light to constitute a monosyllabic foot, a syllable like <Ranu**koh**>, however, was heavy enough. The minimality constraint for graphematic feet is expressed in (36) above.

According to (36), a graphematic foot is either a sequence of two g-syllables or of one heavy g-syllable. The structure of the heavy syllable in a monosyllabic foot is restricted, cf. (36ii.a). The structural restriction for optimal monosyllabic g-feet states that a monosyllabic graphematic foot dominates at least one syllable with a rhyme dominating at least two segments.

It is, of course, trivial to determine the head in a monosyllabic foot, but, in a bisyllabic foot there are two options. In German and English, graphematic and phonological feet are head-initial.

(37) TROCHEE: Graphematic and phonological feet are head-initial (cf. e.g. McCarthy & Prince 1993b).

Taken together, the constraints in (36) and (37) determine two basic types of the graphematic foot in English and German:[22]

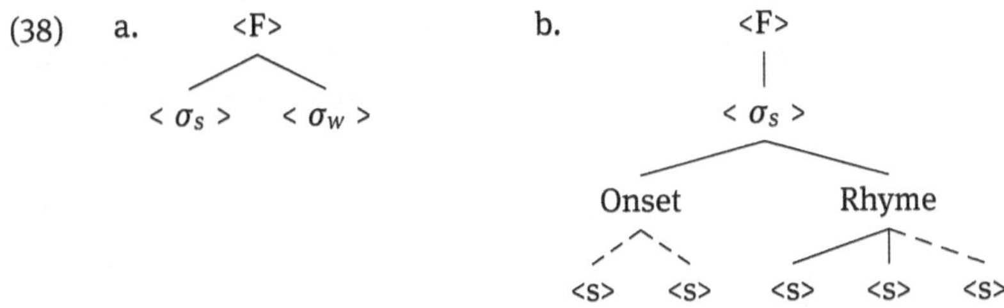

Conditions: (1) Associations represented by continuous lines are obligatory.
(2) One of the associations represented by dashed lines is obligatory.
(3) All other associations are facultative.

The structure in (38a) is a bisyllabic foot, cf. (36i), the first syllable is strong, cf. (37). The weights of the syllables in (38a) are not specified. The structure in (38b) is a monosyllabic foot, cf. (36ii). Since the foot in (38b) consists of only one syllable, this syllable is the head of the foot (37), and needs to have at least three segments contributing to weight in order to be ablte to constitute a foot of its own (36ii.b). The two segments associated with the rhyme with solid lines in the figure are obligatory. Every monosyllabic foot needs to dominate at least one syllable with a rhyme dominating at least two letters, cf. (36ii.a). In order to comply to the

22 <s> is a variable for any segment in (38).

minimality constraint, there must be at least a third segment. Whether third segment is dominated by the onset or by the rhyme is irrelevant, what is relevant is that there is a third segment.

Let us consider the foot structures of some graphematic words. The structures in (39) are examples of basic types of g-feet in English and German.

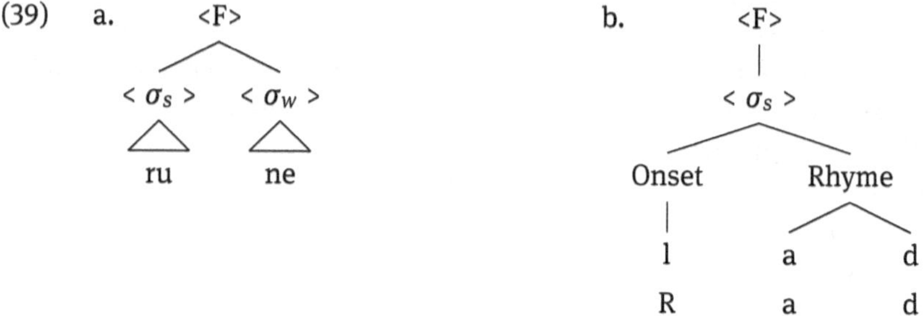

The foot structure in (39a) is an example of a bisyllabic foot. The structures for <rune> and its German counterpart <Rune> are identical. The first syllable is the head of the foot and thus strong, the second syllable is weak. The structure in (39b) is an example of a monosyllabic foot. All letters of the English example <lad> and the German example <Rad> 'wheel' are dominated by one syllable node, which is the only syllable of the foot. This syllable is thereby the head of the foot and thus strong. Let us have a look at the foot assignment of <rune>, cf. tableau 4.26.

Tab. 4.26

<ru.ne>	TROCHEE	MINIMALITY
☞ a. $(\text{ru}_s\ \text{ne}_w)_F$		
b. $(\text{ru}_w\ \text{ne}_s)_F$	*!	
c. $(\text{ru}_s)_F\ (\text{ne}_s)_F$		*!*
d. ru $(\text{ne}_s)_F$		*!
e. $(\text{ru}_s)_F$ ne		*!

The foot in candidate b. is not a trochee, i.e. its head is not foot-initial but -final. In candidate c., both syllables constitute own feet. However, neither syllable is heavy enough to constitute a foot of its own. the candidate thus incurs two violations of MINIMALITY. The same reasoning is valid for candidates d. and e., only that these candidates each comprise only one monosyllabic foot and therefore only incur one violation of Minimality each. Candidate a. does not violate any of the constraints under discussion. Both syllables are parsed into one head-initial foot; candidate a. is thus the winner of the evaluation.

In tableau 4.26, I left one plausible candidate out, that is the candidate, which is not footed at all. In this evaluation, such a candidate would perform as well as the winning candidate since an unfooted candidate incurs no violations of the constraints in discussion.

That being said, there is no (strong) word that is not footed. In optimality theoretic approaches towards phonological feet and words, this fact is often captured by the constraint LxWd=PrWd, which demands that every lexical word corresponds to a prosodic (phonological) word (Prince & Smolensky 1993: 101, cf. §4.3.2). Given the Phonological Hierarchy, this means that every lexical word corresponds to a phonological word, which comprises at least one phonological foot. The minimal phonological word is thus exactly equal to one phonological foot.

As we have discussed in §4.3.2, we do not differentiate between lexical and non-lexical words (for instance, function words) but between strong and weak words, where strong words are words which do not occur in a phonologically reduced form. I thus propose the following graphematic counterpart to the phonological constraint sketched above:

(40) StrWd=GrWd:
Every strong word corresponds to a graphematic word.

The consequences of this constraint are analogous to the consequences of its phonological counterpart: Given the graphematic hierarchy presented in chapter 1, StrWd=GrWd means that every strong word corresponds to a graphematic word, which comprises at least one foot. The minimal graphematic word is thus exactly equal to one graphematic foot. I assume that although this constraint is violable, it outranks most constraints. Constraints that are higher-ranking than StrWd=GrWd are IO-faithfulness constraints which demand that certain words are not footed if this is specified in the input (this may apply, for instance, in non-native words such as *Bö* 'gust', as we have seen in §4.3.2).

Let us consider the remaining candidates of the evaluation of <ru.ne> and the evaluation of the word <lad>, cf. Tableaux 4.27 and 4.28.

The structures of the winning candidates are similar in that all their syllables are dominated by a foot-node; in other words, all syllables are exhaustively parsed into feet. This is not always the case. Under certain circumstances, syllables may be dominated directly by the word-node. I will illustrate what this looks like in bisyllabic g-words: The figures in (41) illustrate the structures contributing

Tab. 4.27

<ru.ne>	StrWd=GrWd	Trochee	Minimality
☞ a. (ru$_s$ ne$_w$)$_F$			
b. ru ne	*!		

Tab. 4.28

<lad>	StrWd=GrWd	Trochee	Minimality
☞ a. (lad$_s$)$_F$			
b. lad	*!		

to graphematic weight in <agree> and <Magie> 'magic'. Note that the illustration in (41) is incomplete since the foot-level is missing; this is indicated by the dashed lines.

(41)

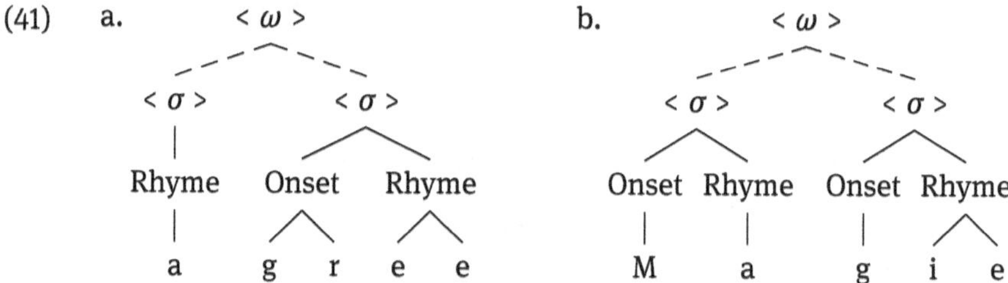

Both the German and the English word have light first g-syllables. The first g-syllable of <a.gree> consists of only one letter dominated by the rhyme. The first g-syllable of <Ma.gie> comprises two letters. The second g-syllables <gree> and <gie> differ in their onsets. <gree> has a complex onset, which dominates two letters, and <gie> has a simple onset, which dominates one letter. The rhyme of both syllables are structurally identical: both rhymes dominate two v-letters. According to the minimality constraint for monosyllabic graphematic feet, both syllables are heavy enough to constitute separate feet. Both syllables also meet the second condition for monosyllabic feet, which demands that the rhyme of a monosyllabic foot must dominate at least two letters.

According to the minimality constraint in (36), two foot structures are possible for words like in (41). The first possible structure is a bisyllabic foot; the second possible structure is a final monosyllabic foot with an unparsed first syllable. Two monosyllabic feet as a third possibility is ruled out by (36ii) since the first syllables are too light in order to constitute separate feet.

These two possibilities are conflicting, as for a word cannot have two foot structures at once. This conflict is caused by two constraints which are well-established in optimality theoretic works on phonological feet (cf. §1.2.2), PARSE-σ and the weight-to-stress-principle (WSP):

(42) PARSE-σ (Prince & Smolensky 1993, McCarthy & Prince 1993):
Syllables are parsed by feet.

(43) WEIGHT-TO-STRESS-PRINCIPLE (Prince & Smolensky 1993):
A heavy syllable is stressed.

The notion of stress is, of course, not feasible in a theory of graphematic feet. I therefore propose the following constraint, which captures the essence of WSP but can be employed in a foot theory of any language medium:

(44) WEIGHT-TO-HEAD-PRINCIPLE (WHP)
Heavy syllables are heads of feet.

The constraint PARSE-σ demands that all syllables of a word must be exhaustively parsed into feet. This constraint therefore promotes the first theoretically possible foot structure for <a.gree>, a bisyllabic foot. The second constraint demands that the heaviest syllable of a foot domain must be the head of a foot, it thus promotes the second possibility, a word-final foot and an unparsed first syllable (a third possible candiate that comprises a head-final bisyllabic foot is ruled out by TROCHEE as I will show below).

If both syllables in a bisyllabic word are of equal weight or if the first syllable is heavier than the second one, the constraints in (42) and (44 are not conflicting. In words such as <a.gree> and <Ma.gie>, where the second g-syllable is heavier than the first g-syllable, cf. (41), however, they do conflict. Since there is no free variation in foot structure, there must be a ranking of the constraints in question.

If PARSE-σ was ranked higher than MINIMALITY and WHP, all bisyllabic g-words would be head-initial. In the phonology of German and English, there are words which have a final word stress, i.e. a word-final monosyllabic foot. Since phonological and graphematic forms map onto each other, it is sensible to assume that some words in the writing systems of English and German also have foot structures with word-final heads. I therefore assume that all constraints discussed so far dominate PARSE-σ. The foot structures of the words in (41) are illustrated in (45).

(45)

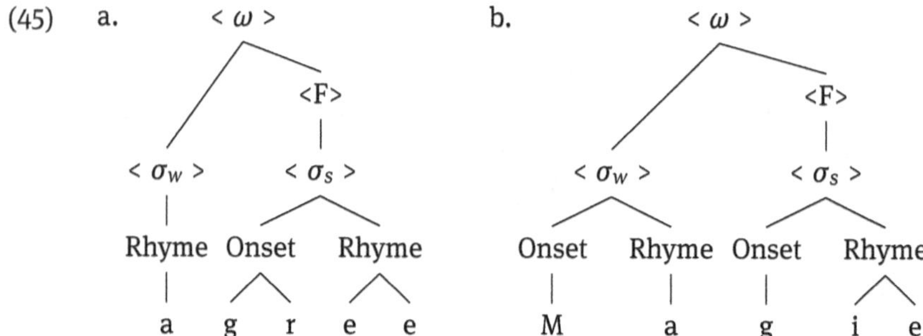

Since PARSE-σ is dominated by WHP, the heaviest syllables are the heads of the feet in (45). The remaining first syllables are too light to constitute feet of their own, which means that they are not parsed into any foot: they cannot be part of the feet the second syllables constitute due to TROCHEE and they cannot constitute own feet due to the minimality constraint in (36ii). Tableau 4.29 exemplifies these considerations with the evaluation of <a.gree>.

Tab. 4.29

<a.gree>	TROCHEE	MINIMALITY	WHP	PARSE-σ
☞ a. a $(\text{gree}_s)_F$				*
b. $(\text{a}_w\ \text{gree}_s)_F$	*!			
c. $(\text{a}_s\ \text{gree}_w)_F$			*!	
d. $(\text{a})_F\ (\text{gree})_F$		*!		

Note that the graphematic representations of words like *agree* and *Magie* are transparent with respect to their foot structure. The prominent syllable is clearly indicated by syllable weight. The phonological representation is not as transparent since both syllables are stressable in principle.[23] The German example [maˈgiː] is especially revealing in this matter. Both p-syllables have the same weight, there is no phonological indication (neither segmental cues nor cues based on syllable

23 Note that the reduction of weak syllables in English is often analysed as an epiphenomenon of foot structure assignment.

weight) that the last syllable is stressed, thus, words like [ma'giː] are often analysed as lexical exceptions (e.g. Féry 1998). The graphematic representation, however, displays a reliable hint as to the structure of this word: graphematic syllable weight.

As we have seen in §4.1, there are words like <meter>, which are canonical trochees; however, if we take only weight into account, the second syllable is heavier than the first syllable and meets the weight and structural condition for a monosyllabic foot, cf. tableau 4.30.

Tab. 4.30

<me.ter>	TROCHEE	MINIMALITY	WHP	PARSE-σ
(☞) a. me $(\text{ter}_S)_F$				*
☞ b. $(\text{me}_S\ \text{ter}_W)_F$			*!	

The data we have seen in §3.2.1.2 and §4.1 strongly suggest that this analysis is wrong. Like in <ru**ne**>, <me**ter**> is a reduced graphematic syllable. In §3.2.1.2, I presented heuristics to identify reduced graphematic syllables. Let us recall them here:

(46) *Heuristics for reduced graphematic syllables*
  i. Reduced g-syllables have <e> as sole v-letter in their V-position.
  ii. Reduced g-syllables have no more than two segments in their rhyme.
  iii. In a sequence of two syllables where the last syllable has the properties described in i. and ii., the second syllable is a reduced syllable.

Exceptions for these heuristics are scarce. They include words like *(to) rebel, hotel* and *Hotel* 'hotel' (but cf. the canonical words *gravel, hazel, model, etc.* and *Engel* 'angel', *Bengel* 'rascal').

In phonology, reduced syllables are excluded from being heads of feet by a constraint like NONHEAD(ə) that states that syllables whose V-position is occupied by schwa cannot be heads of feet (cf. e.g. Féry 1998 for German). Taking the heuristics for reduced graphematic syllables into account, I propose the following constraint:

(47) NONHEAD(RGS): Reduced graphematic syllables cannot be heads of graphematic feet.

Now we can reconsider tableau 4.30 as tableau 4.31.

Tab. 4.31

<me.ter>	NONHEAD	TROCHEE	MINIMALITY	WHP	PARSE-σ
a. me $(\text{ter}_s)_F$	*!				*
☞ b. $(\text{me}_s\ \text{ter}_w)_F$				*	

The words considered so far consist of graphematic syllables either of different weight (light vs. heavy) or of different type (full vs. reduced). What if a bisyllabic word consists of two (equally) heavy syllables? Consider, for example, words like *coffee*, *shampoo*, and *Kaffee* 'coffee'. Graphematically, these words consist of two heavy syllables; if we disregard onset weight, they are of exactly the same weight (if we take onset weight into consideration, the first g-syllable of *shampoo* is slightly heavier than its last syllable). An analysis with the constraints we have considered so far yields an optimal candidate consisting of two monosyllabic graphematic feet. I will demonstrate the evaluation of graphematic words consisting of two heavy g-syllables with the help of the German example *Kaffee*.

Tab. 4.32

<Kaf.fee>	TROCHEE	MINIMALITY	WHP	PARSE-σ
☞ a. (Kaf) (fee)				
b. $(\text{Kaf}_s\ \text{fee}_w)$			*!	
c. $(\text{Kaf}_w\ \text{fee}_s)$	*!		*	
d. Kaf (fee)			*!	*
e. (Kaf) fee			*!	*

The analysis in tableau 4.32 suggests that words consisting of two heavy graphematic syllables comprise two monosyllabic graphematic feet which are underspecified in their prominence relation. A look at the corresponding phonological foot structures of the earlier mentioned words supports this assumption: [ˈkɒfɪ] is a head-initial trochee, [ʃam.ˈpuː] has an unparsed first syllable followed by a word-final monosyllabic trochee, and *Kaffee* is attested as [ˈkafe̞] and [kaˈfeː]. I thus conclude that if there is a graphematic constraint *CLASH, which is proposed in phonological literature (e.g. Alber 1997, Kager 1999) and requires that strong syllables do not occur adjacently, it is ranking below WHP. However, it is also possible that this constraint is not relevant in graphematic foot assignment at all.

Let us turn now to trisyllabic graphematic words. In §4.1 we discussed the foot assignment of the word <divine>. As we have seen earlier, the word consists of three equally light graphematic syllables. Each syllable is too light to constitute a monosyllabic foot, thus there must be one bisyllabic foot and one unparsed g-syllable in <di.vi.ne>. With respect to the constraints so far, both structures, <(di.vi).ne> and <di.(vi.ne)>, perform equally well, cf. tableau 4.33.

Tab. 4.33

<di.vi.ne>	TROCHEE	MINIMALITY	WHP	PARSE-σ
☞ a. di (vi$_s$ ne$_w$)$_F$				*
☞ b. (di$_s$ vi$_w$)$_F$ ne				*
c. di (vi$_w$ ne$_s$)$_F$	*!			*
d. (di$_w$ vi$_s$)$_F$ ne	*!			*
e. (di$_s$)$_F$ (vi$_s$ ne$_w$)$_F$		*!		
f. (di$_s$ vi$_w$)$_F$ (ne$_s$)$_F$		*!		
g. (di$_s$)$_F$ (vi$_s$)$_F$ (ne$_s$)$_F$		*!**		

McCarthy & Prince (1993b) propose alignment constraints which demand that feet are aligned to the right (ALIGN-FOOT-RIGHT) and to the left (ALIGN-FOOT-LEFT) edge of a prosodic word. I thus propose the following graphematic counterparts:

(48) ALIGN-GFOOT-RIGHT
Align (Graphematic word, Right; graphematic Foot, Right)
Every graphematic word ends with a foot.

(49) ALIGN-GFOOT-LEFT
Align (Graphematic word, Left; graphematic Foot, Left)
Every graphematic word begins with a foot.

Like in phonology, ALIGN-GFOOT-RIGHT dominates ALIGN-GFOOT-LEFT in English and German.[24] Let us have a look at the tableau again, this time with the alignment constraints (note that in the tableaux, the names of the constraints are shortened to ALIGNR and ALIGNL).

---

24 For a slightly different analysis of phonological feet in German and English cf. §1.2.2.

Tab. 4.34

<di.vi.ne>	TROCH.	MIN.	WHP	ALIGNR	ALIGNL	PARSE-σ
☞ a. di (vi$_s$ ne$_w$)$_F$					*	*
b. (di$_s$ vi$_w$)$_F$ ne				*!		*
c. di (vi$_w$ ne$_s$)$_F$	*!					*
d. (di$_w$ vi$_s$)$_F$ ne	*!					*
e. (di$_s$)$_F$ (vi$_s$ ne$_w$)$_F$		*!				
f. (di$_s$ vi$_w$)$_F$ (ne$_s$)$_F$		*!				
g. (di$_s$)$_F$ (vi$_s$)$_F$ (ne$_s$)$_F$		*!**				

Note that the evaluation is also valid for German graphematic words of the same (or similar) make-up, e.g. <Ma(ri.ne)> 'navy', <Si(re.ne)> 'siren', <Mu(rä.ne)> 'moray', <Ka(ra.te)> 'karate', etc.

Let us now have a look at a trisyllabic graphematic word with a final heavy graphematic syllable, for instance, a word with a g-diphthong in its ultimate syllable, such as <devotee>. If <devotee> had a light final syllable, like, for instance <devote>, the evaluation would be identical to that of <divine>. The foot assignment in graphematic word with a final heavy syllable, differs substantially, however, cf. tableau 4.35.

Tab. 4.35

<de.vo.tee>	TROCH.	MIN.	WHP	ALIGNR	ALIGNL	PARSE-σ
☞ a. (de$_s$ vo$_w$)$_F$ (tee$_s$)$_F$						
b. de (vo$_s$ tee$_w$)$_F$			*!		*	*
c. de (vo$_w$ tee$_s$)$_F$	*!				*	*
d. (de$_w$ vo$_s$)$_F$ (tee$_s$)$_F$	*!					
e. de vo (tee$_s$)$_F$					*!	**
f. (de$_s$)$_F$ vo (tee$_s$)$_F$		*!				*
g. de (vo$_s$)$_F$ (ee$_s$)$_F$		*!			*	*

Note that if there was not the additional graphematic weight of the ultimate syllable, as e.g. in <divine> or <devote>, candidate b. would have been the winner of the evaluation. However, since the ultimate g-syllable in <de.vo.tee> is heavy, a foot structure as in candidate b. violates WHP.

Again, the evaluation in German is identical, cf. for instance, <(Kana)(pee)> 'sofa', <(Komi)(tee)> 'committee', <(Aza)(lee)> 'azalea'.

Note that in tableau 4.35 the prominence relation of the foot is underspecified. As we have seen in §4.3, there are two diametrical tendencies observable. While monosyllabic feet with syllables comprising g-diphthongs tend to be heads, the data from the experiments in which graphematic weight was increased with the help of additional c-letters suggest that word-final monosyllabic head-feet are dispreferred. These tendencies could be accounted for by two constraints: one constraint demanding that head-feet are aligned with the left edge of graphematic words and by a higher ranking constraint demanding that syllables with g-diphthongs are heads of head-feet. Such an analysis, however, is only supported by experimental data from German; for English graphematic feet there is no evidence for a left-sided head-foot alignment constraint. Further experimental research with English participants and English pseudowords is thus a desideratum.

This section demonstrated that the assignment of graphematic foot structure is well implementable in an OT-framework and that graphematic weight and reduced graphematic syllables are reliable cues to graphematic foot structures. In the following sections, I will present a model of encoding and decoding graphematic feet in the framework of Optimality Theory.

4.4.2 Foot correspondences

In the previous section, I demonstrated how graphematic foot structure is assigned in an OT-model. Graphematic foot structure maps onto phonological foot structure, which means that heads of graphematic feet are also heads of phonological feet (cf. the experimental evidence in §4.3.1). This relation is expressed in the violable constraint HEAD-MATCH (cf. McCarthy 1995).

(50) HEAD-MATCH: If α is the head of a foot and α corresponds to β, then β is the head of a foot.

Graphematic foot structure does encode not only phonological foot structure and by that stress, but it also encodes other supra-segmental properties, such as vowel quantity and ambisyllabicity, which is connected with the foot as we have seen in the sections on the canonical and non-canonical foot, cf. §4.1 and §4.2. In this section, I will present an OT-model of coding and decoding those supra-segmental properties connected to the foot based on the analyses provided in §4.1 and §4.2. Note that the words coding and decoding are not meant in a procedural manner. This OT-Analysis is about the correspondences between structures of different modalities and not about reading and writing processes.

I introduced the constraints dealing with the (de)coding of supra-segmental properties in the writing systems of English and German in the preceding sections and in chapter 3, they are repeated in (51) for convenience.

(51) i. UNARYBINARY
Unary vowel ↔ v-letter in an closed and strong g-syllable.
Binary vowel ↔ v-letter in an open and strong g-syllable.

ii. GEMINATE
An ambisyllabic consonant is coded by gemination of the letter that is the regular correspondent of this consonant (cf. Eisenberg 2006 for German).
The first letter of the gemination is dominated by the nuclear C-position of the first g-syllable; the second letter is dominated by the onset of the following g-syllable.

Note that the constraints UNARYBINARY is applicable in the coding and in the decoding perspective since it describes bidirectional correspondences. The constraint GEMINATE in iii. has the form of a logical implication. The antecedent is a phonological condition and the consequence is graphematic. By logical contraposition, we can infer that the absence of a graphematic geminate decodes the absence of an ambisyllabic consonant, cf. §4.1.

In the preceding sections, we have noted the systematicity of graphematic gemination in canonical bisyllabic trochees: if a foot is canonical and bisyllabic in both representations, the phonological and the graphematic one, the gemination of an intervocalic c-letter corresponds very regularly to an ambisyllabic p-consonant. However, in non-canonical structures, ambisyllabicity coding is not as regular as in canonical structures – especially in the case of English.

In OT literature, there are two approaches towards variation that is connected to certain structures:

(a) The *co-phonology approach* captures variation by splitting up the grammar into two or more constraint hierarchies, or *co-phonologies*, which apply to different lexical classes or constructions (cf. e.g. Orgun 1998, Inkelas 1998, Orgun & Inkelas 2002; for a related but not identical approach cf. stratal OT, Kiparsky 2000).

(b) In the *indexed constraint approach* only one fixed constraint ranking (per language) is employed. Certain constraints are split up into different indexed versions. Each version applies to a different lexical class or construction (cf. e.g. McCarthy & Prince 1995, Pater 2000).

The approaches are similar to a considerable degree and equally capable to account for the difference between non-canonical and canonical structures in German and English writing systems (for an overview and a comparison of these approaches in general cf. Inkelas & Zoll 2007). In this work, I will account for the differences in non-canonical and canonical structures with regard to ambisyllabicity (de)coding with the help of an indexed constraint, cf. (52).[25]

(52) GEMINATE*can*
In canonical bisyllabic p-feet and g-feet:
An ambisyllabic consonant is coded by a gemination of the letter that is the regular correspondent of this consonant.
The first letter of the gemination is dominated by the nuclear C-position of the first g-syllable; the second letter is dominated by the onset of the following g-syllable.

The constraints GEMINATE and the indexed constraint GEMINATE*can* differ in one point: GEMINATE*can* has an initial condition: GEMINATE*can* applies only if the phonological *and* the graphematic representation of a word are canonical bisyllabic feet. Additionally, they may also differ in their ranking in the constraint hierarchy.

I will argue in the analyses below that the geminate constraints are tied in German. Since GEMINATE, the more general constraint, is violated if GEMINATE*can* is violated, I will leave out the constraint in the illustrations of German evaluations for the sake of simplicity.

The constraint GEMINATE*can* is a specific instance of the more general constraint GEMINATE. The former therefore ranks at least as high as the latter.

The constraints in (51) and (52) are correspondence constraints. The violation of one of these correspondence constraints may be associated with a violation of another correspondence constraint. Consider, for example, the input [swɪm̩ə˞]

25 The co-phonology, or rather co-graphematics that can account for the variation found in English would look like this:
(i) Canonical structures: HEADMATCH, UNBIN, GEM ≫MAX ≫DEP
(ii) Non-canonical structures: HEADMATCH, UNBIN ≫MAX ≫DEP ≫GEM

with ambisyllabic [m] and the candidate *<swi.mer>. This candidate does not conform to GEMINATE$_{can}$ since the corresponding c-letter <m> is not geminated. Because there is no c-letter geminate, the first v-letter of the candidate is in an open and strong g-syllable. Since the corresponding phonological syllable houses a unary p-vowel, the candidate also violates UNARYBINARY.

Another class of constraints are faithfulness constraints such as DEP and MAX. These constraints are violated if the output is not identical to the input with respect to segments. I introduced these constraints earlier; they are repeated here for convenience.

(53) a. MAX:
Input segments must have output correspondents. ('No deletion')
i. MAX(G-INPUT/P-OUTPUT)
ii. MAX(P-INPUT/G-OUTPUT)
iii. MAX(G-INPUT/G-OUTPUT)
iv. MAX(P-INPUT/P-OUTPUT)
b. DEP:
Output segments must have input correspondents. ('No insertion')
i. DEP(G-INPUT/P-OUTPUT)
ii. DEP(P-INPUT/G-OUTPUT)
iii. DEP(G-INPUT/G-OUTPUT)
iv. DEP(P-INPUT/P-OUTPUT)

The list in (53) shows that the faithfulness constraints MAX and DEP are actually bundles of constraints. Whether the constraint in i. or ii. applies, depends on whether the coding or decoding perspective is taken. The constraints in iii. and iv. apply when the modality of the input and output are identical.

The third set of constraints rules out ill-formed structures.

(54) GSYLL-WELL-FORMEDNESS
Graphematic syllables must be well-formed.

(55) PSYLL-WELL-FORMEDNESS
Phonological syllables must be well-formed.

These well-formedness constraints are actually bundles of many constraints. These bundles include violable markedness constraints like ONSET and *CODA (cf. e.g. Prince & Smolensky 1993) but also undominated constraints like the graphematic syllable peak restriction stating that every g-syllable has a v-letter in its V-position, cf (2) in §3.1. This means that it is possible that two candidates incurring one violation of the well-formedness constraints each may actually perform differently well in a more elaborate analysis. In the interests of simplicity I will leave out an elaborate syllable analysis as long as there is a better performing candidate that does not violate any of the well-formedness constraints.[26] Instead of listing all possible constraints here, I will discuss them when the need arises.

There is one specific graphematic well-formedness constraint I would like to single out given the fact that this constraint is not uniformly ranked in English and German. We have noted in §3.3 that in morphologically simple words, word division in English and German is guided by different principles. While English word division is mainly guided by UNARYBINARY, German word division is guided by the so called *one grapheme rule*. We introduced this constraint in §4.1.2.

(56) SYLLABIFY: A graphematic syllable starts with exactly one grapheme.

In chapter 3, I presented a first approach to coding and decoding vowel quantity within an optimality theoretic model. This approach is limited to mono- and bisyllabic words (both graphematically and phonologically) since we ignored foot structure in this chapter. We can now broaden the analysis by including polysyllabic words.

The constraints and their rankings are identical in the coding and the decoding perspective. I will demonstrate the coding and decoding perspective in the following subsections.

4.4.2.1 Canonical feet

As we have seen in §4.4.1, foot structures can be assigned in an OT-model. In the following analyses, however, I will focus on other supra-segmental properties connected with the graphematic foot aside from the foot structure itself. I will thus leave the assignment of graphematic foot structure out for the sake of simplicity. The (non-)canonicity of the input is hinted at in subscript in the input, although it is not part of the input in the strict sense (as shown in the previous section). Canonical structures are indicated by subscript *can*, non-canonical structures are indicated by subscript *nc*.

4.4.2.1.1 English cases

Let us begin our discussion with English cases. In §3.2.2, I presented the cases *late* and *lad* in both directions of correspondence. Both words are canonical in the graphematic and phonological representation. Phonologically, they are monosyllabic and graphematically, <la.te> is bisyllabic and <lad> is monosyllabic.

26 For elaborate analyses of the phonological syllable within the OT-framework cf. e.g. Hammond 1999, Kager 1999, Féry & van de Vijver 2003, Zec 2007.

I will begin with two similar cases, [ˈlæt̬ɚ] – <lat.ter> and [ˈleɪ̯.tɚ] – <la.ter>. The graphematic words <la.ter> and <lat.ter> have in common that each of them comprises one bisyllabic canonical graphematic foot that ends in a reduced graphematic syllable. They differ with respect to one crucial point: as opposed to the first g-syllable of <la.ter>, the first g-syllable of <lat.ter> is closed by the first letter of a c-letter geminate.

Let us begin with the phonological form [ˈlaɪ̯.tɚ]; consider tableau 4.36.

Tab. 4.36

[ˈleɪ̯.tɚ]$_{can}$	HEAD-MATCH	GWELL	UNBIN	GEM$_{can}$	MAX	DEP	GEM
a. lat.ter			*!			*	
b. la.tter		*!				*	
c. latt.er			*!			*	
☞ d. la.ter							
e. lat.er			*!				
f. la.te.re	*!		*			*	

As we can see, evaluating the graphematic correspondent of a canonical foot structure with a binary vowel in an open first syllable is trivial. The winning candidate does not violate any constraint while other plausible candidates violate at least one constraint. Candidate d. is hence the intrinsic winner of this evaluation.

Let us see how the same set of candidates performs when we change the input: let us consider the word [ˈlæt̬ɚ] with a unary first p-vowel and an ambisyllabic consonant.

As sketched in the introduction to this section, the GEMINATE constraints are in conflict with MAX and DEP. The two faithfulness constraints militate against epentheses and deletions of segments. The GEMINATE constraints, on the other hand, cause a segmental mismatch between the output and the input: one ambisyllabic consonant corresponds to two c-letters; cf. tableau 4.37.

The input in tableau 4.37 is a bisyllabic canonical trochee. All candidates are canonical bisyllabic trochees as well, with the exception of candidate f. which is a structure ending in a canonical bisyllabic constraint. All candidates conform to HEADMATCH – except for candidate f. Candidate f., *<la(tere)>, has the same structure as, e.g., <se(vere)> - [sɪˈvɪə]; its first g-syllable is not parsed and the last

Tab. 4.37

[ˈlæṭə˞]$_{can}$	HEAD-MATCH	GWELL	UNBIN	GEM$_{can}$	MAX	DEP	GEM
☞ a. lat.ter						*	
b. la.tter		*!	*	*		*	*
c. latt.er				*!		*	*
d. la.ter			*!	*			*
e. lat.er				*!			*
f. la.te.re	*!			*		*	*

two syllables build up a final bisyllabic g-foot. However, the input specifies that the phonological head of [ˈlæṭə] is the first syllable. Thus, candidate f. violates HEAD-MATCH. All other candidates conform to this constraint.[27]

Candidates b. and. d. violate UNARYBINARY. Both have an open first g-syllable but correspond to a unary p-vowel (additionally, candidate b. is graphematically ill-formed because its second g-syllable begins with a c-geminate). Candidates b., c., d., and e. violate GEMINATE$_{can}$: d. and e. do not comprise a c-letter gemination of the regular correspondent of the ambisyllabic consonant (/t/ ↔ <t>); and although b. and c. each comprise a geminated c-letter, <t>, the first letter of the geminate, is not dominated by the nuclear C-positions of the first g-syllables.

The winning candidate a. conforms to all constraints but DEP. This violation is natural for candidates that conform to GEMINATE$_{can}$ and/ or GEMINATE. The gemination constraints demands that a c-letter is doubled and one of the c-letters of the geminate has of course no correspondent in the phonological input.

Let us switch the perspectives and consider tableau 4.38. Note that the graphematic syllable boundary is only indicated for convenience; the boundary does not need to be specified in the input since it is unambiguously coded by the c-letter geminate.

Let us discuss the violations of the candidates in order of the constraints. Candidate e. has an unfooted first syllable and a final monosyllabic foot. In the input, however, the first syllable is the head of a bisyllabic foot. Candidate e. thus violates HEAD-MATCH. Note that apart from this violation, candidate e. performs quite well since GEMINATE$_{can}$ (shortened to GEM$_{can}$ in the tableaux) does not apply in the decoding perspective (it could be argued that the candidate additionally

27 Even if we assume that the foot structure of this candidate is <(la.te).re>, it would still be ruled out by GEMINATE$_{can}$.

Tab. 4.38

<(lat$_s$.ter$_w$)$_F$ >$_{can}$	HEAD-MATCH	PWELL	UNBIN	GEM$_{can}$	MAX	DEP	GEM
☞ a. 'læt̩ɚ					*		
b. 'læ.tɚ		*!			*		
c. 'læt.ɚ		*!			*		
d. 'leɪ̯.tɚ			*!		*		
e. lə.'tɛr	*!				*		

violates UNARYBINARY; however, this would not change anything). Candidate b. and c. violate PWELL. Candidate b. is phonologically ill-formed since its first syllable is strong and ends in a unary p-vowel. Candidate c. is not ill-formed but at least more marked than candidate a. since the second syllable does not have an onset. Candidate d. violates UNARYBINARY (shortened in the tableaux as UNBIN): In the input, there is a strong closed g-syllable, but in the first syllable of the candidate is a unary p-vowel. All candidates violate MAX. In English, there are no phonological consonantal geminations, thus every phonologically well-formed candidate must violate MAX, if there is a c-letter geminate in the input. Since all candidates equally violate MAX, this constraint is not relevant for this analysis.

Now let us compare the evaluation from above with c-letter geminate with a similar case without c-letter geminate, <later>. In a word like that, the graphematic syllable boundary is ambiguous: both, <lat.er> and <la.ter> are plausible graphematic syllable boundaries. The graphematic syllable boundary, however, is essential for the application of the constraint UNARYBINARY. This means that if we do not know the graphematic syllable boundary of a word, the mapping constraints UNARYBINARY cannot apply.

It is, however, possible to decode such a word with the help of GEMINATE. This constraint states that ambisyllabic consonants are coded with c-letter geminates. The absence of a c-letter geminate thus decodes the absence of ambisyllabicity. This means that a candidate that features an ambisyllabic consonant violates the GEMINATE if there is no c-letter geminate in the input, cf. 4.39.

Let us now have a look at words whose phonological form comprises an ambisyllabic consonant that does not map onto a c-letter geminate. Consider the word ['lʌv̩ə] – <lover>. The consonant [v] is ambisyllabic, yet the regular correspondent of this consonant, <v>, is not geminated. As we have seen in §4.1, this is due to a high-ranking constraint *<vv> militating against the gemination of the letter <v>. This constraint ranks higher than GEMINATE$_{can}$. Consider tableau 4.40.

Tab. 4.39

<la.ter>*can*	HEAD-MATCH	PWELL	UNBIN	GEM*can*	MAX	DEP	GEM
a. ˈlæṭə˞				*!			*
b. ˈlæ.tə˞		*!					
c. ˈlæt.ə˞		*!					
☞ d. ˈlaɪ̯.tə˞							
e. lə.ˈtɛr	*!						

Tab. 4.40

[ˈlʌṿər]*can*	HEAD-MATCH	*<vv>	UNBIN	GEM*can*	MAX	DEP	GEM
☞ a. lov.er				*			*
b. lo.ver			*!	*			*
c. lov.ver		*!				*	

Candidate c. incurs a fatal violation of *<vv>. The other candidates violate GEMINATE*can* and GEMINATE. They differ, however, regarding their performance with respect to UNARYBINARY. The first g-syllable of candidate a. is closed and the first g-syllable of candidate b. is open. Since the v-letters correspond to a unary p-vowel in the onset, candidate b. incurs a violation of UNARYBINARY, while candidate a. does not. Candidate a. is thus the winner of the evaluation.

The analysis of words with an ambisyllabic consonant corresponding to a complex grapheme, i.e. [ˈbrʌðər] – <brother>, is similar to the analysis presented in tableau 4.40 above. Of course, *<vv> is not responsible for the fact that there is no gemination in such a word. In §4.1 we argued for the following constraint:

(57) *GEMINATE-COMPLEX: Complex graphemes are not geminated.

Consider tableau 4.41 in which this constraint is employed (in the tableaux, *GEMINATE-COMPLEX is shortened to GEM-COMPL).

Non-identical geminates, such as <ch> – <tch> or <k> – <ck> (Rollings 2004: 66) must be accounted for by special mapping constraints, for instance ‘the geminate corresponding to [k] is <ck>’. Constraints like these override the general gemination constraints. Aside from that, the evaluations of the coding of words with identical and non-identical geminates do not differ.

Tab. 4.41

['brʌḍər]$_{can}$	HEAD-MATCH	GEM-COMPL	UNBIN	GEM$_{can}$	MAX	DEP	GEM
☞ a. broth.er				*			*
b. bro.ther			*!	*			*
c. broth.ther		*!				*	

Let us switch the perspective and have a look at the evaluation of the correspondents of words with c-letters that are not geminated but correspond to an ambisyllabic consonant, cf. tableau 4.42

Tab. 4.42

<broth.er>$_{can}$	HEAD-MATCH	PWELL	UNBIN	GEM$_{can}$	MAX	DEP	GEM
☞ a. 'brʌḍər				(*)			(*)
b. 'brʌ.ðər		*!					
c. 'brʌð.ər		*!					
d. 'broʊ.ðər			*!				

The evaluation above is valid for the evaluation of correspondents of words like <lover> as well. As we can see, the evaluation yields the desired result, however, this is only the case if the graphematic syllable boundary is known. If the graphematic syllable boundary is not specified, a candidate like candidate d., ['broʊ.ðər], with binary first p-vowel would win (cf. tableau 4.39).

It is not clear, however, if candidates like ['brʌḍər] and ['lʌṿər] really violate the GEMINATE constraints in the decoding perspective since complex graphemes and <v> cannot be geminated (hence the asterisks in brackets). If they do not violate these constraints, candidates with unary p-vowels and candidates with binary p-vowel would perform equally well. This might explain contrasts like *liver* vs. *diver* and *gather* vs. *father*.

4.4.2.1.2 German cases

Let us now turn to German cases. Consider the word <Mat. te> – [maṭə] 'mat' (I will skip the evaluation of a similar word with binary vowel, like e.g. *Mate* 'maté' or *Tage* 'days.' For a detailed discussion of the evaluations of such words cf. §3.2.2 and the following section §4.4.3.2). The canonical phonological foot [maṭə] comprises an ambisyllabic consonant, [t]. Like in English, there are c-geminates in German. This means that there is a mismatch between the number of graphematic and phonological segments in cases of ambisyllabicity. We can therefore conclude that GEMINATE is higher ranking than MAX and DEP in German as well. Let us begin with a phonological input, consider tableau 4.43.

Tab. 4.43

['maṭə]$_{can}$	HEAD-MATCH	SYLL	GWELL	GEM	MAX	DEP	UNBIN	MINSYLL
☞ a. Mat.te						*		*
b. Ma.tte		*!	*	*		*	*	*
c. Matt.e		*!		*		*		*
d. Ma.te				*!			*	*
e. Mat.e		*!		*				*
f. Mat.tee	*!					**		*

Let us have a look at the most important, i.e. fatal violations. Candidates b., c. and e. have second syllables that do not begin with exactly one grapheme. These candidates therefore violate SYLLABIFY. Moreover, candidate b., <Ma.tte>, is graphematically ill-formed. No syllable may begin with a c-letter geminate according to the length sequencing principle (LSP, Fuhrhop et al. 2011: 283; §3.1.2). Candidate d. fatally violates GEMINATE because this candidate does not feature a c-letter geminate at all (the violations of candidates b. and c. are caused by their violations of the structural condition of GEMINATE). Finally, candidate f. has a final heavy g-syllable, thus its foot structure is very likely to be different from the foot structure in the input and the candidate therefore incurs a violation of HEADMATCH. Even if we do not assume the foot structures to be different from the input, candidate f. loses against candidate a. since f. incurs one violation more of DEP. Thus, candidate a., <Mat.te>, is the optimal output for the input ['maṭə]$_{can}$.

Let us turn now to graphematic inputs. <Mat.te> is a canonical graphematic structure with a c-letter geminate. The second g-syllable of that graphematic word is reduced, cf. tableau 4.44.

Let us have a look at the fatal violations. Candidate e. has an unparsed initial syllable, the final syllable is a monosyllabic foot. Since the graphematic input is a bisyllabic trochee, candidate e. fatally violates HEAD-MATCH. Candidates b. and c. violate phonological well-formedness constraints. Candidate b. comprises

Tab. 4.44

<Mat.te>*can*	HEAD-MATCH	PWELL	GEM	MAX	DEP	UNBIN
☞ a. ˈmaṭə				*		
b. ˈma.tə		*!		*		
c. ˈmat.ə		*!		*		
d. ˈmaː.tə				*		*!
e. ma.ˈteː	*!			*		

a strong syllable that is open but ends in a unary vowel and the second syllable of candidate c. does not have an onset. Thus, both candidates are more marked than candidate a. and d.; their violations of PWELL are therefore fatal.

The decisive difference between candidates a. and d. is their performance regarding UNARYBINARY. The c-letter geminate closes the first syllable in the input, thus only a candidate with a corresponding unary p-vowel in the first syllable can conform to UNARYBINARY.

Let us now have a look at not geminated correspondents to ambisyllabic consonants, i.e. complex graphemes. Like in tableau 4.41 for English, the responsible constraint for blocking the gemination of complex graphemes is *GEMINATE-COMPLEX. Consider the evaluation for the correspondent of [vaʃ̣ən] '(to) wash' in tableau 4.45 (cf. also tableau 4.9 in §4.1.2).

Tab. 4.45

[ˈvaʃ̣ən]*can*	HEAD-MATCH	GEM-COMPL	SYLL	GEM	MAX	DEP	UNBIN
a. wasch.en		*!	*	*			
☞ b. wa.schen			*	*		*	
c. wasch.schen	*!				*		

Comparing this evaluation with the evaluation of the similar English case, *brother*, cf. tableau 4.41, we see that SYLLABIFY is the decisive constraint in German, while in English, the optimal candidate is determined ultimately by UNARYBINARY. This difference in ranking explains the difference in graphematic syllable boundaries, cf. e.g. <broth.er> vs. <wa.schen>.[28]

Decoding words with complex graphemes corresponding to ambisyllabic consonants in German poses similar, even more serious problems than in English; consider table 4.46.

Tab. 4.46

<wa.schen>*can*	HEAD-MATCH	PWELL	GEM	MAX	DEP	UNBIN
a. ˈvaʃ̣ən						*
b. ˈva.ʃən		*!				*
c. ˈvaʃ.ən		*!				*
☞ d. ˈvaː.ʃən						

German words like <wa.schen> are opaque with respect to vowel quantity coding; the word <du.schen> '(to) shower', for instance, is attested with unary and binary vowel. In contrast to words such as <broth.er> in English, line breaks do not give reliable cues to vowel quantity decoding in German words with complex graphemes corresponding to ambisyllabic consonants.

4.4.2.2 Non-Canonical Feet

As we have seen, the evaluations of bisyllabic canonical trochees in the coding perspective are quite straight forward in German and English; in the decoding perspective, however, the evaluations are a bit more problematic when complex graphemes (or <v>) are involved. Let us now turn to non-canonical bisyllabic and polysyllabic words. Note that the constraint GEMINATE*can* does not apply if the input or the output is non-canonical.

28 Note that in English, there is also a constraint stating that suffixes are hyphenated. The word division of monomorphemic words such as <bish.op> (cf. Gove 2002), however, prove the relevance of UNARY-BINARY in English word division, cf. §3.3.

4.4.2.2.1 English cases

Let us begin with English cases. As we have seen in §4.2 above, ambisyllabicity (decoding) is unsystematic in non-canonical graphematic structures in English. Basically, there are two ways of modelling this property in an OT-model. One way is say that ambisyllabicity (de)coding by c-letter geminates is regular in non-canonical structures in English and that the absence of c-letter geminations in g-words corresponding to words with ambisyllabic consonant is lexically determined. The other way would be to state the opposite by saying that ambisyllabicity (de)coding by c-letter geminates is irregular in non-canonical structures in English and that every instance of c-letter gemination is lexically determined.

Let us pursue the latter way and say that c-letter gemination in non-canonical structures in English are irregular and that every occurence of c-letter geminates is specified in the lexicon (we will explore the other way of modelling irregularities in the German cases). Consider the word *limit* with the phonological form ['lɪm̩ɪt] and the graphematic form <lim.it>. The phonological form is a bisyllabic trochee with a reduced syllable ([ɪ] is licensed in reduced phonological syllables in English, cf. §1.2); the [m] is ambisyllabic.

The regular correspondent of [ɪ] is <i>. This means that although ['lɪm̩ɪt] ends in a reduced phonological syllable, the graphematic correspondent <lim.it> does not end in a reduced graphematic syllable and is thus non-canonical. The constraint GEMINATE$_{can}$ does therefore not apply; consider tableau 4.47.

Tab. 4.47

['lɪm̩ɪt]$_{can}$	HEAD-MATCH	GWELL	UNBIN	GEM$_{can}$	MAX	DEP	GEM
☞ a. lim.it							*
b. li.mit			*!				*
c. lim.mit						*!	
d. li.mmit		*!	*			*	*
e. limm.it						*!	*
f. lim.meat	*!					*	*

Let us discuss the fatal violations in the order of the constraints. The g-diphthong in candidate f. constitutes an own monosyllabic g-foot; the input, however, has an initial head. The candidate thus violates HEADMATCH. The second syllable of candidate d. begins with <mm>, the syllable is thus graphematically ill-formed (cf.

LSP, Fuhrhop et al. 2011). Candidate b. violates UNARYBINARY, its first g-syllable is open, while the first p-syllable of the input houses a unary p-vowel. Candidates c. and e. fatally violate DEP. Thus, candidate a. wins the evaluation.

Let us have a look at the two best performing candidates: the winner <lim.it> and the second best but not optimal candidates <lim.mit>. If the graphematic form was canonical and thereby GEMINATE$_{can}$ applied, <lim.mit> would have been optimal like in the evaluation of ambisyllabicity decoding in canonical word structures, cf. tableau 4.37; however, as GEMINATE$_{can}$ does not apply, it is the c-letter gemination itself that makes the candidate lose. A c-letter gemination always incurs a violation of DEP since it involves the epenthesis of a graphematic segment that has no correspondent in the input (<limm.it> is for the same reason sub-optimal; however, a form like <limm.it> is always sub-optimal compared to either of the two forms). The winning candidate <lim.it>, on the other hand, codes the unarity of the input p-vowel properly without violating DEP.

Spellings with c-letter geminates corresponding to ambisyllabic consonants in non-canonical word structures are irregular in the analysis proposed here. The occurrence of c-letter geminates in such structures cannot be explained by GEMINATE$_{can}$ as shown above. It thus needs to be lexically specified. In §3.2.2, I already gave an example how a unidirectional OT-analysis can account for lexical exceptions: The non-predictable information, i.e. that what makes a word exceptional, is specified in the input and an IDENT-IO constraint ensures the realisation of this additional piece of information (cf. Wiese 2004: 324f. for a similar OT-model for unpredictable spellings in German).

In the case of a non-canonical bisyllabic trochee like [ˈbæl̩ət]$_{nc}$, the additional information in the input is that the graphematic correspondent of the ambisyllabic consonant must be doubled in the graphematic output. This means as well as the phonological form, in this case [ˈbæl̩ət], [l] → <ll> is also specified in the input.

The relevant faithfulness constraint is a MAX-constraint relating to a graphematic input and a graphematic output, MAX(G-INPUT/ G-OUTPUT), cf. (53) for MAX-constraints. This constraint demands that every graphematic element in the input must have a graphematic correspondent in the output. Note that this constraint operates only on the segmental level, in contrast to the GEMINATE constraints, which require that doubled letters have to be dominated by certain syllabic constituents, consider tableau 4.48.

Note that it is not necessary to rank MAX(G-INPUT/ G-OUTPUT) differently than MAX(P-INPUT/ G-OUTPUT). For this reason, I subsumed both MAX-constraints under the label MAX in the tableau above.

Tab. 4.48

[ˈbæḷət]$_{nc}$, <ll>	HEAD-MATCH	GWELL	UNBIN	GEM$_{can}$	MAX	DEP	GEM
a. bal.ot					*!		*
b. ba.lot			*!		*		*
☞ c. bal.lot						*	
d. ba.llot		*!	*			*	*
e. bal.loot	*!						*

The only differences to tableau 4.47 are thus the additional MAX(G-INPUT/ G-OUTPUT) violations caused by the mismatch between the graphematic input and the graphematic candidates a. and b.

Let us turn now to graphematic inputs, consider tableau 4.49.

Tab. 4.49

<lim.it>$_{nc}$	HEAD-MATCH	PWELL	UNBIN	GEM$_{can}$	MAX	DEP	GEM
☞ a. ˈlɪṃɪt							*
b. ˈlaɪ̯.mɪt			*!				
c. ˈlɪm.ɪt		*!					
d. ˈlɪ.mɪt		*!					
e. lɪ.ˈmaɪ̯t	*!						

Two of the five candidates are phonologically marked: the second syllable in candidate c. has no onset and the first syllable in d. is strong but ends in a unary p-vowel. This leaves three candidates that are phonologically unmarked: a. [ˈlɪṃɪt], b. [ˈlaɪ̯.mɪt] and e. [lɪ.ˈmaɪ̯t]. Candidate e., [lɪ.ˈmaɪ̯t], ends in a final monosyllabic foot as opposed to the input; this candidate thus violates HEADMATCH. Candidate b. has a binary p-vowel in its first syllable, the corresponding syllable in the input, however, is closed and strong. Thus, candidate b. violates UNARYBINARY. Candidate a. violates the logical contraposition of GEMINATE: [ˈlɪṃɪt] comprises an ambisyllabic consonant but a c-letter geminate in the input is missing. Candidate a. still performs better than the other candidates and is the winner of the evaluation.

The evaluation of the correspondents of non-canonical g-words that have a non-geminated letter corresponding to an ambisyllabic consonant is identical to the evaluation of correspondents of words that have other non-geminated graphematic elements such as complex graphemes or <v> corresponding to an ambisyllabic consonant, cf. tableau 4.42. Like in the case of <broth.er> or <lov.er> it is essential to know whether the first syllable is graphematically closed or not, cf. for instance the contrast between *cubit* (with binary first vowel) and *limit*.

Now let us see how the correspondents of bisyllabic non-canonical trochees with irregular c-letter geminates are evaluated, cf. tableau 4.50.

Tab. 4.50

<bal.lot>*nc*	HEAD-MATCH	PWELL	UNBIN	GEMcan	MAX	DEP	GEM
☞ a. ˈbæl̩ət					*		
b. ˈbeɪ̯.lət			*!		*		
c. ˈbæl.ət		*!			*		
d. ˈbæ.lət		*!			*		
e. bə.ˈlɒt	*!				*		

As we can see in the tableau above, there is no difference to the evaluation of correspondents of non-canonical trochees without c-letter gemination. In both evaluations, the best candidates are the ones with a unary vowel in the first p-syllable and the ones with a binary p-vowel in the first p-syllable. In tableau 4.49 and 4.50 the decisive constraint is UNARYBINARY, which is responsible for the selection of a candidate with a unary vowel in the first p-syllable such as [ˈbæl̩ət]. The only difference is that the c-letter gemination of <bal.lot> unambiguously determines the graphematic syllable boundary.

Let us now turn to polysyllabic words. We have seen in §4.4.1 how foot structures are assigned to graphematic words comprising three g-syllables. In cases like <devotee> it is the graphematic weight that gives reliable cues to graphematic foot structures. Obviously, the constraint UNARYBINARY cannot account for the mapping of graphematic diphthongs onto binary p-vowels in closed g-syllables. In the example <de.vo.tee>, for instance, the g-diphthong is in a closed and strong syllable and thus should map onto a unary vowel according to UNARYBINARY. I thus propose the following mapping constraint, which is employed in tableau 4.51[29]:

(58) GDIPH: Graphematic diphthongs map onto binary phonological vowels.

Tab. 4.51

<(de.vo)(tee)>$_{nc}$	HEAD-MATCH	GDIPH	UNBIN	MAX	DEP	GEM
☞ a. ˈˈdɛ.və.ˈtiː			*			
b. ˈˈdɛ.və.ˈtɪ		*!				
c. də.ˈvəʊ.tə	*!	*	*			

We have seen in §4.4.1 how the graphematic foot structure is assigned to <de.vo.tee>. The heads of the feet in this graphematic word are the first and the last g-syllable. The first syllable is the head of a bisyllabic g-foot, the last syllable is the head of a monosyllabic g-foot. Candidate c. [də.ˈvəʊ.tə] thus violates UNARYBINARY since a weak syllable, <gi> is mapped onto a strong p-syllable with a binary vowel. Additionally, this candidate violates GDIPH since the g-diphthong in the input does not map onto a binary p-vowel. Candidate a. and b. have the same foot structure. While the last p-syllable of candidate b. has a unary p-vowel, the last syllable of candidate a. has a binary vowel. Candidate a. thus violates UNARYBINARY but conforms to the higher ranking constraint GDIPH.

Let us now turn to the coding perspective. There are generally two graphematic marking devices for final monosyllabic feet: First, a monosyllabic foot can be coded as shown above with the help of a g-diphthong. The second possibility is to code the monosyllabic foot with a canonical bisyllabic trochee with reduced g-syllable, as, for instance, in <de(vote)> and <di(vine)>. The choice of the means of coding a final monosyllabic p-foot depends above all on phonological syllable structure: A binary p-vowel in a phonologically open syllable which forms a final monosyllabic p-foot is regularly coded as a g-diphthong (e.g. *agree, devotee, engineer*), while a binary p-vowel in a phonologically closed syllable which forms

29 For the sake of clarity, I left out the constraint GEMINATE$_{can}$ since it is not relevant for non-canonical inputs.

a monosyllabic p-foot is regularly coded as a canonical g-foot (e.g., *devote, calculate*, cf. Rollings 2004: 87, 90). Vowel quality coding can also play a role, as in *alone* vs. *balloon* (for an elaborate study on vowel quality coding cf. Rollings 2004).

4.4.2.2.2 German cases

Compared to English, ambisyllabicity (de)coding with c-letter geminates is very frequent in non-canonical graphematic structures in German, cf. §4.2. The evaluations of regular cases such as *Komma* 'comma' are therefore (nearly) identical to the cases discussed in the previous section. Consider tableaux 4.52 and 4.53.

Tab. 4.52

['kɔm̩a]$_{nc}$	HEAD-MATCH	SYLL	GWELL	GEM	MAX	DEP	UNBIN
☞ a. Kom.ma						*	
b. Ko.mma		*!	*	*		*	*
c. Komm.a		*!		*		*	
d. Ko.ma				*!			*
e. Kom.a		*!		*			
f. Kom.maa	*!					**	

The evaluation in tableau 4.52 does not differ from the evaluation of a canonical structure with ambisyllabic consonant in tableau 4.43 (except that the constraint MINSYLL does not apply to tableau 4.52).

Tab. 4.53

<Kom.ma$_{nc}$ >	HEAD-MATCH	PWELL	GEM	MAX	DEP	UNBIN
☞ a. 'kɔm̩a				*		
b. 'kɔ.ma		*!		*		
c. 'kɔm.a		*!		*		
d. 'koː.ma				*		*!
e. kɔ.'maː	*!			*		

The evaluation illustrated in tableau 4.53 does not differ substantially from the evaluation illustrated in tableau 4.44. The crucial difference between the two best performing candidates in tableau 4.53 is not their performance with respect to GEMINATE but with respect to UNARYBINARY.

Let us now examine irregular words without c-letter gemination. The irregular absence of c-letter geminations must be specified in the input and an input output faithfulness constraint blocks the gemination. We use the word *Limit* as a representative example of such cases. The additional information in the input is that the correspondent of [m] is <m> (and not <mm>). The constraint that blocks the gemination is DEP-G-INPUT/G-OUTPUT, which is violated if there are graphematic insertions additional to the graphematic input (cf. Wiese 2004: 324; and cf. (53)).

The German word *Limit* is quite similar to its English cognate. The phonological form is identical, it is ['lɪṃɪt]. Regarding the graphematic representation <Limit>, however, there is one important difference. While in English, the graphematic syllable boundary is <lim.it>, the German word division yields the graphematic boundary <Li.mit>.

As we have seen in §3.3, this is due to different word division constraint rankings in English and German. In morphologically simple words in English, word division is mainly guided by the constraint UNARYBINARY: Hyphenated g-syllables must be able to map correctly onto their phonologically correspondents. The English word <limit> is hyphenated <lim-it> (cf. Gove 2002); this hyphenation ensures that the first syllable maps onto a unary p-vowel. If it was hyphenated *<li-mit>, it would be decoded with a binary p-vowel, probably like [laɪ̯.mɪt], cf. §3.3.

In German, however, the most important constraint with respect to word division in morphologically simple words is the so called one-grapheme-rule: the last grapheme between two v-letters belongs to the g-syllable of the second v-letter. We have introduced the constraint SYLLABIFY that corresponds to this rule in §4.1. <Limit> is hyphenated <Li-mit> in compliance with SYLLABIFY but in violation of UNARYBINARY, cf. tableau 4.54.

Tab. 4.54

['lɪṃɪt]$_{nc}$, <m>	SYLL	DEP-GI/GO	GEM	MAX	DEP	UNBIN
☞ a. Li.mit			*			*
b. Lim.it	*!		*			
c. Lim.mit		*!			*	

Constraint DEP-G-INPUT/G-OUTPUT is ranked higher than the GEMINATE constraint; it thus blocks c-letter gemination: The only candidate displaying c-letter gemination fatally violates DEP-G-INPUT/G-OUTPUT.

Let us now switch the perspective and consider the evaluation of correspondents of non-canonical graphematic trochees without c-letter gemination corresponding to words with ambisyllabic consonants.

If we compare the coding of a non-canonical word with a unary p-vowel in the first syllable, like e.g. [ˈlɪm̩ɪt], with the coding of a non-canonical word with a binary p-vowel in the first syllable, like e.g. [ˈpuː.ma], we do not see any differences in the graphematic structure of these words. Consider tableau 4.55, where the evaluation of the correspondent of [ˈpuː.ma] 'cougar' is illustrated.

Tab. 4.55

[ˈpuː.ma]*nc*	SYLL	GEM	MAX	DEP	UNBIN
☞ a. Pu.ma					
b. Pum.a		*!			*

As we can see, the evaluation of coding the non-canonical structures [ˈlɪm̩ɪt] and [ˈpuː.ma] do not differ, although the former has a unary p-vowel in its first syllable and an ambisyllabic consonant, while the latter has a binary p-vowel in its first syllable and no ambisyllabic consonant. The few exceptions to ambisyllabicity (de)coding must thus also have lexically specified additional information in the input. If not, a word like <Li.mit> should be decoded with a binary first p-vowel, like in e.g., <Pu.ma>, cf. 4.56.

Tab. 4.56

<Pu.ma>*nc*	GEM	MAX	DEP	UNBIN
☞ a. ˈpuː.ma				
b. ˈpum̩a				*!

The lexically specified phonological information in the input is that the first phonological vowel of *Limit* is unary (cf. tableau 3.24 for another analysis where it is lexically specified that a vowel is unary). Consider tableau 4.57.

Tab. 4.57

<Li.mit>$_{nc}$, 1st syll.: /UN/	I-IO[UNBIN]	GEM	MAX	DEP	UNBIN
a. ˈlɪmɪt					*
☞ b. ˈliː.mɪt	*!				

Let us now turn to polysyllabic words in German. Once the foot structure is assigned to a trisyllabic word (cf. §4.4.1), the mapping is quite easy. The only plausible candidates for the decoding of a graphematic word like <(Ka.na).(pee)> are a phonological one-foot and a phonological two-foot structure, *(Ka. na).(pee)* or *Ka.(na. pee)*. The decisive constraint in this evaluation is HEADMATCH. Thus *(Ka. na).(pee)* is selected.

Tables 4.58 and 4.59 summarise the final rankings of the constraints under discussion. Each column in these tables represents one stratum within the constraint hierarchy.

Tab. 4.58: Ranking for German

HEADMATCH *GEMINATE-COMPL PWELL GWELL SYLLABIFY IDENT-IO[UNBIN] (IDENT-OO[UNBIN]) DEP(GI/GO)	GEMINATE (GEMINATE$_{can}$)	DEP MAX	UNARYBINARY (MINSYLL)

Tab. 4.59: Ranking for English

HEADMATCH *GEMINATE-COMPL PWELL GWELL UNARYBINARY *<VV> (MINSYLL)	GEMINATE$_{can}$	MAX	DEP	GEMINATE

The rankings are quite similar in German and English. There are five strata within the hierarchies. In both languages, the first stratum contains most of the constraints. There are some constraints in brackets. These constraints are not relevant for the analysis at hand, but since they were introduced in §3.2.1 they are mentioned here in order to get a full ranking. Moreover there are some constraints that do not appear in both rankings. The IDENT-IO-constraints and DEP(G-INPUT/G-OUTPUT) are not mentioned in the English evaluations since they are simply not necessary. In the analysis of irregular bisyllabic words with single c-letters corresponding to ambisyllabic consonants such as *Limit* in German, for instance, an IDENT-IO constraint ensures that the lexically specified information that the first v-letter maps onto a binary phonological vowel is realised in the output. In the corresponding analysis of English, this constraint is not needed since the syllable boundary in connection with a high-ranking constraint UNARYBINARY ensures the correct mapping relation. The fact that the constraints do not appear in the final ranking of English does not mean that they do not exist in English, it only means that they are not relevant and that their ranking in the constraint hierarchy is thus not of interest. Other constraints that do not appear are the different versions of MAX and DEP. Only instances of MAX and DEP that rank differently from the other faithfulness constraints are mentioned separately in the table. This is why DEP(GI/GO) appears in the ranking of German but not in the ranking of English.

Comparing the two rankings, we can see that there are some constraints which are undominated in both languages. These are HEADMATCH, GEMINATE-COMPL, PWELL and GWELL. There are two crucial differences in the ranking. First, UNARYBINARY is undominated in English, while it is in the lowest stratum of the German hierarchy. However, this does not render UNARYBINARY irrelevant in German. In the decoding perspective it plays an important role, cf. tableau 4.53. We have found this difference in rankings also earlier in §3.2.2.

The second difference concerns the GEMINATE constraint. Given the results from the CELEX search concerning ambisyllabicity coding in bisyllabic words in §4.1 and §4.2, it is plausible to assume that GEMINATE is a high-ranking constraint in German, both in canonical and non-canonical structures. A model like this produces least lexical exceptions. In the analysis of the ambisyllabicity (de)coding in English, we accounted for the difference between canonical and non-canonical structures by ranking the indexed version of GEMINATE differently from the general version of GEMINATE. The indexed version GEMINATE_{can} ranks equally high as the GEMINATE constraint family in German. The general version, however, ranks lowest of the relevant constraints presented here.

The approach presented above is a working optimality theoretic model of correspondences of graphematic and phonological feet in English and German. However, it is quite cumbersome to evaluate the coding and the decoding perspective separately, although they are clearly interdependent. The bidirectional character of some of the constraints presented above (for instance, UNARYBINARY) suggest that writing systems are not optimised for one perspective only but for both perspectives simultaneously.

Employing the framework of *bidirectional Optimality Theory* (biOT), I will present an optimality theoretic approach that will address the issues raised above in the following section.

4.4.3 A Bidirectional OT-approach

In the previous subsections, I presented an analysis in a unidirectional Optimality Theory framework. In a unidirectional analysis, the evaluation can either take the perspective graphematics to phonology or phonology to graphematics. That is, either we evaluate the coding or decoding of a graphematic word.

We have already seen in the analyses in this chapter and in chapter 3 that there are constraints which are applicable to both perspectives; UNARYBINARY, for example, is a bidirectional constraint, which captures the coding and decoding perspectives simultaneously. Moreover it is sensible to assume that writing systems are not optimised unidirectionally for readers or writers but for both perspectives at the same time. Thus, a bidirectional analysis seems to be a very reasonable approach to a formal analysis of writing systems.

The framework of bidirectional Optimality theory (Blutner 2000, 2002; Jäger 2002) is such a formal framework for a bidirectional analysis. After a basic introduction to bidirectional OT, I will present an analysis of the graphematic foot in English and German within this framework.

4.4.3.1 Bidirectional OT

Bidirectional OT was applied first in the semantics/pragmatics interface. In order to make the basic concepts of bidirectional optimality theory more accessible, I will briefly summarise the main ideas of Blutner's (2000, 2002) bidirectional approach with respect to the semantics/pragmatics interface.

Analyses in unidirectional OT in phonology, morphology, or syntax generally have an abstract input. The candidates, which are evaluated, are realisations of this input. The output is the optimal realisation. Thus, in these analyses a production perspective is taken (cf. Blutner 2002: 159-160). While most OT-approaches in syntax, morphology, and phonology have a production perspective, most OT-approaches in semantics have an interpretative perspective, i.e. interpretations of a concrete input are competing.

Blutner (2000: 193), however, points out that "in the case of syntax, we cannot explain interpretative preferences when we take the production perspective alone. In the case of semantics/pragmatics we cannot explain blocking effects when we take the comprehension perspective alone."

One example of a blocking effect is the lexical blocking of 'conceptual grinding.' Conceptual grinding denotes the phenomenon that some countable nouns acquire a mass noun reading denoting the material the individual objects are made of. For instance, the word *fish* can denote countable animals as in *fish live underwater* but also the flesh of fish as in *fish is on the menu.*

Some specialised mass terms, e.g. *pork, beef, wood,* usually block conceptual grinding of related count nouns, e.g. *pig, cow, tree* (Blutner 2000: 193).

(59) a. I ate pork/?pig.
b. Some persons are forbidden to eat beef/?cow.
c. The table is made of wood/?tree.

This blocking effect is not explicable by taking only the perception perspective into account. Blutner (2000) argues, however, that this effect can be explained by a bidirectional model, which takes the production *and* perception point of view into consideration. A proper OT-treatment of semantics/pragmatics therefore has to consider both perspectives at the same time: an expression is blocked with regard to a certain interpretation if this interpretation can be generated more economically by an alternative expression.

In bidirectional OT, the production and comprehension perspective is taken simultaneously by evaluating pairs of objects. In the case of the semantic/syntactic interface, a pair is formed by a linguistic expression, A, and an interpretation, τ. A pair $\langle A, \tau \rangle$ is evaluated by constraints which may apply to one part of the pair, or to a relationship, such as a mapping-relationship, between the parts of a pair (cf. Blutner 2000, Jäger 2002 for a formal definition of the bidirectional framework).

Blutner (2000) formulates two versions of the bidirectional OT (biOT), the strong and the weak biOT. In the strong biOT, exactly one winner is selected. Consider the following definition of the strong version of the bidirectional Optimality Theory:

(60) *Bidirectional OT (strong Version)* (cf. Blutner 2000: 199-200, Beaver & Lee 2004: 123)
$\langle A, \tau \rangle$ is strong optimal iff
a. $\langle A, \tau \rangle \in$ **Gen**
b. there is no $\langle A', \tau \rangle \in$ **Gen** such that $\langle A, \tau \rangle \succ \langle A', \tau \rangle$, and
c. there is no $\langle A, \tau' \rangle \in$ **Gen** such that $\langle A, \tau \rangle \succ \langle A, \tau' \rangle$.

In the definition above, $\langle A, \tau\rangle \succ \langle A', \tau\rangle$ means that relative to τ, A' is more harmonic than A, and $\langle A, \tau\rangle \succ \langle A, \tau'\rangle$ means that relative to A, τ' is more harmonic than τ. A pair $\langle A, \tau\rangle$ thus satisfies condition b. in the definition above if A is an optimal production that can be generated starting with τ, while a pair $\langle A, \tau\rangle$ satisfies condition c. in the definition above if τ is an optimal outcome of interpreting A. In other words, a pair $\langle A, \tau\rangle$ is strong optimal if there is no better A' than A relative to τ, and there is no better τ' than τ relative to A.

This definition exhibits the major difference to unidirectional OT: the constraints of unidirectional OT evaluate candidates, i.e. possible output forms in relation to the input. In bidirectional OT, however, the perspective is interchangeable; the input can be seen as output and vice versa. Thus, the input *and* the output are evaluated at the same time. The winner of an evaluation is an input-output pair that performs better than the other pairs in the evaluation.

I will demonstrate an evaluation in strong biOT with the help of an abstract example. Let us assume that there are two constraints called F and C. F is a constraint on linguistic forms, in other words, a markedness constraint; C is a constraint on resulting contexts and refers to coherence and informativeness. These constraints are not ranked. A_1 and A_2 are two linguistic forms that are semantically equivalent. τ_1 and τ_2 are two interpretations. Let us say that A_1, but not A_2, satisfies F and that τ_1, but not τ_2, satisfies C.

Tab. 4.60: Example of an evaluation in strong bidirectional OT (Blutner 2000: 201)

Forms		F	C		F	C
A_1	☞➸			☞		★
A_2	➸	★			★	★
Interpretations		τ_1			τ_2	

Consider the Tableau above. The symbol ☞ marks the optimal candidate when the production perspective is taken, ➸ indicates the optimal candidate when the perception perspective is taken. The pair $\langle A_1, \tau_1\rangle$ is strong optimal, i.e. it is optimal in both perspectives and blocks form A_2 in all its (semantically admissible) interpretations.

A strong biOT-analysis like this can be used to describe *total blocking*. For example, a form like **fallacity* does not exist because it is blocked by the form *fallacy*.

Blocking, however, is not always total. One example of partial blocking is the use of productive (periphrastic) causatives (61b) versus the use of lexical causatives (61a) (Blutner 2000: 202).

(61) a. Black Bart killed the sheriff.
b. Black Bart caused the sheriff to die.

The form in (61a) is usually used in a stereotypical causative situation (direct, unmediated causation through physical action), while the form in (61b) is usually used in a more marked situation, e.g. an indirect action, for instance when Black Bart caused the sheriff's gun to backfire by stuffing it with cotton (Blutner 2000: 202). An expression like (61b) is blocked in a stereotypical causative situation.

The bidirectional OT model presented so far cannot explain *partial* blocking. The strong version of bidirectional OT assumes that a form-interpretation pair $\langle A, \tau \rangle$ is bidirectionally optimal only if two conditions are met: (i) τ is optimal for A and A is optimal for τ, and (ii) the bidirections of optimization are independent of each other, in other words, one perspective does not influence the other perspective (Blutner 2000: 203). If we drop the second condition, i.e., if we allow the mutual influence of perspectives, bidirectional OT can describe partial blocking; consider the following recursive definition of a weak version of bidirectional Optimality Theory:

(62) *Bidirectional OT (weak version)* (cf. Blutner 2000, Jäger 2000)

$\langle A, \tau \rangle$ is super-optimal iff
a. $\langle A, \tau \rangle \in$ **Gen**,
b. There is no super-optimal $\langle A', \tau \rangle \in$ **Gen** such that $\langle A', \tau \rangle \succ \langle A, \tau \rangle$, and
c. There is no super-optimal $\langle A, \tau' \rangle \in$ **Gen** such that $\langle A, \tau' \rangle \succ \langle A, \tau \rangle$.

A super-optimal pair $\langle A, \tau \rangle$ is thus a pair that has no competitor that is itself super-optimal and comprises either A or τ. Reconsider the example from above in the weak version of OT, cf. Tableau 4.61.

Tab. 4.61: Example of an evaluation in weak bidirectional OT (Blutner 2000: 204)

Forms		F	C		F	C
A_1	☞➵					*
A_2		*		☞➵	*	*
Interpretations		τ_1			τ_2	

Let us have a look at the A_1-row (perception perspective). Since τ_1 satisfies C while τ_2 does not, ➻ selects τ_1. Now we switch the perspective and start with τ_1: A_1 performs better than A_2 and is therefore selected by ☞. This means that just like in the strong version, the pair $\langle A_1, \tau_1 \rangle$ is *super-optimal.*

Let us switch the perspectives again. We start with A_2. The unmarked form A_1 blocks $\{\tau_1\}$ (cf. 62). ➻ therefore selects τ_2. An analogous argument applies to the production perspective starting with τ_2. ☞ has to select A_2 since τ_1 blocks A_1. In contrast to the strong bidirectional OT, there are two *super-optimal* candidates in weak bidirectional OT, in this case $\langle A_1, \tau_1 \rangle$ and $\langle A_2, \tau_2 \rangle$.

That there is a second super-optimal pair $\langle A_2, \tau_2 \rangle$ might be confusing at first glance; after all, both elements of the pair are marked. In order to illustrate weak biOT better, let us examine the case of partial blocking mentioned above, cf. (61).

There are two linguistic forms, A_1: *kill* and A_2: *cause to die*, and there are two interpretations, τ_1: 'direct causation' and τ_2: 'indirect causation.' Thus there are four pairs that will be evaluated:

(63) i. ⟨ *kill*, direct causation ⟩
ii. ⟨ *kill*, indirect causation ⟩
iii. ⟨ *cause to die*, direct causation ⟩
iv. ⟨ *cause to die*, indirect causation ⟩

Let us consider two constraints, BeBrief and BePrecise (cf. Krifka 2002). BeBrief demands that simple and short linguistic forms are used and BePrecise demands that the interpretation must be as informative/ specific as possible. Let us assume that the interpretation 'direct causation' satisfies BePrecise while 'indirect causation' does not. We will use a notation system based on unidirectional OT-tableaux, consider the following tableau:

Tab. 4.62: First round of the evaluation

	BeBrief	BePrecise
✌$_1$ a. ⟨ *kill*, direct causation ⟩		
b. ⟨ *kill*, indirect causation ⟩		*
c. ⟨ *cause to die*, direct causation ⟩	*	
d. ⟨ *cause to die*, indirect causation ⟩	*	*

A super-optimal candidate is indicated by ✌; subscript numbers indicate in which round of the evaluation the candidate was selected. The 1 in this example thus indicates that the pair ⟨*kill*, direct causation⟩ is the super-optimal candidate of the first round of the evaluation. In a strong bidirectional OT, the evaluation would be complete; in the weak model, the evaluation takes another round.

The winning candidate is removed from the tableau. In addition, all blocked candidates are also removed. In this case, candidates b. and c. are blocked. Candidate b. is blocked because A_1, *kill*, has already found its optimal partner with τ_1 in candidate a. Candidate c. is blocked because τ_1, direct causation, is part of the super-optimal pair in candidate a. This leaves candidate d. for the second round of the evaluation.

Tab. 4.63: Second round of the evaluation

	BEBRIEF	BEPRECISE
✌$_2$ a. ⟨*cause to die*, indirect causation ⟩	*	*

Since there are no other (plausible) candidates left and since ⟨*cause to die*, indirect causation⟩ does not comprise any element of the first super-optimal pair, it is the winner of the second round of the evaluation.
The second super-optimal candidate thus is a marked form for a marked interpretation and the first super-optimal candidate is an unmarked form for an unmarked interpretation. BiOT is therefore a suitable model for the emergence of the marked in the sense of Horn (1984) (Blutner 2000).

After this basic introduction to bidirectional OT, we will employ the framework of weak bidirectional OT in analysing the graphematic foot in English and German. One obvious difference to the analysis of the semantics/pragmatics interface is that there are no form-meaning pairs in graphematics but pairs composed of graphematic and phonological representations. Moreover, the following analysis is about the correspondences of two modalities and not like in the examples above about speakers and hearers.

4.4.3.2 Graphematic Feet in biOT

For an analysis of the graphematic foot in bidirectional OT we will adopt the constraints discussed in the previous sections. A few constraints need reconsideration, though. In the analyses in §4.4.2 we employed the constraints MAX and DEP. These constraints are violated if segments of the input are not realised in the output (MAX) or if segments in the output do not have correspondents in the input

(Dep). We formulated four Max and Dep constraints in (53) in §4.4.2. Since the notions of input and output are interchangeable in bidirectional OT, we can drop two of these constraints and reformulate the remaining ones:

(64) a. MaxP:
All phonological segments correspond to graphematic segments.
b. MaxG:
All graphematic segments correspond to phonological segments.

Note that it is not necessary to formulate Max *and* Dep constraints. Because the coding and decoding perspective is interchangeable in a bidirectional analysis, a distinction between Dep and Max is not meaningful: The constraint MaxP is equivalent to a constraint DepG and the constraint MaxG is equivalent to a constraint DepP.

Let us begin with the examination of the (de)coding of vowel quantity in English. We consider three graphematic and three phonological forms, cf. table 4.64.[30]

Tab. 4.64: Parts of candidates in tableau 4.65

Graphematic forms	Phonological forms
g1: <mad>	*p1*: /mæd/
g2: <ma.de>	*p2*: /meɪd/
g3: <ma>	*p3*: /mɑː/

These forms can be combined to 3 × 3 = 9 pairs. In the first step of the evaluation, we determine the pair that performs best with respect to the constraints and relative to the other pairs.
In tableau 4.65 there are two candidates that perform equally well, thus there are two super-optimal pairs, a. and i. There is no better partner for <mad> than /mæd/ and vice versa because all of the other pairs that comprise one of the two elements perform worse than ⟨<mad>, /mæd/⟩. For the same reason <ma> is the optimal partner for /mɑː/ and vice versa.

Since these two pairs are super-optimal, they block other pairs which comprise at least one of their elements. This means, every pair that comprises /mɑː/, /mæd/, <mad>, or <ma> is blocked, cf. tableau 4.66.

30 Note that I use tableau with rotated constraint labels for the illustrations of biOT evaluations in order to optically separate them from illustrations of unidirectional OT evaluations.

Tab. 4.65: First round of the evaluation

			UnBin	MaxP	MaxG
✌$_1$	a.	⟨ <mad>, /mæd/ ⟩			
	b.	⟨ <mad>, /meɪd/ ⟩	*		
	c.	⟨ <mad>, /mɑ:/ ⟩	*		*
	d.	⟨ <ma.de>, /mæd/ ⟩	*		*
	e.	⟨ <ma.de>, /meɪd/ ⟩			*
	f.	⟨ <ma.de>, /mɑ:/ ⟩			**
	g.	⟨ <ma>, /mæd/ ⟩	*	*	
	h.	⟨ <ma>, /meɪd/ ⟩		*	
✌$_1$	i.	⟨ <ma>, /mɑ:/ ⟩			

Tab. 4.66: Second round of the evaluation

			UnBin	MaxP	MaxG
✌$_1$	a.	⟨ <mad>, /mæd/ ⟩			
	b.	~~⟨ <mad>, /meɪd/ ⟩~~	*		
	c.	~~⟨ <mad>, /mɑ:/ ⟩~~	*		*
	d.	~~⟨ <ma.de>, /mæd/ ⟩~~	*		*
✌$_2$	e.	⟨ <ma.de>, /meɪd/ ⟩			*
	f.	~~⟨ <ma.de>, /mɑ:/ ⟩~~			**
	g.	~~⟨ <ma>, /mæd/ ⟩~~	*	*	
	h.	~~⟨ <ma>, /meɪd/ ⟩~~		*	
✌$_1$	i.	⟨ <ma>, /mɑ:/ ⟩			

This leaves one pair, candidate e. The evaluation thus yields three super-optimal pairs: ⟨<mad>, /mæd/⟩, ⟨<ma>, /mɑ:/⟩ and ⟨<ma.de>, /meɪd/⟩. The analysis thus predicts correctly the graphematic-phonological pairs in vowel quantity (de)coding in English.

In §3.2.2, we discussed why in graphematic words such as <ma.de> the first syllable is opened by <e> and not by another v-letter. The reasoning was as follows: only <e> is licensed in the peak of a reduced graphematic syllable. Among reduced graphematic syllables there is a particular class of g-syllables called minimal syllables. These g-syllables end in <e> and have the property that their nuclei do not correspond to phonologically nuclei. Syllables ending in another v-letter, e.g. <o>, are not minimal reduced g-syllables, their nuclei thus correspond to phonological nuclei.

This property of the minimal reduced g-syllable is expressed by the constraint MINSYLL stating that the nucleus of a minimal g-syllable does not correspond to a phonological nucleus and by the constraint DEPNUC stating that every nucleus in the output corresponds to a nucleus in the input. While in unidirectional analyses two constraints are needed, one for the coding, one for the decoding perspective, bidirectional analyses can do with one constraint, consider the following tableau:

Tab. 4.67

			UNBIN	MINSYLL	MAXP	MAXG
☞1	a.	⟨ <ma.do>, /ˈmɑː.dəʊ/ ⟩				
	b.	⟨ <ma.do>, /ˈmeɪd/ ⟩				*
	c.	⟨ <ma.de>, /ˈmɑː.dəʊ/ ⟩		*		
☞2	d.	⟨ <ma.de>, /ˈmeɪd/ ⟩				*

Candidate a. does not violate any constraint, this pair is thus super-optimal and blocks every other candidate which comprises either the graphematic form <ma.do> or the phonological form /mɑː.dəʊ/. Thus, the candidates b. and c. are blocked and candidate d. is the second super-optimal candidate of this evaluation.

The best competitor of candidate d., candidate b. is blocked by the super-optimal pair a. In a bidirectional OT-analysis, we can therefore at least give up one of the two constraints needed in a unidirectional analysis (either DEPNUC or MINSYLL).

Let us now move on to ambisyllabicity (de)coding. The forms in table 4.68 are the basis for the forthcoming evaluation in tableau 4.69.
There are three graphematic and two phonological forms, we thus evaluate $3 \times 2 = 6$ pairs in tableau 4.69.

Tab. 4.68: Parts of candidates in tableau 4.69

Graphematic forms	Phonological forms
g1: <la.ter>	*p1*: /laṭər/
g2: <lat.er>	*p2*: /leɪ.tər/
g3: <lat.ter>	

Tab. 4.69

			UNBIN	GEM$_{can}$	MAXP	MAXG	GEM
☞$_1$	a.	⟨ <la.ter>, /ˈleɪ.tər/ ⟩					
	b.	⟨ <la.ter>, /ˈlaṭər/ ⟩	*	*			*
	c.	⟨ <lat.er>, /ˈleɪ.tər/ ⟩	*				
	d.	⟨ <lat.er>, /ˈlaṭər/ ⟩		*			*
	e.	⟨ <lat.ter>, /ˈleɪ.tər/ ⟩	*			*	
☞$_2$	f.	⟨ <lat.ter>, /ˈlaṭər/ ⟩				*	

As we have seen above, a pair like ⟨<la.ter>, /leɪ.tər/⟩ does not violate any of the relevant constraints; as there is no better partner for either of the two elements of the pair, it is super-optimal. The super-optimal pair a. thus blocks every candidate comprising any of its parts: candidates b., c., and e. This leaves two candidates, d. and f. These two candidates are competitors since they comprise the same phonological form. This means that only one of them can be super-optimal.

Candidate f. performs better than candidate d. Thus, the graphematic form <lat.ter> is the best partner for the phonological form /ˈlaṭər/; in other words, d. is the second super-optimal candidate.

Let us now turn to canonical structures in German. We begin with a case similar to the one evaluated above; consider the German words *Matte* 'mat' and *Mate* 'maté' with the graphematic forms <Mat.te> and <Ma.te> and the phonological forms /maṭə/ and /maːtə/, cf. table 4.70.
Like in the evaluation above, there are three graphematic and two phonological forms, we thus evaluate 3 × 2 = 6 pairs in tableau 4.71.

Tab. 4.70: Parts of candidates in tableau 4.71

Graphematic forms	Phonological forms
g1: <Ma.te>	*p1*: /maːtə/
g2: <Mat.e>	*p2*: /maṭə/
g3: <Mat.te>	

Tab. 4.71

			Gem	Syllabify	MaxP	MaxG	UnBin	MinSyll
✌$_1$	a.	⟨ <Ma.te>, /ˈmaːtə/ ⟩						*
	b.	⟨ <Ma.te>, /ˈmaṭə/ ⟩	*				*	*
	c.	⟨ <Mat.e>, /ˈmaːtə/ ⟩		*			*	*
	d.	⟨ <Mat.e>, /ˈmaṭə/ ⟩	*	*				*
	e.	⟨ <Mat.te>, /ˈmaːtə/ ⟩				*	*	*
✌$_2$	f.	⟨ <Mat.te>, /ˈmaṭə/ ⟩				*		*

The super-optimal pair ⟨<Ma.te>, /ˈmaːtə/⟩ blocks candidates b., c., and e. leaving candidates d. and f. These candidates share the same phonological form, this means that they cannot be simultaneously super-optimal. However, because of d.'s violations of Geminate, candidate f. performs better and is thus the second super-optimal pair and blocks the competing candidate d.

This evaluation resembles the evaluations we have seen in English above. Let us thus consider a case in which German and English differ more: the (de)coding of monosyllabic words with binary phonological vowels (cf. tableau 4.66 for the analysis of the (de)coding of English monosyllabic words with binary phonological vowel). Let us reconsider the word <Tag> – /taːk/ 'day'.

A bidirectional analysis similar to the one proposed for English or the German case above, would yield ⟨<Tag>, /ˈtak/⟩ with a unary p-vowel in the phonological form as super-optimal pair. This super-optimal pair would block any other pair which comprises the graphematic form <Tag>; thus also the pair ⟨<Tag>, /ˈtaːk/⟩, which is the actual pair found in German. An analysis like that therefore seems to be incorrect and needs some consideration.

In §3.2.2 we argued that the reason why words such as <Tag> are decoded with a binary vowel can be explained by paradigmatic leveling. Paradigmatic leveling denotes the tendency that morphologically related units, such as stems, have identical representations. A word like <Tag> has syllabic suffixes in its inflectional paradigm: all plural forms (and optionally Genitive and Dative Singular) have a syllabic suffix, e.g. *Tag+e*. Due to onset maximation (cf. §1.2), the syllabic structure is [taː.gə] with an open and strong syllable. Because no strong syllable ends with a unary p-vowel, the first syllable of [taː.gə] has a binary p-vowel. As a result of paradigmatic leveling, all p-vowels of the paradigm have the same form. Because unary vowels are not licensed in open and strong syllables, all p-vowels of the paradigm have a binary p-vowel in the first syllable. This reasoning applies for most of monosyllabic words with a single final consonant which have an inflectional paradigm with syllabic suffixes (cf. table 3.21 for the phonological and graphematic paradigm of *Tag*).

In the unidirectional approach in §3.2.2, paradigmatic leveling is seen as output-output faithfulness relation. In the input, there are two graphematic forms, one form without a syllabic suffix and one form with syllabic suffix; accordingly there are two phonological forms in the output. The constraint IDENT-OO[UnBin] is violated when the vowels in the output differ with respect to their status as being unary or binary.

Let us transfer this unidirectional model into a bidirectional model. First, the graphematic-phonological pair must be expanded. The phonological and the graphematic element must consist of at least two forms each, e.g. ⟨<Tag, Ta.ge>, /ˈtaːk, ˈtaː.gə/⟩. Second, the constraint must be reformulated since input and output are irrelevant notions in a bidirectional OT approach:

(65) IDENT-P[UnBin]:
Let α be a phonological vowel in p-form$_1$ and β be its correspondent in p-form$_2$. If α is unary, then β is unary and if α is binary, then β is binary.

Let us also consider a constraint accounting for stem constancy of the graphematic form:

(66) IDENT-G[Gem]:
Let α be a c-letter in g-form$_1$ and β be its correspondent in g-form$_2$. If α is geminated, then β is geminated.

The next step is to consider the parts which make up the candidate pairs. We will examine two variables: graphematic forms can either display c-letter gemination or not and phonological forms may have a unary vowel in their first syllables or not (note that a unary vowel in a strong first syllable within a bisyllabic foot correlates with ambisyllabicity if there is only one intervocalic consonant). Table 4.72 gives an overview of the parts the candidate pairs are composed of.

Tab. 4.72: Parts of candidate pairs in tableau 4.73

Graphematic Forms				***Phononological Forms***			
Variable	Form	Variable	Form	Variable	Form	Variable	Form
Gem –	*Tag*	Gem –	*Ta.ge*	Bin –	tak	Bin –	tag̣ə
Gem –	*Tag*	Gem +	*Tag.ge*	Bin –	tak	Bin +	ta:.gə
Gem +	*Tagg*	Gem –	*Ta.ge*	Bin +	ta:k	Bin –	tag̣ə
Gem +	*Tagg*	Gem +	*Tag.ge*	Bin +	ta:k	Bin +	ta:.gə

We will examine every possible combination of these parts without judging their likeliness a priori. There are four combinations for the graphematic part of the candidate pairs and four combinations for the phonological part of the candidate pair; this means that there are 4 × 4 = 16 pairs we need to consider in tableau 4.73.[31]

This rather complicated looking evaluation in tableau 4.73 needs some explanation. There are 16 candidate pairs in tableau 4.73. These pairs are all the possible combinations of the parts in table 4.72. The pair performing best with respect to the constraints and relative to the other candidates is candidate d. It only incurs one violation of UNARYBINARY because the first form of the graphematic part of the pair, <Tag>, has a closed (first) g-syllable, while the corresponding p-syllable, /ta:k/, has a binary p-vowel. Thus there is no better partner for <Tag, Ta.ge> than /ta:k, ta:.gə/ and vice versa; the pair is super-optimal.

The super-optimal pair blocks every pair with the graphematic part <Tag, Ta.ge>, i.e. candidates a, b. and c., and every pair with the phonological part /ta:k, ta:.gə/, i.e. candidates h., l., and p. (keep in mind that the parts of the pairs are treated like one unit although the parts consists of more than one element). Let us have a look at the next tableau in which all candidates blocked by the first super-optimal pair are indicated, cf. tableau 4.74.

31 I left the constraint SYLLABIFY out since no candidate incurs a violation of it.

Tab. 4.73: First round of the evaluation

			IDENT-P[UNBIN]	IDENT-G[GEM]	GEM	MAXP	MAXG	UNBIN	MINSYLL
	a.	⟨<Tag, Ta.ge>, /tak, tag̣ə/⟩			*			*	*
	b.	⟨<Tag, Ta.ge>, /tak, taː.gə/⟩	*						*
	c.	⟨<Tag, Ta.ge>, /taːk, tag̣ə/⟩	*		*				*
✌$_1$	d.	⟨<Tag, Ta.ge>, /taːk, taː.gə/⟩						*	*
	e.	⟨<Tag, Tag.ge>, /tak, tag̣ə/⟩		*			*		*
	f.	⟨<Tag, Tag.ge>, /tak, taː.gə/⟩	*	*			*	*	*
	g.	⟨<Tag, Tag.ge>, /taːk, tag̣ə/⟩	*	*			*	*	*
	h.	⟨<Tag, Tag.ge>, /taːk, taː.gə/⟩		*			*	**	*
	i.	⟨<Tagg, Ta.ge>, /tak, tag̣ə/⟩		*	*		*	*	*
	j.	⟨<Tagg, Ta.ge>, /tak, taː.gə/⟩	*	*			*		*
	k.	⟨<Tagg, Ta.ge>, /taːk, tag̣ə/⟩	*	*	*		*	*	*
	l.	⟨<Tagg, Ta.ge>, /taːk, taː.gə/⟩		*			*	*	*
	m.	⟨<Tagg, Tag.ge>, /tak, tag̣ə/⟩					**		*
	n.	⟨<Tagg, Tag.ge>, /tak, taː.gə/⟩	*				**	*	*
	o.	⟨<Tagg, Tag.ge>, /taːk, tag̣ə/⟩	*				**	*	*
	p.	⟨<Tagg, Tag.ge>, /taːk, taː.gə/⟩					**	**	*

Of the pairs that are not blocked by the first super-optimal pair, candidate m. performs best. This pair is thus super-optimal and blocks candidates e., i., n., and o. The only remaining pairs are candidates f., g., j., and k. In the next tableau displaying the third round of the evaluation, all candidates that are blocked so far are purged, cf. tableau 4.75.

The best performing candidate of the third round of the evaluation is candidate j. This super-optimal output blocks candidate f. and k. This leaves candidate g., which is thus the super-optimal output of the fourth round of the evaluation.

Tab. 4.74: Second round of the evaluation

			IDENT-P[UNBIN]	IDENT-G[GEM]	GEM	MAXP	MAXG	UNBIN	MINSYLL
	a.	~~⟨<Tag, Ta.ge>, /tak, tag̣ə/⟩~~			*			*	*
	b.	~~⟨<Tag, Ta.ge>, /tak, taː.gə/⟩~~	*						*
	c.	~~⟨<Tag, Ta.ge>, /taːk, tag̣ə/⟩~~	*		*				*
☞$_1$	d.	⟨<Tag, Ta.ge>, /taːk, taː.gə/⟩						*	*
	e.	⟨<Tag, Tag.ge>, /tak, tag̣ə/⟩		*			*		*
	f.	⟨<Tag, Tag.ge>, /tak, taː.gə/⟩	*	*			*	*	*
	g.	⟨<Tag, Tag.ge>, /taːk, tag̣ə/⟩	*	*			*	*	*
	h.	~~⟨<Tag, Tag.ge>, /taːk, taː.gə/⟩~~		*			*	**	*
	i.	⟨<Tagg, Ta.ge>, /tak, tag̣ə/⟩		*	*		*	*	*
	j.	⟨<Tagg, Ta.ge>, /tak, taː.gə/⟩	*	*			*		*
	k.	⟨<Tagg, Ta.ge>, /taːk, tag̣ə/⟩	*	*	*		*	*	*
	l.	~~⟨<Tagg, Ta.ge>, /taːk, taː.gə/⟩~~		*			*	*	*
☞$_2$	m.	⟨<Tagg, Tag.ge>, /tak, tag̣ə/⟩					**		*
	n.	⟨<Tagg, Tag.ge>, /tak, taː.gə/⟩	*				**	*	*
	o.	⟨<Tagg, Tag.ge>, /taːk, tag̣ə/⟩	*				**	*	*
	p.	~~⟨<Tagg, Tag.ge>, /taːk, taː.gə/⟩~~					**	**	*

Let us examine the super-optimal pairs of the evaluation more closely. The first super-optimal pair, ⟨<Tag, Ta.ge>, /taːk, taː.gə/⟩ is the actual (de)coding of *Tag, Tage*. The other pairs do not occur in German. How can we interpret these results if these examples do not occur in the examined language?

The answer to this question lies within the definition of super-optimality: If there *was* a paradigm /tak, tag̣ə/ it would be coded <Tagg, Tag.ge>. and if there *were* the paradigms /tak, taː.ge/ and /taːk, tag̣ə/, they would be coded <Tag, Tag.ge> and <Tagg, Ta.ge> respectively; or taking the other perspective, if there were the related graphematic forms <Tagg, Tag.ge> they would be decoded /tak, tag̣ə/ and if there were the related graphematic forms <Tag, Tag.ge> and <Tagg,

Tab. 4.75: Third round of the evaluation

			IDENT-P[UNBIN]	IDENT-G[GEM]	GEM	MAXP	MAXG	UNBIN	MINSYLL
✌$_1$	d.	⟨<Tag, Ta.ge>, /ta:k, ta:.gə/⟩						*	*
✌$_2$	m.	⟨<Tagg, Tag.ge>, /tak, tag̣ə/⟩					**		*
	f.	⟨<Tag, Tag.ge>, /tak, ta:.gə/⟩	*	*			*	*	*
✌$_4$	g.	⟨<Tag, Tag.ge>, /ta:k, tag̣ə/⟩	*	*			*	*	*
✌$_3$	j.	⟨<Tagg, Ta.ge>, /tak, ta:.gə/⟩	*	*			*		*
	k.	⟨<Tagg, Ta.ge>, /ta:k, tag̣ə/⟩	*	*	*		*	*	*

Ta.ge>, they would be decoded /tak, ta:.gə/ and /ta:k, tag̣ə/ respectively. The biOT-analysis thus shows how the system works and which forms conform to the system; if these forms are used in a language is another question.

We can therefore regard the unused super-optimal pairs as predictions or patterns: for the pattern ⟨<Tagg, Tag.ge>, /tak, ˈtag̣ə/⟩ we can find the real example ⟨<nass, nas.se>, /nas, naṣə/⟩ ‘wet’. This pair is an example of ambisyllabicity (de)coding and graphematic stem constancy in a bisyllabic (canonical) structure in German.

There are no examples, however, for the third and fourth super-optimal candidates. This is explicable by their very unlikely phonological paradigms: both paradigms do not display paradigmatic leveling. We can interpret the prediction of the biOT-evaluation as follows: if there were words in German without paradigmatic leveling, they would be (de)coded like the candidates g. and j. in tableau 4.75.

Now that we have discussed canonical structures, let us move on to noncanonical ones. Let us begin with English cases. We begin with bisyllabic words, consider the forms in 4.76.

Tab. 4.76: Parts of candidates in tableau 4.77

Graphematic forms	Phonological forms
g1: <li.mit>	*p1*: /lɪṃɪt/
g2: <lim.mit>	*p2*: /laɪ.mɪt/
g3: <li.mit>	

Like in the analyses of ambisyllabicity (de)coding in canonical structures above, there is an asymmetry between the number of phonological and graphematic forms. There are three graphematic forms and two phonological forms, which can be combined into six pairs. The asymmetry will mean that one graphematic form will be blocked by the super-optimal candidates, cf. tableau 4.77.[32]

Tab. 4.77

			HeadMatch	UnaryBinary	MaxP	MaxG	Gem
✌$_2$	a.	⟨ <lim.it>, /ˈlɪṃɪt/ ⟩					*
	b.	⟨ <lim.it>, /ˈlaɪ.mɪt/ ⟩		*			
	c.	⟨ <lim.mit>, /ˈlɪṃɪt/ ⟩				*	
	d.	⟨ <lim.mit>, /ˈlaɪ.mɪt/ ⟩		*		*	
	e.	⟨ <li.mit>, /ˈlɪṃɪt/ ⟩		*			*
✌$_1$	f.	⟨ <li.mit>, /ˈlaɪ.mɪt/ ⟩					

The best performing pair is candidate f.; it does not incur any violation. It is super-optimal and blocks thus candidates b., d., and e. Of the remaining candidates, the pair in a. performs best; it incurs only one violation of Geminate because its phonological part features an ambisyllabic consonant but there is no c-letter gemination in the graphematic part of the pair. This super-optimal pair blocks the last remaining candidate c.

32 Note that I have left out the irrelevant constraint Geminate$_{can}$.

Let us compare the evaluation above with a similar evaluation in German. We will consider the following parts of pairs in the forthcoming evaluation, cf. table 4.78.

Tab. 4.78: Parts of candidates in tableau 4.79

Graphematic forms	Phonological forms
g1: <Kom.ma>	*p1*: /ˈkɔṃa/
g2: <Ko.ma>	*p2*: /ˈkoː.ma/
g3: <Kom.a>	

We consider three plausible graphematic forms and two plausible phonological forms. Thus, there are six pairs we will examine in tableau 4.79.

Tab. 4.79

			GEM	SYLLABIFY	MAXP	MAXG	UNBIN
✌$_2$	a.	⟨ <kom.ma>, /ˈkɔṃa/ ⟩				*	
	b.	⟨ <kom.ma>, /ˈkoː.ma/ ⟩				*	*
	c.	⟨ <ko.ma>, /ˈkɔṃa/ ⟩	*				*
✌$_1$	d.	⟨ <ko.ma>, /ˈkoː.ma/ ⟩					
	e.	⟨ <kom.a>, /ˈkɔṃa/ ⟩	*	*			
	f.	⟨ <kom.a>, /ˈkoː.ma/ ⟩		*			*

Candidate d. in tableau 4.79 does not violate any constraint and since there is no better partner for either element of the pair in d., it is super-optimal. It blocks candidates b., c., and f. leaving candidates a. and e. Since the graphematic form of candidate e. violates GEMINATE and the SYLLABIFY it performs worse than candidate a., which is thus the second super-optimal candidate.

Lexical exceptions such as <Li.mit> mapping on /ˈlɪṃɪt/ in German are not discussed in this bidirectional OT analysis of the graphematic foot. The reason is that bidirectional OT analyses reveal systematic patterns. Exceptional patterns thus cannot be captured by an analysis within bidirectional OT (but cf. §4.4.2 for an analysis of such exceptions within a unidirectional OT analysis).

Let us now turn to evaluations in which graphematic weight has an influence. Up until now we have regarded graphematic foot structure for granted, but like in the unidirectional analysis above, it is not a problem to integrate the constraints for graphematic foot structure assignment into the evaluation. I will demonstrate this with the following cases. Let us begin with bisyllabic words in German. This time we will not only consider segmental differences in the graphematic form but also differences in foot structure; cf. table 4.80, in which phonological and (potential) graphematic forms of the words *Arme* 'arms' and *Armee* 'army' are displayed.

Tab. 4.80: Parts of candidates in tableau 4.81

Graphematic forms	Phonological forms
g1: <(Ar.me)>	*p1*: /ˈar.mə/
g2: <Ar.(me)>	*p2*: /ar.ˈmeː/
g3: <(Ar.mee)>	
g4: <Ar.(mee)>	

The first syllables in the round brackets are the heads of the feet the brackets indicate. Note that we examine the most plausible foot structures only, head-final foot structures, for instance, are disregarded.

Tab. 4.81

			WHP	MINIMALITY	HEADMATCH	MAXP	MAXG
☞	a.	⟨ <(Ar.me)>, /ˈar.mə/ ⟩					
	b.	⟨ <(Ar.me)>, /ar.ˈmeː/ ⟩			*		
	c.	⟨ <Ar.(me)>, /ˈar.mə/ ⟩	*	*	*		
	d.	⟨ <Ar.(me)>, /ar.ˈmeː/ ⟩	*	*			
	e.	⟨ <(Ar.mee)>, /ˈar.mə/ ⟩	*				*
	f.	⟨ <(Ar.mee)>, /ar.ˈmeː/ ⟩	*		*		*
	e.	⟨ <Ar.(mee)>, /ˈar.mə/ ⟩			*		
☞	f.	⟨ <Ar.(mee)>, /ar.ˈmeː/ ⟩					

There are two super-optimal candidates in tableau 4.81. These two candidates do not violate any of the relevant constraints and block all other candidates. Tableau 4.81 thus nicely shows how the constraints for graphematic foot assignment can be integrated into a bidirectional analysis.
Let us now examine an evaluation of English words in which graphematic weight plays a role and that may feature graphematic forms with unparsed g-syllables, consider table 4.82.

Tab. 4.82: Parts of candidates in tableau 4.83

Graphematic forms	Phonological forms
g1: <de(vo.te)>	*p1*: /dɪˈvəʊ̯t/
g2: <(de.vo)te>	*p2*: /ˈˈdɛ.vəʊ̯.ˈtiː/
g3: <(de.vo)(tee)>	
g4: <de(vo.tee)>	
g5: <(de.vo)tee>	

Note that the graphematic forms in table 4.82 differ only in one segment: *g1* and *g2* end in <e>, *g3*, *g4*, and *g5* end in <ee>. The foot structure of the graphematic forms is indicated by round brackets, the first graphematic syllables in the brackets are the heads of the feet the brackets indicate.

Candidate f. performs best in tableau 4.83, this pair only incurs one violation of MaxG since one v-letter of the final graphematic diphthong is mute. This super-optimal pair blocks candidate e. and every candidate comprising the phonological form /ˈˈdɛ.vəʊ̯.ˈtiː/.
Of the remaining candidates, candidate a. performs best. This pair is the second super-optimal candidate and blocks the rest of the candidates since all other candidates either comprise the same graphematic form (this is the case in candidate b.) or the same phonological form.

4.4.4 Summary

The aim of this section was to show that graphematic feet in German in English can be analysed within a formal Optimality Theory framework.

In the first two subsections the graphematic foot was analysed within a unidirectional OT framework. In the first subsection, foot assignment was discussed. The OT-analysis revealed that there are no differences between the foot assignment of graphematic feet in English and in German. In both writing sys-

Tab. 4.83

			WHP	MINIMALITY	HEADMATCH	ALIGNR	ALIGNL	MAXP	MAXG	PARSE-σ
☞2	a.	⟨ <de(vo.te)>, /dɪˈvəʊ̯t/ ⟩					*		*	*
	b.	⟨ <de(vo.te)>, /ˈˈdɛ.vəʊ̯.ˈtiː/ ⟩			*		*		*	*
	c.	⟨ <(de.vo)te>, /dɪˈvəʊ̯t/ ⟩			*	*			*	*
	d.	⟨ <(de.vo)te>, /ˈˈdɛ.vəʊ̯.ˈtiː/ ⟩			*	*			*	*
	e.	⟨ <(de.vo)(tee)>, /dɪˈvəʊ̯t/ ⟩			**				**	
☞1	f.	⟨ <(de.vo)(tee)>, /ˈˈdɛ.vəʊ̯.ˈtiː/ ⟩							*	
	e.	⟨ <de(vo.tee)>, /dɪˈvəʊ̯t/ ⟩	*				*		**	*
	f.	⟨ <de(vo.tee)>, /ˈˈdɛ.vəʊ̯.ˈtiː/ ⟩	*		**		*		*	*
	g.	⟨ <(de.vo)tee>, /dɪˈvəʊ̯t/ ⟩	*		**	*			**	*
	h.	⟨ <(de.vo)tee>, /ˈˈdɛ.vəʊ̯.ˈtiː/ ⟩	*		*	*			*	*

tems, graphematic foot structure assignment is mainly guided by the constraint TROCHEE stating that every g-foot is head-initial, by the constraint MINIMALITY stating that feet must either consists of two graphematic syllables or of at least one heavy g-syllable, by WEIGHT-HEAD-PRINCIPLE stating that heavy g-syllables are head of g-feet, and by an alignment constraint stating that every graphematic word ends with a foot. These constraints result in graphematic foot structures which match phonological foot structures very well. However, the foot structures are assigned on basis of these graphematic constraints alone and not by correspondence to phonological foot structures. The influence of purely graphematic weight, which cannot be linked to phonological weight, on graphematic foot structure assignment plays a key role in proving this claim.

In the second subsection a unidirectional OT analysis of the mapping relation of graphematic feet to phonological feet was presented. The constraint HEAD-MATCH, which states that the position of heads of feet must be identical in the input and the output, ensure the correct (de)coding of foot structure. The correct mapping of heads of feet is crucial for foot-sensitive constraints like UNARYBINARY and GEMINATE. Graphematic foot structure is thus indirectly responsible for the correct (de)coding of ambisyllabicity and vowel quantity.

The last subsection showed that the bidirectional OT framework is a suitable framework for graphematics. In unidirectional OT, candidates, i.e. potential outputs, are evaluated with respect to constraints and in relation to the input. Bidirectional OT, on the other hand, considers pairs; in the case of supra-segmental graphematics, pairs of graphematic and phonological structures. This means that the notions of input and output are meaningless in biOT since they are interchangeable. The analysis presented in the last subsection showed that biOT is not only a suitable framework but also a conceptually intuitive one since it can account for the reasonable assumption that writing systems are optimised for the writing and reading perspective alike.

4.5 Summary of this Chapter

In this chapter, I introduced the graphematic foot. It is defined as a sequence of at least one and at most two graphematic syllables. Exactly one syllable of this sequence is the head of the foot. In English and German, graphematic (and phonological) feet are trochaic, that is, they are head-initial.

In both languages, there is a distinction between canonical and non-canonical structures. Canonical feet in English and German are trochees; if they are bisyllabic, they end in a reduced syllable. Canonical words end in a trochee with a reduced syllable. Non-canonical feet, on the other hand, are bisyllabic but do not end in a reduced syllable and non-canonical words either consist of exactly one non-canonical foot or they consist of more than one foot and end in a monosyllabic foot. This definition holds for phonological and graphematic structures.

The graphematic representation of ambisyllabicity and its correlate, i.e., a unary vowel, is different in canonical and non-canonical structures. In canonical structures, ambisyllabicity is systematically represented by c-letter geminates. The absence of c-letter geminates indicates the absence of ambisyllabic consonants, cf. e.g. *later* vs. *latter*, *beten* '(to) pray' vs. *Betten* 'beds'.

As shown in chapter 3, graphematic syllables are often opened by reduced graphematic syllables, especially by minimal graphematic syllables, i.e. graphematic syllables ending in <e>, as in e.g. *mate, late, waste, noble, single, owe*, etc. These minimal syllables, together with the preceding syllable, constitute a canonical trochee. In polysyllabic graphematic words they thus indicate graphematic foot structure, e.g. in *di(vine), re(mote), se(rene), cal(culate), fabri(cate), turpen(tine).*

The representation of binary vowels by g-diphtongs such as <ee> as in *meet*, *Meer* 'sea' is not productive in canonical graphematic structures. In non-canonical structures, however, g-diphthongs are productive and indicate graphematic foot structure by graphematic weight.

Experimental data from pseudoword reading tasks confirm this analysis. The experiments show that the increase of purely graphematic weight (by mute letters) influences the assignment of graphematic foot structure and by that the selection of phonological foot structure. In both experiments presented in this chapter, the graphematic weight of the ultimate syllable of a trisyllabic pseudoword was increased, which led to an enhanced proportion of antepenultimate and ultimate stress. Antepenultimate stress is only explicable by foot structure: the increased weight of the ultimate graphematic syllable leads to the emergence of a monosyllabic final foot and an initial bisyllabic foot.

Data retrieved in the CELEX (Baayen et al. 1995) database show the relevance of graphematic weight for a minimality condition of graphematic feet. Although there are strong phonological monosyllabic words that have only one segment in their rhyme, there are virtually no monosyllabic strong graphematic words with only one segment in the rhyme, cf. e.g. *See* 'sea' but **Se*, *Kuh* 'cow' but **Ku*, *sea*, *bee*, *owe*. This observation leads to the conclusion that there is a minimality constraint for graphematic words as well. Since graphematic words consist of graphematic feet, a monosyllabic graphematic word consists of exactly one monosyllabic foot. The experimental data supports this hypothesis, for example, the experiment of Evertz & Primus (2013) shows that the last graphematic syllable in experimental items such as <Ra.nu.ko> does not constitute a foot of its own, the last syllable in <Ra.nu.koh>, however, does. The database based evidence also shows that the graphematic onset contributes to graphematic syllable weight – at least in German.

In the last section of this chapter, an analysis of the graphematic foot within the framework of Optimality Theory was given. The analysis was given in two models of Optimality Theory, in unidirectional and bidirectional OT. This section shows that OT – especially biOT – is a suitable framework for graphematic feet and other supra-segmental units within the writing systems of English and German.

5 Conclusion

This work examined the graphematic foot in English and German and the properties of subordinate units of the graphematic hierarchy connected with the graphematic foot. I hope that this work, together with the previous works of Primus (2010) and Evertz & Primus (2013), will fill a gap in supra-segmental writing system research by making it possible to establish a complete graphematic counterpart to the phonological hierarchy that contains all major categories from the segment to the graphematic word. This graphematic hierarchy – built on purely graphematic considerations – is hopefully the foundation of further research and might also be relevant for didactic considerations.

In this last chapter, I will address remaining issues and compare the English and German writing system with respect to the graphematic foot.

5.1 Non-linear vs. Linear Approaches

An objection to a supra-segmental analysis like the one presented in this work could be to claim that existing linear analyses can describe and explain the phenomena under discussion (vowel quantity (de)coding, ambisyllabicity (de)coding) with less effort but with the same explanatory strength. Let us discuss if that is true.

A linear account for vowel quantity (de)coding in English is proposed, for example, by Venezky (1999: 83): "In the wordfinal pattern VCe, where V is a stressed, single-letter vowel spelling and C is a simple (consonant) functional unit, <e> generally indicates the free pronunciation of V." In Venezky's terminology, *free* corresponds to binary and *checked* corresponds to unary. Other approaches with a similar line of explanation include Albrow (1972) and Cook (2004).

As Evertz & Primus (2013: 8) point out, linear approaches like these leave many aspects of mute <e> unexplained. First, Venezky's (1999) VCe-rule offers no explanation for the restriction to a single intervening c-grapheme (a functional C unit in Venezky's terms). Second, the stress sensitivity of this pattern is not explicable in a linear model. Third, cases such as *tittle, single, table, noble, waste* and *chaste* cannot be accounted for because there are two or more intervening consonants.

Let us see whether the approach presented here can explain these aspects. As I have argued throughout this work, the presence of 'mute' <e> has structural reasons: the <e> creates a canonical graphematic foot together with the immediately preceding graphematic syllable. As I have shown in §4.1, syllables containing <e>

https://doi.org/10.1515/9783110583441-005

thus give reliable cues to graphematic foot structure. Because graphematic foot structure bidirectionally corresponds to phonological foot structure, these syllables also give reliable cues to phonological foot structure. This explains the stress sensitivity of mute <e>.

With no intervening morphological boundaries, a single graphematically intervocalic c-letter is prone to graphematic onset maximisation, in other words, the c-letter is part of the second syllable in such a configuration and, hence, opens the first g-syllable, cf. e.g. <ma.te>, <ga.te>, <re.mo.te>. In cases in which there are more than one graphematically intervocalic c-letters, two structures are possible. First, in words such as <no.ble>, <ta.ble>, <ti.tle>, <ri.fle> the two intervocalic c-letters can build well-formed onsets and thus are the onsets of the reduced syllable due to graphematic onset maximisation. Just like in the case of <ma.te>, the first graphematic syllable is open and hence maps onto a phonological vowel with a binary p-vowel. Second, if the intervocalic c-letters cannot build well-formed onsets, e.g. <nst> or <tt>, these letters are split up between the syllables, cf. <mon.ster>, <cut.ter>. The first syllable is closed and strong and thus maps onto a phonological syllable with a unary phonological vowel.

This shows that the model presented here can account for cases in which there are more than one c-letters between mute <e> and another v-letter, and it can make reliable predictions about the mapping relation of strong syllables.

The supra-segmental approach presented here and in Primus (2010) and Evertz & Primus (2013) can also explain why there is an <e> in words such as <noble>, <tittle>, <theatre>, etc. Every graphematic syllable needs to have a v-letter in its peak; we dubbed this the graphematic peak constraint in §3.1. Thus, a graphematic form like <nobl> would be graphematically monosyllabic (cf. the graphematically monosyllabic word *Dirndl* 'dirndl dress').

As for gemination, Venezky (1999: 87) states that a "geminate consonant cluster regularly marks a checked correspondent for a preceding vowel." This statement, however, does not capture the foot sensitivity of c-letter geminates.

This foot-sensitivity is twofold, as we have seen in chapter 4. First, the presence of c-letter geminates is connected with ambisyllabicity (cf. Eisenberg 2006). This claim is supported by psycholinguistic studies which report that participants linked the presence of c-letter geminates with the presence of ambisyllabic consonants (cf. Derwing 1992, Treiman & Danis 1988, Treiman et al. 2002, Zamuner & Ohala 1999).[1]

1 Interestingly, Elzinga & Eddington (2013) report an effect of age and education level: the older and the better educated the participants were, the more often did they connect ambisyllabicity to c-letter geminates. Their findings are in line with earlier findings of Treiman et al. (2002) and

Ambisyllabicity, in turn, is linked with foot structure, as shown in §1.2: because the nuclei of stressed syllables are required to branch, syllables with a unary p-vowel need a closing consonant. Together with onset maximisation of the following syllable, this may lead to ambisyllabicity.

The GEMINATE constraint proposed in this work captures the link of c-letter geminates with ambisyllabicity and thus foot structure. It states that an ambisyllabic p-consonant is coded by the gemination of the regular correspondent of that consonant. Furthermore, it specifies that the first element of the c-letter geminate is dominated by the rhyme of the first g-syllable and the second c-letter of the geminate is dominated by the onset of the immediately following g-syllable, cf. §4.1.2.

Second, ambisyllabicity coding is more robust in canonical structures than in non-canonical ones, as shown in §4.1 and §4.2. Linear rules like the one presented above are blind for such differences, but in the analysis offered in §4.4 this difference could be accounted for by two variants of the GEMINATE constraint: an indexed one that applies only to canonical structures and that is highly ranked in the constraint hierarchy, and an unindexed one that applies to all structures and that is relatively low ranking in English (note that these constraints are tied in German, as will be repeated in the last section).

The occurrence of c-letter geminates in graphematically monosyllabic words can partially be explained by an IDENTITY constraint requiring that graphematic representations of paradigms need to be as similar as possible. This tendency, also known as stem constancy, was demonstrated in §4.4.3.2.

Evertz & Primus (2013: 8) point to yet another weakness of linear approaches. Linear approaches like that of Venezky suggest a long-distance backwards marking: mute <e> is claimed to signal a binary vowel backwards across an intervening C-unit; c-gemination is supposed to represent a preceding unary vowel. In contrast, structural analyses like that of Evertz & Primus (2013) and the one presented here claim that these devices are local: mute <e> creates the nucleus of the reduced syllable it belongs to, c-gemination signals the ambisyllabicity of the corresponding consonant. The other functions are explicable by further constraints that govern the distribution of ambisyllabicity, reduced vowels, and their correlates in canonical structures.

Fallows (1981), who both observed a similar interaction for younger children when compared to older children and adults. Elzinga & Eddington (2013) hypothesise that older and more educated speakers may perceive geminates differently, either because they are more likely to have learned the responsible graphematic constraint to the effect that c-letter geminates should be split among syllables, or because their greater experience with the written language means they have had more exposure to written materials that hyphenate between geminate consonants.

In sum, a non-linear model offers the appropriate structural units as explananda for these facts: foot structure and its connection to word structure, stress and syllable structure (cf. Evertz & Primus 2013), while linear approaches like the one sketched above fail to cover the same range of analysis.

5.2 Graphematic syllable boundaries

It is worthwhile to give a thought on whether and how graphematic syllables agree with syllables that emerge in word division. Especially interesting for this matter is <ck>. Rollings (2004: 66) refers to <ck> as a *non-identical geminate* in English. Likewise, Eisenberg (2006) regards <ck> as a c-letter geminate in German although <ck> is indivisible in word division in contemporary German. German orthography prior to the spelling reform in 1996, however, prescribed the hyphenation of <ck> as <k-k> like in <Zuk-ker> 'sugar'. Given the fact that words such as <Zu-cker> are most likely decoded with a unary vowel and with an ambisyllabic consonant in canonical foot structures, we could assume that in some cases, the graphematic syllable boundary differs from the syllable boundary prescribed by orthography. The cause might be the constraint SYLLABIFY that *distorts* the graphematic syllable boundary in orthographically correct word division.

We find a similar situation in the coding of ambisyllabic velar nasals in English. In §3.3 and §4.1.2, I pointed to the example <sing-er>. This word is a bisyllabic canonical trochee featuring an ambisyllabic velar nasal. However, this word is not morphologically simple, but features a suffix. Differently from the situation found in German word division, suffixes are hyphenated at the end of the line in English. This led to the (tentative) assumption in §4.1.2 that the graphematic syllable boundary and the boundary that emerges in word division may not match in this case. Responsible for this mismatch is the morphological word division constraint requiring suffixes to be hyphenated in English.

The English and German examples, however, differ in two important points. First, unlike the cases of words with <ng> in English, there is no variation in German words with <ck>: in all words, <ck> is indivisible. Second, for the mismatch found in English, we can find a morphological reason, for German such a reason cannot be found. The second reason is especially important because only morphological reasons are considered to be legitimate intervening factors in the word division of both languages, cf. §3.3.

Although it is tempting to stipulate a mismatch between the graphematic syllable boundary and the syllable boundary that emerges in word division for the case of <ck> in German, such a stipulation has far reaching consequences. In §2.3, for example, we argued that one reason for regarding <sch> as a complex grapheme of German is the fact that it is indivisible in word division. If we state that syllables emerging in word division are not necessarily identical with graphematic syllables although there is no intervening morphological reason, this argument for <sch> as one complex grapheme is void.[2]

Linked to the discussion there is a small passage in Fuhrhop & Peters (2013) in which it is discussed whether syllable boundaries that emerge in word division are valid arguments for identifying complex graphemes in German. Their main reason to cast doubt on this line of argument is that they are not sure how "natural" word division is, given the fact that for a long time people were instructed to hyphenate according to syllable boundaries that emerge when a word is spoken slowly. They conclude that it remains an open question whether <sch> is a complex grapheme or not, although they tend to regard it as consisting of <s> and <ch> (Fuhrhop & Peters 2013: 206). I will join them in their verdict that the question is still open, although I tend to regard <sch> as one grapheme, cf. §2.3 for a discussion.

5.3 English and German compared

As shown throughout this work, German and English are similar to a considerable degree in structural graphematic terms. The canonical foot structures are trochees ending in reduced syllables in both languages.

In both languages, vowel quantity and ambisyllabicity are coded with similar means: with the foot structures discussed in chapter 4. In canonical structures, ambisyllabicity, and connected with that, vowel quantity, is coded with the presence or absence of c-letter geminates, cf. e.g. <Rat.te> – <ra.te> 'rat', '(I) guess' and <lat.ter> – <la.ter>. The coding of binary vowels with c-letter geminates is not productive in canonical foot structures, as opposed to non-canonical structures. In non-canonical structures, both languages code binary phonological vowels in strong syllables as graphematic diphthongs, cf. <a.(gree)>, <(en.gi.)(neer)>; <(Ma.)(gie)> 'magic', <(Ka.na.)(pee)> 'sofa.'

As shown in the data and in the OT-analysis in chapter 4, German and English differ with respect to the coding of vowel contrast by syllable structure. In English, closed strong g-syllables reliably decode a unary vowel, as, for instances, in <mad>, <nod>, while open strong g-syllables reliably decode a binary phono-

2 This discussion shall not imply that <ck> is a complex grapheme. The indivisibility of this geminate might be caused by the <c>: this letter is not a legitimate g-syllable coda, which might also explain why <k-k> substituted <ck> in German word division prior to 1996.

logical vowel, e.g. <ma.de>, <no.de>. These correspondences also hold in non-canonical structures and seem to be the guiding principle of word division in morphologically simple words in English, e.g. <fu.ture>, <mod.ern>.

We have seen in chapter 3 that this vowel contrast is coded with the help of *minimal syllables* in English. Minimal graphematic syllables are reduced g-syllables that end in <e>. The nuclei of these syllables do not map onto phonological nuclei, in other words, the <e> is mute. With the help of minimal syllables, the prosodic properties of a word can be coded in a minimally invasive way since a minimal g-syllable neither changes the phonological syllable structure nor adds phonological material, cf. §4.1. Minimal syllables create canonical feet and thereby may open g-syllables, as, for instance in <ma.te>, <no.ble>, <di.(vi.ne)>.

Unlike in English, there are no graphematic syllables in German that have mute nuclei. The vowel contrast under discussion is not represented by open vs. closed graphematic syllables in monosyllabic p-words. The words *weg* 'away' with a unary p-vowel and *Weg* 'way' with a binary p-vowel are revealing in this matter. Because *Weg* is part of a paradigm comprising bisyllabic forms, such as *Wege* 'ways', *paradigmatic leveling*, i.e. the tendency that related word forms have the same representation, can be seen as responsible for the vowel being binary. However, paradigmatic leveling is not coded in the graphematic form. Without additional morphological knowledge, monosyllabic graphematic words with a single c-letter closing the syllable are opaque with respect to the vowel contrast under discussion in German.

Another point in which German and English differs is ambisyllabicity coding in non-canonical foot structures. While ambisyllabicity coding is rather unpredictable in non-canonical foot structures in English, there are only few exceptions to GEMINATE in bisyllabic non-canonical foot structures in German. Because of this reason, the constraints GEMINATE and GEMINATE$_{can}$ were analysed as tied in German but differently ranking in English. It has to be noted, however, that the empirical data on which this decision was based on is only fragmentary. While it is true that ambisyllabicity coding in bisyllabic non-canonical words is robust in German, it is possible that this is different in words comprising more than two syllables. Words such as *Kamera* 'camera', *Anorak* 'anorak', *Ananas* 'pineapple', *Kamerad* 'comrade' and *Kapitel* 'chapter' point in this direction.

These examples show that both languages have in common the fact that ambisyllabicity coding in non-canonical structures is less systematic than in canonical structures; the languages differ, however, in the degree of unsystematicity in ambisyllabicity coding in non-canonical structures.

Yet another difference is word division. Word division in morphologically simple words in English is mainly guided by UNARYBINARY. The division of German morphologically simple words, however, is guided by SYLLABIFY, a constraint demanding that a hyphenated syllable begins with exactly one grapheme. Thus, a word like *limit* is hyphenated <lim-it> in English and <Li-mit> in German.

Summarising, we can say that English and German are very similar with respect to supra-segmental properties of their writing systems. The differences addressed in this work can be accounted for by constraint ranking in OT-analyses such as the ones provided here. However, especially with respect to the question of how regular ambisyllabicity coding in non-canonical structures really is, further research is needed.

Bibliography

Alber, Birgit. 1997. Quantity sensitivity as the result of constraint interaction. In G. Booij & J. van de Weijer (eds.), *Phonology in Progress - Progress in Phonology. HIL Phonology Papers III*, 1–45. Holland Academic Graphics.

Albrow, Kenneth Harold. 1972. *The english writing system: Notes towards a description.* London: Longman.

Althaus, Hans Peter. 1980. Graphetik. In H. P. Althaus, H. Henne & E. Wiegand (eds.), *Lexikon der germanistischen Linguistik*, 138–142. Tübingen: Niemeyer.

Anderson, John. M. & Charles Jones. 1974. Three theses concerning phonological representations. *Journal of Linguistics* 10. 1–26.

Aronoff, Mark. 1985. Orthography and linguistic theory. *Language* 61. 28–72.

Augst, Gerhard. 1980. Die graphematische Dehnungsbezeichnung und die Möglichkeiten einer Reform. *Deutsche Sprache* 4. 306–326.

Baayen, R. Harald, Richard Piepenbrock & Leon Gulikers. 1995. *The CELEX Lexical Database (CD-ROM).* Philadelphia, PA: Linguistic Data Consortium, University of Pennsylvania.

Badecker, William. 1996. Representational properties common to phonological and orthographic systems. *Lingua* 99. 55–83.

Baroni, Antonio. 2013. Eye Dialect and Casual Speech Spelling: Orthographic Variation in OT. *Writing Systems Research* 5(1). 24–53.

Beaver, David I. & Hanjung Lee. 2004. Input-Output Mismatches in OT. In Reinhard Blutner & Henk Zeevat (eds.), *Optimality Theory and Pragmatics*, 112–153. Basingstoke: Palgrave/Macmillan.

Berg, Kristian. 2012. Identifying graphematic units. Vowel and consonant letters. *Written Language & Literacy* 15(1). 26–45.

Berg, Kristian, Franziska Buchmann, Katharina Dybiec & Nanna Fuhrhop. 2014. Morphological spellings in English. *Written Language and Literacy* 17(2). 282–307.

Berg, Kristian & Nanna Fuhrhop. 2011. Komplexe Silbenkernschreibungen im Englischen im Vergleich mit dem Deutschen. *Linguistische Berichte* 228. 443–466.

Berg, Kristian, Beatrice Primus & Lutz Wagner. 2016. Buchstabenmerkmal, Buchstabe, Graphem. In Beatrice Primus & Ulrike Domahs (eds.), *Laut – Gebärde – Buchstabe*, 337–355. Berlin/ New York: De Gruyter.

Bleser, Ria de. 1991. Formen und Erklärungsmodelle der erworbenen Dyslexien. In G. Blanken (ed.), *Einführung in die linguistische Aphasiologie. Theorie und Praxis*, 329–347. Freiburg i. Br.: HochschulVerlag.

Bloomfield, Leonard. 1933. *Language.* New York: Henry Holt & Co.

Blutner, Reinhard. 2000. Some Aspects of Optimality in Natural Language Interpretation. *Journal of Semantics* 17. 189–216.

Blutner, Reinhard. 2002. Bidirektionale Optimalitätstheorie. *Kognitionswissenschaft* 9. 158–168.

Bollwage, Max. 2010. *Buchstabengeschichte(n).* Graz: Akademische Druck- und Verlagsanstalt.

Booji, Geert. 1996. Cliticization as a Prosodic Integration: The Case of Dutch. *The Linguistic Review* 13. 219–242.

Bredel, Ursula. 2008. *Die Interpunktion des Deutschen. Ein kompositionelles System zur Online-Steuerung des Lesens.* Tübingen: Niemeyer.

https://doi.org/10.1515/9783110583441-006

Bredel, Ursula. 2009. Das Interpunktionssystem des Deutschen. In Angelika Linke & Helmuth Feilke (eds.), *Oberfläche und Performanz*, 117–135. Tü bingen: Niemeyer.

Brekle, Herbert E. 1994. Die Buchstabenformen westlicher Alphabetschriften in ihrer historischen Entwicklung. In H. Günther & O. Ludwig (eds.), *Schrift und Schriftlichkeit. Ein interdisziplinäres Handbuch internationaler Forschung*, vol. 1, 171–204. Berlin/ New York: de Gruyter.

Brekle, Herbert E. 1999. *Die Antiqualinie von ca. –1500 bis ca. +1500. Untersuchungen zur Morphogenese des westlichen Alphabets auf kognitivistischer Basis.* Münster: Nodus.

Brekle, Herbert E. 2001. Zur handschriftlichen und typographischen Geschichte der Buchstabenligatur ß aus gotisch-deutschen und humanistisch-italienischen Kontexten. In Peter Amelung, Irmgard Bezzel, Otto Böcher & Aloys Ruppel (eds.), *Gutenberg-Jahrbuch 2001*, 67–76. Mainz: Gutenberg-Gesellschaft.

Brentari, Diane. 2012. Phonology. In Roland Pfau, Markus Steinbach & Bencie Woll (eds.), *Sign Language. An International Hanbdbook*, 21–54. Berlin/ New York: de Gruyter.

Briere, Eugene J., Russell M. Campbell & Marmo Soemarmo. 1968. A need for the syllable in contrastive analysis. *Journal of Verbal Learning and Verbal Behavior* 7. 384–389.

Burzio, Luigi. 1994. *Principles of English Stress.* Cambridge: Cambridge University Press.

Burzio, Luigi. 2005. Sources of Paradigm Uniformity. In Laura J. Downing, T. Alan Hall & Renate Raffelsiefen (eds.), *Paradigms in Phonological Theory*, 65–106. Oxford: Oxford University Press.

Butt, Matthias & Peter Eisenberg. 1990. Schreibsilbe und Sprechsilbe. In Christian Stetter (ed.), *Zu einer Theorie der Orthographie*, 33–64. Tü bingen: Niemeyer.

Caramazza, Alfonso & Gabriele Miceli. 1990. The structure of graphemic representations. *Cognition* 37. 243–297.

Carney, Edward. 1994. *A Survey of English Spelling.* London: Routledge.

Chomsky, Noam & Moris Halle. 1968. *The Sound Pattern of English.* New York: Harper & Row.

Clements, George N. 1990. The Role of the Sonority Cycle in Core Syllabification. In John Kingston & Mary Beckman (eds.), *Papers in Laboratory Phonology I*, 283–333. Cambridge: Cambridge University Press.

Clements, George N. & Samuel J. Keyser. 1983. *CV phonology.* Cambridge/Mass.: MIT Press.

Cook, Vivian. 2004. *The English Writing System.* London: Routledge.

Coueignoux, Philippe. 1981. La reconnaissance des charactères. *La recherche* 126(12). 1094–1103.

Coulmas, Florian. 1996. *The Blackwell Encyclopedia of Writing Systems.* Oxford: Blackwell.

Cuetos, Fernando & Edith Labos. 2001. The autonomy of the orthographic pathway in a shallow language: Data from an aphasic patient. *Aphasiology* 15(4). 333–342.

Davis, Stuart. 1988. Syllable onsets as a factor in stress rules. *Phonology* 5. 1–10.

Derwing, Bruce L. 1992. A 'pause-break' task for eliciting syllable boundary judgments from literate and illiterate speakers: Preliminary results for five diverse languages. *Language and Speech* 35. 219–235.

Dogil, Grzegorz. 1989. Phonologische Konfigurationen, natü rliche Klassen, Sonorität und Syllabizität. In Martin Prinzhorn (ed.), *Phonologie*, 198–222. Opladen: Westdeutscher Verlag.

Domahs, Frank, Ria de Bleser & Peter Eisenberg. 2001. Silbische Aspekte segmentalen Schreibens - neurolinguistische Evidenz. *Linguistische Berichte* 185. 13–30.

Domahs, Ulrike, Ingo Plag & Rebecca Carroll. 2014. Word stress assignment in German, English and Dutch: Quantity-sensitivity and extrametricality revisited. *Journal of Comparative Germanic Linguistics* 17(1). 59–96.

Domahs, Ulrike & Beatrice Primus. 2015. Laut – Gebärde – Buchstabe. In Ekkehard Felder & Andreas Gardt (eds.), *Sprache und Wissen*, 125–142. Berlin/ New York: de Gruyter.

Domahs, Ulrike, Richard Wiese, Ina Bornkessel-Schlesewsky & Matthias Schlesewsky. 2008. The processing of German word stress: evidence for the prosodic hierarchy. *Phonology* 25. 1–36.

Dudenredaktion. 1996. *Duden. Rechtschreibung der deutschen Sprache.* Mannheim: Dudenverlag.

Dudenredaktion (ed.). 2000. *Duden. Das Aussprachewörterbuch.* Mannheim: Dudenverlag.

Dudenredaktion. 2015. *Duden – Deutsches Universalwörterbuch* 4th edn. Mannheim: Dudenverlag.

Dürscheid, Christa. 2012. *Einführung in die Schriftlinguistik. Grundlagen und Theorien* 4th edn. Göttingen: Vandenhoek & Ruprecht.

Eden, Murray & Morris Halle. 1961. The characterization of cursive handwriting. In C. Cherry (ed.), *Information theory: Fourth london symposium*, 187–299. Washington: Butterworths.

Eisenberg, Peter. 1989. Die Schreibsilbe im Deutschen. In Peter Eisenberg & Hartmut Günther (eds.), *Schriftsystem und Orthographie*, 57–84. Tü bingen: Niemeyer.

Eisenberg, Peter. 1991. Syllabische Struktur und Wortakzent: Prinzipien der Prosodik deutscher Wörter. *Zeitschrift für Sprachwissenschaft* 10. 37–64.

Eisenberg, Peter. 1999. Vokallängenbezeichung als Problem. *Linguistische Berichte* 179. 343–349.

Eisenberg, Peter. 2005. Der Buchstabe und die Schriftstruktur des Wortes. In Dudenredaktion (ed.), *Duden. die grammatik*, Mannheim: Duden-Verlag 7th edn.

Eisenberg, Peter. 2006. *Grundriß der deutschen Grammatik. Bd. 1: Das Wort* 3rd edn. Stuttgart: J.B. Metzler.

Elzinga, Dirk & David Eddington. 2013. An Experimental Approach to Ambisyllabicity in English. *http://linguistics.byu.edu/faculty/eddingtond/ambisyllabicity%20paper.pdf*.

Everett, Dan & Keren Everett. 1984. On the Relevance of Syllable Onsets to Stress Placement. *Linguistic Inquiry* 15(4). 705–711.

Evertz, Martin. 2016. Graphematischer Fuß und graphematisches Wort. In Beatrice Primus & Ulrike Domahs (eds.), *Laut – Gebärde – Buchstabe*, 377–397. Berlin/ New York: de Gruyter.

Evertz, Martin & Beatrice Primus. 2013. The graphematic foot in English and German. *Writing Systems Research* 5(1). 1–23.

Faber, Alice. 1992. Phonemic Segmentation as Epiphenomenon: Evidence from the History of Alphabetic Writing. In S. D. Lima, M. Noonan & P. Downing (eds.), *The linguistics of literacy (typological studies in language, 21),*, 111–134. Amsterdam: Johns Benjamins.

Fallows, Deborah. 1981. Experimental evidence for English syllabification and syllable structure. *Journal of Linguistics* 17. 309–317.

Féry, Caroline. 1986. Metrische Phonologie und Wortakzent im Deutschen. *Studium Linguistik* 20. 16–43.

Féry, Caroline. 1998. German word stress in Optimality Theory. *Journal of Comparative Linguistics* 2. 101–142.

Féry, Caroline & Ruben van de Vijver (eds.). 2003. *The Syllable in Optimality Theory.* Cambridge: Cambridge University Press.

Fronek, Josef. 1982. *Thing* as a function word. *Linguistics* 20. 633–654.

Fuhrhop, Nanna. 2005. *Orthografie*. Heidelberg: Winter.

Fuhrhop, Nanna. 2008. Das graphematische Wort (im Deutschen): Eine erste Annäherung. *Zeitschrift für Sprachwissenschaft* 27. 189–228.

Fuhrhop, Nanna & Franziska Buchmann. 2009. Die Längenhierarchie: Zum Bau der graphematischen Silbe. *Linguistische Berichte* 218. 127–155.

Fuhrhop, Nanna & Franziska Buchmann. 2016. Graphematische Silbe. In Beatrice Primus & Ulrike Domahs (eds.), *Laut – Gebärde – Buchstabe*, 356–376. Berlin/ New York: de Gruyter.

Fuhrhop, Nanna, Franziska Buchmann & Kristian Berg. 2011. The length hierarchy and the graphematic syllable: Evidence from German and English. *Written Language & Literacy* 14.2. 275–292.

Fuhrhop, Nanna & Jörg Peters. 2013. *Einführung in die Phonologie und Graphematik*. Stuttgart: J. B. Metzler.

Gallmann, Peter. 1985. *Graphische Elemente der geschriebenen Sprache. Grundlagen für eine Reform der Orthographie*. Niemeyer.

Geilfuss-Wolfgang, Jochen. 2007. Stammkonstanz ohne Stützformen. *Zeitschrift für Sprachwissenschaft* 26. 133–154.

Giegerich, Heinz J. 1985. *Metrical phonology and phonological structure: German and English*. Cambridge: Cambridge University Press.

Giegerich, Heinz J. 1992. *English phonology: An introduction*. Cambridge: Cambridge University Press.

Goldsmith, John A. 1999. *Phonological theory: The essential readings*. Malden, MA: Blackwell.

Gove, Philip Babcock (ed.). 2002. *Webster's third new international dictionary of the English language, unabridged*. Springfield, Mass.: Merriam-Webster.

Günther, Hartmut. 1988. *Schriftliche Sprache: Strukturen geschriebener Wörter und ihre Verarbeitung beim Lesen*. Tü bingen: Narr.

Günther, Hartmut. 1992. Re-re-plik. Zur linguistischen Rekonstruktion und zur anwenderorientierten Formulierung der orthographischen Worttrennungsregel im Deutschen. *Deutsche Sprache* 20. 244–255.

Gussenhoven, Carlos. 1986. English plosive allophones and ambisyllabicity. *Gramma* 10. 119–141.

Hall, Robert A. 1964. *Introductory linguistics*. Philadelphia: Chilton Books.

Hall, Tracy A. 1999. Phonotactics and the Prosodic Structure of German Function Words. In Tracy Hall & Ursula Kleinhenz (eds.), *Studies on the Phonological Word*, 99–131. Amsterdam: John Benjamins.

Hammond, Michael. 1999. *The Phonology of English. A Prosodic Optimality-Theoretic Approach*. Oxford: Oxford University Press.

Harris, Roy. 1995. *Signs of Writing*. London: Routledge.

Harris, Roy. 2009. Speech and Writing. In D. R. Olson & N. Torrance (eds.), *The Cambridge Handbook of Literacy*, Cambridge: University Press.

Hayes, Bruce. 1981. *A metrical theory of stress rules*. Bloomington, Indiana: Indiana University.

Hayes, Bruce. 1982. Extrametricality and English stress. *Linguistic Inquiry* 13. 227–276.

Henderson, Leslie. 1985. On the use of the term 'grapheme'. *Language and Cognitive Processes* 1(2). 135–148.

Hendriks, Petra & Helen de Hoop. 2001. Optimality Theoretic Semantic. *Linguistics and Philosophy* 24(1). 1–32.

Horn, L. R. 1984. Toward a new taxonomy for pragmatic inference: Q-based and R-based implicatures. In D. Schiffrin (ed.), *Meaning, Form, and Use in Context*, 11–42. Washington: Georgetown University Press.

Hume, Elizabeth & David Odden. 1996. Reconsidering [consonantal]. *Phonology* 13. 345–376.

Hurch, Bernhard & Utz Maas. 1998. Morphoprosodie des marokkanischen Arabischen. *Folia Linguistica* 32. 239–263.

Inkelas, Sharon. 1998. The theoretical status of morphologically conditioned phonology: a case study from dominance. In Geert Booij & Jaap van Marle (eds.), *Yearbook of Morphology 1997*, 121–155. Amsterdam: Springer.

Inkelas, Sharon & Cheryl Zoll. 2007. Is grammar dependence real? A comparison between cophonological and indexed constraint approaches to morphologically conditioned phonology. *Linguistics* 45(1). 133–171.

Ito, Junko & R. Armin Mester. 1992. Weak layering and word binarity. Tech. Rep. LRC-92-09 Linguistics Research Center, University of California Santa Cruz.

Jäger, Gerhard. 2002. Some notes on the formal properties of bidirectional optimality theory. *Journal of Logic, Language and Information* 11. 427–451.

Janssen, Ulrike. 2003. *Untersuchungen zum Wortakzent im Deutschen und Niederländischen*. PhD thesis, University of Düsseldorf.

Jessen, Michael. 1999. German. In Harry van der Hulst (ed.), *Word Prosodic Systems in the Languages of Europe*, 515–545. Berlin/ New York: de Gruyter.

Jones, Daniel. 2006. *Cambridge English pronouncing dictionary* 17th edn. Cambridge: Cambridge University Press.

Kabak, Bariş & René Schiering. 2006. The Phonology and Morphology of Function Word Contractions in German. *Journal of Comparative Germanic Linguistics* 9. 53–99.

Kager, René. 1989. *A metrical theory of stress and destressing in English and Dutch*. Berlin/ New York: de Gruyter.

Kager, René. 1999. *Optimality Theory*. Cambridge: Cambridge University Press.

Kahn, Daniel. 1976. *Syllable-based generalizations in English phonology*: MIT dissertation.

Kaltenbacher, Erika. 1994. Typologische Aspekte des Wortakzents: Zum Zusammenhang von Akzentposition und Silbengewicht im Arabischen und Deutschen. *Zeitschrift für Sprachwissenschaft* 13. 20–55.

Kelly, Michael H. 2004. Word onset patterns and lexical stress in English. *Journal of Memory and Language* 50. 231–244.

Kenstowicz, Michael. 1996. Base-identity and uniform exponence: alternatives to cyclicity. In Jacques Durand & Bernard Laks (eds.), *Current Trends in Phonology: Models and Methods*, 363–393. European Studies Research Institute and University of Salford.

Kiparsky, Paul. 1979. Metrical Structure Assignment is Cyclic. *Linguistic Inquiry* 10. 421–441.

Kiparsky, Paul. 1982. Lexical Morphology and Phonology. In *Linguistics in the Morning Calm*, 3–91. Seoul: Hansin.

Kiparsky, Paul. 2000. Opacity and cyclicity. *The Linguistic Review* 17. 351–367.

Kirchhoff, Frank. 2016. Interpunktion und Intonation. In Beatrice Primus & Ulrike Domahs (eds.), *Laut – Gebärde – Buchstabe*, 398–417. Berlin/ New York: de Gruyter.

Kluge, Friedrich. 1999. *Etymologisches Wörterbuch der deutschen Sprache*. Berlin/ New York: de Gruyter.

Knaus, Johannes & Ulrike Domahs. 2009. Experimental evidence for minimal and optimal metrical structures of German word prosody. *Lingua* 119. 1396–1413.

Kohrt, Manfred. 1985. *Problemgeschichte des Graphembegriffs und des frühen Phonembegriffs*. Tü bingen: Niemeyer.
Krifka, Manfred. 2002. Be brief and vague! And how Bidirectional Optimality Theory allows for verbosity and precision. In D. Restle & D. Zaefferer (eds.), *Sounds and systems: studies in the structure and change*, 439–458. Berlin/ New York: de Gruyter.
Lavoie, Lisa M. 2001. *Consonant Strength*. New York, London: Garland.
Legendre, Geraldine, Jane Grimshaw & Sten Vikner. 2001. *Optimality-theoretic syntax*. Cambridge: MIT Press.
Liberman, Mark. 1975. *The Intonational System of English*: MIT Cambridge, MA dissertation.
Liberman, Mark & Alan S. Prince. 1977. On stress and linguistic rhythm. *Linguistic Inquiry* 8. 249–336.
Lyons, John. 1972. Human language. In R. A. Hinde (ed.), *Non-Verbal Communication*, Cambridge: University Press.
Maas, Utz. 1992. *Grundzüge der deutschen Orthografie*. Tübingen: Niemeyer.
Maas, Utz. 1999. *Phonologie. Einführung in die funktionale Phonetik des Deutschen*. Opladen: Westdeutscher Verlag.
McCarthy, John J. 1982a. Nonlinear Phonology: An Overview. *GLOW Newsletter* 8. 63–77.
McCarthy, John J. 1982b. Prosodic Templates, Morphemic Templates, and Morphemic Tiers. In Harry van der Hulst & Norval Smith (eds.), *The Structure of Phonological Representations I*, 191–224. Dordrecht: Foris.
McCarthy, John J. 1995. Faithfulness in prosodic morphology and phonology: Rotuman revisited. In *Ms., University of Massachusetts, Amherst. ROA-110, Rutgers Optimality Archive*, .
McCarthy, John J. & Alan S. Prince. 1993a. Generalized Alignment. In G. Booij & J. van Marle (eds.), *Yearbook of Morphology 1993*, 79–153. Dordrecht: Kluwer.
McCarthy, John J. & Alan S. Prince. 1993b. *Prosodic Morphology I: Constraint Interaction and Satisfaction* RuCCS-TR. Center for Cognitive Science.
McCarthy, John J. & Alan S. Prince. 1995a. Faithfulness and reduplicative identity. In Jill Beckman, Laura Dickey & Suzanne Urbanczyk (eds.), *University of Massachusetts Occasional Papers in Linguistics 18: Papers in Optimality Theory*, 249–384. Amherst: GLSA.
McCarthy, John J. & Alan S. Prince. 1995b. Prosodic Morphology. In John Goldsmith (ed.), *The Handbook of Phonological Theory*, Blackwell.
McMahon, April. 2001. *An introduction to english phonology*. Edinburgh: University Press.
Miceli, Gabriele, Barbara Benvegnù, Rita Capasso & Alfonso Caramazza. 1997. The Independence of Phonological and Orthographic Lexical Forms: Evidence from Aphasia. *Cognitive Neuropsychology* 14(1). 35–69.
Morais, José, Jesus Alegria & Alain Content. 1987. The relationship between segmental analysis and alphabetic literacy: An interactive view. *European Journal of Cognitive Psychology* 7. 415–438.
Moulton, William G. 1962. *The sound of English and German*. Chicago: University of Chicago Press.
Muthmann, Gustav. 1996. *Phonologisches Wörterbuch der deutschen Sprache*. Tübingen: Niemeyer.
Naumann, Carl Ludwig. 1989. *Gesprochenes Deutsch und Orthographie*. Frankfurt a.M.: Peter Lang.
Neef, Martin. 2000. Die Distribution des [h] im Deutschen: Schriftaussprache und Phonologie. *Convivium 2000* 271–286.

Neef, Martin. 2002. Das Maß aller Dinge: Sonorität. In Michael Bommes, Christina Noack & Doris Tophinke (eds.), *Sprache als Form. Festschrift für Utz Maas zum 60. Geburtstag*, 32–48. Wiesbaden: Westdeutscher Verlag.

Neef, Martin. 2005. *Die Graphematik des Deutschen*. Tübingen: Niemeyer.

Neef, Martin. 2010. Die Schreibung nicht-nativer Einheiten in einer Schriftsystemtheorie mit einem mehrschichtigen Wortschatzmodell. In Anke Holler & Carmen Scherer (eds.), *Strategien der Integration und Isolation nicht-nativer Einheiten und Strukturen*, 11–29. Berlin/ New York: de Gruyter.

Neef, Martin & Beatrice Primus. 2001. Stumme Zeugen der Autonomie - Eine Replik auf Ossner. *Linguistische Berichte* 187. 353–378.

Nespor, Marina & Irene Vogel. 1986. *Prosodic Phonology*. Fordrecht: Foris.

Noel, Patrizia Aziz Hanna. 2002. 'Dromedar oder Drome'dar? Eine Untersuchung des deutschen Simplexakzents anhand von Wörtern mit doppeltem Akzentmuster. *Sprachwissenschaft* 27. 423–446.

Nottbusch, Guido, Rüdiger Weingarten & Udo Will. 2005. Syllabic structures in typing: Evidence from deaf writers. *Reading and Writing* 18(6). 497–526.

Olson, David R. 1993. How writing represents speech. *Language & Communication* 13(1). 1–17.

Olson, David R. 1994. *The world on paper*. Cambridge: Cambridge University Press.

Orgun, Cemil Orhan. 1998. Cyclic and noncyclic effects in a declarative grammar. In Geert Booij & Jaap van Marle (eds.), *Yearbook of Morphology 1997*, 179–218. Amsterdam: Springer.

Orgun, Cemil Orhan & Sharon Inkelas. 2002. Reconsidering bracket erasure. In Geert Booij & Jaap van Marle (eds.), *Yearbook of Morphology 2001*, 115–146. Amsterdam: Springer.

Ossner, Jakop. 1996. Silbifizierung und Orthographie des Deutschen. *Linguistische Berichte* 165. 369–400.

Ossner, Jakop. 2001. Das <h>-Graphem im Deutschen. *Linguistische Berichte* 187. 325–351.

Pater, Joe. 2000. Non-uniformity in English secondary stress: The role of ranked and lexically specific constraints. *Phonology* 17. 236–274.

Pelli, Denis G., Catherine W. Burns, Bart Farell & Deborah C. Moore-Page. 2006. Feature detection and letter identification. *Vision Research* 46. 4646–4674.

Perlmutter, David M. 1992. Sonority and syllable structure in American Sign Language. *Linguistic Inquiry* 23. 407–442.

Picard, Marc. 1984. English aspiration and flapping revisited. *Canadian Journal of Linguistics* 29. 42–57.

Pompino-Marschall, Bernd. 1993. Die Silbe im Deutschen - gesprochen, geschrieben, beschrieben. In Jürgen Baumann, Hartmut Günther & Ulrich Knoop (eds.), *homo scribens. Perspektiven der Schriftlichkeitsforschung*, 43–65. Tübingen: Niemeyer.

Pompino-Marschall, Bernd. 1995. *Einführung in die Phonetik*. Berlin/ New York: de Gruyter.

Price, P.J. 1980. Sonority and Syllabicity: Acoustic Correlates of Perception. *Phonetica* 37. 327–343.

Primus, Beatrice. 2000. Suprasegmentale Graphematik und Phonologie: Die Dehnungszeichen im Deutschen. *Linguistische Berichte* 181. 5–30.

Primus, Beatrice. 2003. Zum Silbenbegriff in der Schrift-, Laut- und Gebärdensprache – Versuch einer mediumübergreifenden Fundierung. *Zeitschrift für Sprachwissenschaft* 22. 3–55.

Primus, Beatrice. 2004. A featural analysis of the modern roman alphabet. *Written Language & Literacy* 7.2. 235–274.

Primus, Beatrice. 2006. Buchstabenkomponenten und ihre Grammatik. In Ursula Bredel & Hartmut Günther (eds.), *Orthographietheorie und Rechtschreibunterricht*, 5–43. Tü bingen: Niemeyer.

Primus, Beatrice. 2010. Strukturelle Grundlagen des deutschen Schriftsystems. In Ursula Bredel, Astrid Müller & Gabriele Hinney (eds.), *Schriftsystem und Schrifterwerb: linguistisch – didaktisch – empirisch*, 9–45. Tü bingen: Niemeyer.

Prince, Alan S. 1980. A Metrical Theory for Estonian Quantity. *Linguistic Inquiry* 11. 511–562.

Prince, Alan S. & Paul Smolensky. 1993. *Optimality Theory: constraint interaction in generative grammar.* Ms., Rutgers University (= Rutgers University Center for Cognitive Science Technical Report 2).

Prinz, Michael & Richard Wiese. 1990. Ein nicht-lineares Modell der Graphem-Phonem-Korrespondenz. *Folia Linguistica* 24. 73–103.

Ramers, Karl Heinz. 1992. Ambisilbische Konsonanten im Deutschen. In Peter Eisenberg, Karl Heinz Ramers & Heinz Vater (eds.), *Silbenphonologie des Deutschen*, 246–283. Tübingen: Narr.

Ramers, Karl Heinz. 1998. Minimale Wörter: Prosodische Beschränkungen graphischer Wortstrukturen. In Bernd J. Krögerger (ed.), *Festschrift für Georg Heike*, 25–39. Frankfurt am Main: Forum Phoneticum 66.

Ramers, Karl Heinz. 1999a. Vokalquantität als orthographisches Problem: Zur Funktion der Doppelkonsonanzschreibung im Deutschen. *Linguistische Berichte* 177. 54–64.

Ramers, Karl Heinz. 1999b. Zur Doppelkonsonanzschreibung im Deutschen: Eine Rereplik. *Linguistische Berichte* 179. 350–360.

Restle, David & Theo Vennemann. 2001. Silbenstruktur. In E. König, W. Oesterreicher & W. Raible (eds.), *Language Typology and Language Universals. (=HSK). Volume 2.*, 1310–1336. Berlin/ New York: De Gruyter.

Rogers, Henry. 2005. *Writing Systems: A Linguistic Approach* 3rd edn. Oxford: Blackwell.

Rollings, Andrew G. 2004. *The spelling patterns of English*. München: Lincom Europa.

Röttger, Timo, Ulrike Domahs, Marion Grande & Frank Domahs. 2012. Structural factors affecting the assignment of word stress in german. *Journal of Germanic Linguistics* 24(1). 53–94.

Roubah, Aïcha & Marcus Taft. 2001. The functional role of syllabic structure in French visual word recognition. *Memory & Cognition* 29. 373–381.

Ryan, Des. 2010. *Kre-8-iv Spell!nk: Why constructed homophony is key to understanding patterns of orthographic change.* Edinburgh University MA thesis.

de Saussure, Ferdinand. 1959. *Course in General Linguistics.* New York: McGraw-Hill. Translated by Wade Baskin.

Scharnhorst, Jürgen. 1988. Die graphische Ebene im Modell des Sprachsystems. In D. Nerius & G. Augst (eds.), *Probleme der geschriebenen Sprache. Beiträge zur Schriftlinguistik auf dem XIV. Internationalen Linguistenkongreß 1987 in Berlin*, 87–102. Linguistische Studien, Reihe A, Arbeitsberichte.

Selkirk, Elisabeth O. 1980. The Role of Prosodic Categories in English Word Stress. *Linguistic Inquiry* 11. 563–605.

Selkirk, Elisabeth O. 1981. On the Nature of Phonological Representation. In John Anderson, John Laver & Terry Myers (eds.), *The Cognitive Representation of Speech*, 379–388. Amsterdam: North Holland.

Selkirk, Elisabeth O. 1984. *Phonology and Syntax: The Relation between Sound and Structure.* Cambridge: MIT Press.

Selkirk, Elisabeth O. 1996. The prosodic structure of function words. In James L. Morgan & Katherine Demuth (eds.), *Signal to Syntax*, 187–213. Mahwah, NJ: Lawrence Erlbaum.

Shattuck-Hufnagel, Stefanie & Alice E. Turk. 1996. A Prosody Tutorial for Investigators of Auditory Sentence Processing. *Journal of Psycholinguistic Research* 25(2). 193–247.

Song, Hye Jeong & Richard Wiese. 2010. Resistance to complexity interacting with visual shape – German and Korean orthography. *Writing Systems Research* 2. 87–103.

Sucharowski, Wolfgang. 1996. *Sprache und Kognition. Neuere Perspektiven in der Sprachwissenschaft*. Opladen: Westdeutscher Verlag.

Tillmann, Hans Günther & Phil Mansell. 1980. *Phonetik. Lautsprachliche Zeichen, Sprachsignale und lautsprachlicher Kommunikationsprozess*. Stuttgart: Klett-Cotta.

Treiman, Rebecca, Judith A. Bowey & Derrick Bourassa. 2002. Segmentation of spoken words into syllables by English-speaking children. *Journal of Experimental Child Psychology* 83. 213–238.

Treiman, Rebecca & Catalina Danis. 1988. Syllabification of intervocalic consonants. *Journal of Memory and Language* 27. 87–104.

Treiman, Rebecca & Andrea Zukowski. 1990. Toward an understanding of English syllabification. *Journal of Memory and Language* 29. 66–85.

Trommelen, Mike & Wim Zonneveld. 1999. English. In Harry van der Hulst (ed.), *Word prosodic systems in the languages of Europe*, 478–491. Berlin/ New York: de Gruyter.

Venezky, Richard L. 1970. *The structure of English orthography*. The Hague: Mouton.

Venezky, Richard L. 1999. *The American Way of Spelling: The Structure and Origins of American English Orthography*. New York, London: The Guilford Press.

Vennemann, Theo. 1982. Zur Silbenstruktur der deutschen Standardsprache. In Theo Vennemann (ed.), *Silben, Segmente, Akzente*, 261–305. Tübingen: Niemeyer.

Vennemann, Theo. 1990. Syllable structure and simplex Modern Standard German. *Chicago Linguistic Society* 26(2). 399–412.

Vennemann, Theo. 1991. Skizze der deutschen Wortprosodie. *Zeitschrift für Sprachwissenschaft* 10. 86–111.

Vennemann, Theo. 1995. Der Zusammenbruch der Metrik im Spätmittelalter und sein Einfluss auf die Metrik. In Hans Fix (ed.), *Quantitätsproblematik und Metrik. Greifswalder Symposion zur germanistischen Grammatik*, 185–223. Amsterdam: Radopi.

Vigário, Marina. 1999. On the Prosodic Status of Stressless Function Words in European Portuguese. In Tracy Alan Hall & Ursula Kleinhenz (eds.), *Studies on the Phonological Word*, 255–295. Amsterdam: John Benjamins.

Watt, William C. 1988. What is the proper characterization of the alphabet? Part 4: Union. *Semiotica* 70. 199–241.

Weingarten, Rüdiger. 2004. Die Silbe im Schreibprozess und im Schriftspracherwerb. In Ursula Bredel, Gesa Siebert-Ott & Tobias Thelen (eds.), *Schriftspracherwerb und Orthographie*, 6–21. Baltmannsweiler: Schneider.

Weingarten, Rüdiger, Guido Nottbusch & Udo Will. 2004. Morphemes, syllables and graphemes in written word production. In T. Pechmann & Ch. C. Habel (eds.), *Multidisciplinary approaches to language production*, 529–572. Berlin/ New York: de Gruyter.

Wiese, Richard. 1987. Laut, Schrift und das Lexikon. *Deutsche Sprache* 15. 318–335.

Wiese, Richard. 2000. *The Phonology of German* 2nd edn. Oxford: Oxford University Press.

Wiese, Richard. 2004. How to optimize orthography. *Written Language & Literacy* 7. 305–331.

Wimmer, Heinz, Karin Landerl, Renate Linortner & Peter Hummer. 1991. The relationship between phonemic awareness to reading acquisition: More consequence than precondition but still important. *Cognition* 40. 219–249.

Wurzel, Wolfgang Urlich. 1970. Der Fremdwortakzent im Deutschen. *Linguistics* 56. 87–108.

Wurzel, Wolfgang Urlich. 1980. Der deutsche Wortakzent: Fakten – Regeln – Prinzipien. *Zeitschrift für Germanistik* 1. 299–318.

Zamuner, Tania S. & Diane K. Ohala. 1999. Preliterate children's syllabification of intervocalic consonants. In Annabell Greenhill, Heather Littlefield & Cheryl Tano (eds.), *Proceedings of the 23rd annual Boston Conference on Language Development*, 753–763. Somerville MA: Cascadilla Press.

Zec, Draga. 1993. Rule Domains and Phonological Change. In Sharon Hargus & Ellen Kaisse (eds.), *Studies in Lexical Phonology*, 365–405. New York: Academic Press.

Zec, Draga. 2007. The syllable. In Paul de Lacy (ed.), *The Cambridge Handbook of Phonology*, 161–194. Cambridge University Press.

Zenker, Sven. 2011. *Worttrennung am Zeilenende - Deutsch und Englisch im Vergleich*. University of Cologne Schriftliche Hausarbeit im Rahmen der ersten Staatsprüfung für das Lehramt für die Sekundarstufe II.

Zifonun, Gisela, Ludger Hoffmann & Bruni Strecker (eds.). 1997. *Grammatik der Deutschen Sprache*. Berlin/ New York: de Gruyter.

Appendix

Phonological Constraints

ALING-FOOT-LEFT (ALIGN PRWD, L; FT, L): Every Prosodic Word begins with a foot (McCarthy & Prince 1993).
ALING-FOOT-RIGHT (ALIGN PRWD, R; FT, R): Every Prosodic Word ends with a foot (McCarthy & Prince 1993).
ALLFT-LEFT (ALIGN FT, L; PRWD, L): Every foot stands in initial position in the prosodic word.
FOOT-BINARITY: Feet are binary at a syllabic or moraic level of analysis (Prince & Smolensky 1993).
LEXWD=PRDWD: Every lexical word corresponds to a prosodic word (Prince & Smolensky 1993: 101).
NONFINALITY: The final syllable is not footed (Prince & Smolensky 1993).
PARSE-σ: Syllables are parsed by feet (Prince & Smolensky 1993).
pSYLL-WELL-FORMEDNESS: Phonological syllables must be well-formed.
RIGHTMOST (ALING HEAD-FT, R; PRWD, R): The right edge of the head-foot coincides with the right edge of the prosodic word (Prince & Smolensky 1993).
TROCHEE: Feet are head-initial (Prince & Smolensky 1993).
WSP (Weight-to-Stress Principle): A heavy syllable is stressed (Prince & Smolensky 1993).

Graphematic Constraints

ALIGN-gFOOT-LEFT (Align (Graphematic word, Left; graphematic Foot, Left)): Every graphematic word begins with a foot.
ALIGN-gFOOT-RIGHT (Align (Graphematic word, Right; graphematic Foot, Right)): Every graphematic word ends with a foot.
BRANCHING-gN: The nucleus of a full g-syllable in a prosodically strong position is branching. All other nuclei do not branch.
*COMPL-CgN: The second nuclear position of a g-syllable is barred for complex graphemes (Primus 2003: 40, my translation).
*GEMINATE-COMPLEX: Complex graphemes are not geminated.
gPEAK: Every g-syllable has a v-letter in its peak (Maas 1999: 265, Primus 2003: 31, Evertz & Primus 2013: 5).

https://doi.org/10.1515/9783110583441-007

*GRAPHAMBI: Every graphematic element is exhaustively contained in the superordinate unit of which it is a part.
GSYLL-WELL-FORMEDNESS: Graphematic syllables must be well-formed.
LSP: The graphematic syllable core [i.e., the V-position] is occupied by the most compact grapheme. The length of the segments increases monotonously toward both syllable edges.
MINIMALITY:Graphematic feet are mono- or bisyllabic. If a graphematic foot is monosyllabic it dominates a syllable with a rhyme dominating at least two segments and its syllable has a weight of at least three morae.
NOFREECODA: The coda of a character lacks the feature [free].
NOLEFT: The character is not [leftwards].
NONHEAD(RGS): Reduced graphematic syllables cannot be heads of graphematic feet.
*NUCLEAR-<H>: <h> may only appear in a post-nuclear C-position of a graphematic syllable that immediately follows a nuclear C-position occupied by a vocalic element (Primus 2000: 23, my translation).
PARSE-σ: Syllables are parsed by feet.
STRWD=GRWD: Every strong word corresponds to a graphematic word.
SYLLABIFY: A graphematic syllable starts with exactly one grapheme.
TROCHEE: Graphematic feet are head-initial.
VERTICALHEAD: A non-vertical segment depends on a vertical line; i.e., there is no horizontal line or a dot without a vertical line.
WEIGHT-TO-HEAD-PRINCIPLE (WHP): Heavy syllables are heads of feet.

Faithfulness and Mapping Constraints

BINARY: A binary p-vowel bidirectionally corresponds to a v-letter in an open and strong g-syllable
UNARY: A unary p-vowel bidirectionally corresponds to a v-letter in a closed and strong g-syllable

DEP: Output segments must have input correspondents. ('No insertion')
MAX: Input segments must have output correspondents. ('No deletion')
MAXG: All graphematic segments correspond to phonological segments.
MAXP: All phonological segments correspond to graphematic segments.
DEPNUC: Every nucleus in the output corresponds to a nucleus in the input.

GEMINATE: An ambisyllabic consonant is coded by gemination of the c-letter that is the regular correspondent of this consonant. The first letter of the geminate is dominated by the nuclear C-position of the first g-syllable; the second letter is dominated by the onset of the immediately following g-syllable.
GEMINATE*can*: In canonical bisyllabic p-feet and g-feet: An ambisyllabic consonant is coded by a gemination of the letter that is the regular correspondent of this consonant. The first letter of the gemination is dominated by the nuclear C-position of the first g-syllable; the second letter is dominated by the onset of the following g-syllable.

IDENT-OO[UnBin]: Let α be a phonological vowel in output $form_1$ and β be its correspondent in output $form_2$. If α is unary, then β is unary and if α is binary, then β is binary.
IDENT-IO[UnBin]: Let α be a phonological vowel input $form_1$ and β be its correspondent in output $form_2$. If α is unary, then β is unary and if α is binary, then β is binary.
IDENT-P[UnBin]: Let α be a phonological vowel in p-$form_1$ and β be its correspondent in p-$form_2$. If α is unary, then β is unary and if α is binary, then β is binary.
IDENT-G[Gem]: Let α be a c-letter in g-$form_1$ and β be its correspondent in g-$form_2$. If α is geminated, then β is geminated.

MINSYLL: The nucleus of a minimal g-syllable does not correspond to a phonological nucleus.

www.ingramcontent.com/pod-product-compliance
Lightning Source LLC
Chambersburg PA
CBHW032057230426
43662CB00035B/587